YOUR
HEART,
MY HANDS

YOUR HEART, MY HANDS

An IMMIGRANT'S REMARKABLE JOURNEY
to BECOME ONE of AMERICA'S
PREEMINENT CARDIAC SURGEONS

ᥱ

ARUN K. SINGH, MD

with JOHN HANC

Foreword by DELOS M. COSGROVE, MD

CENTER STREET

New York Nashville

Copyright © 2019 by Arun K. Singh, MD

Cover design by Edward Crawford
Cover photography by Getty Images
Cover copyright © 2019 by Hachette Book Group.

Hachette Book Group supports the right to free expression and the value of copyright. The purpose of copyright is to encourage writers and artists to produce the creative works that enrich our culture.

The scanning, uploading, and distribution of this book without permission is a theft of the author's intellectual property. If you would like permission to use material from the book (other than for review purposes), please contact permissions@hbgusa.com.
Thank you for your support of the author's rights.

Center Street
Hachette Book Group
1290 Avenue of the Americas
New York, NY 10104
centerstreet.com
twitter.com/centerstreet

First Edition: April 2019

Center Street is a division of Hachette Book Group, Inc. The Center Street name and logo are trademarks of Hachette Book Group, Inc.

The publisher is not responsible for websites (or their content) that are not owned by the publisher.

The Hachette Speakers Bureau provides a wide range of authors for speaking events. To find out more, go to www.HachetteSpeakersBureau.com or call (866) 376-6591.

Unless otherwise noted, photos are courtesy of the author.

Library of Congress Cataloging-in-Publication Data.
Names: Singh, Arun K., author. | Hanc, John, author.
Title: Your heart, my hands : an immigrant's remarkable journey to become one of America's preeminent cardiac surgeons / Arun K. Singh, with John Hanc ; foreword by Delos Cosgrove.
Description: First edition. | New York : Center Street, Hachette Book Group, April 2019.
Identifiers: LCCN 2018049847| ISBN 9781546082989 (hardcover) | ISBN 9781546082972 (ebook)
Subjects: | MESH: Singh, Arun K., 1944– | Surgeons | Cardiology | Cardiac Surgical Procedures | Emigrants and Immigrants | United States | India | England | Autobiography
Classification: LCC RD27.35.S515 | NLM WZ 100 | DDC 617.092 [B]—dc23
LC record available at https://lccn.loc.gov/2018049847

ISBN: 978-1-5460-8298-9 (hardcover), 978-1-5460-8297-2 (ebook)

Printed in the United States of America

LSC-C

10 9 8 7 6 5 4 3 2 1

This book is dedicated to my mother, Krishna. Despite all adversity, she instilled in me a positive spirit without which I would have ended up on the streets of India. Also to my wife, Barbara, who helped me in more ways than anyone else over the course of my adult life and pulled me up during my darkest days. Finally, to our two sons, Ari and Michael, for their continued support and love.

I slept and dreamt that life was joy.
I awoke and saw that life was service.
I acted and behold, service was joy.

—RABINDRANATH TAGORE

Contents

CONTENTS

Foreword

Medical school graduates who entered the field of cardiac surgery in the early 1970s have a unique perspective. Our careers have tracked most of the major developments in the field. We've seen the refinement of coronary artery bypass grafting, the development of valve repair, and now the use of minimally invasive and robotic techniques. We helped make cardiac surgery safer and more effective. All of this has contributed to a dramatic fall in mortality from cardiovascular disease and has lengthened life spans across the developed world.

Arun K. Singh, MD, has played a prominent role in this remarkable saga. Over the course of a long and productive career he has performed more than twenty thousand operations, including over fifteen thousand open heart surgeries, and has covered the full range of cardiovascular conditions. The volume and quality of his work are renowned. I have been proud to welcome Dr. Singh into my operating room as an observer over the years. This great surgeon has earned the respect of his peers and the gratitude of his patients. But few know the long road that led to his professional achievements.

Your Heart, My Hands tells the powerful story of Dr. Singh's life and career. It begins in India, where he faced many headwinds as a child and young man. These included cultural and familial issues, as well as his own rebellious temperament.

Most seriously, he endured two bone-shattering accidents

and years of arduous rehabilitation. These injuries left him with permanent disabilities that would seem to disqualify him from any profession that required use of the hands. But the very determined Dr. Singh developed work-arounds and went on to succeed in a role that calls for manual dexterity of the highest order.

Less obviously, Dr. Singh also has dyslexia—a congenital neurological condition that affects how you learn. Those of us who have dyslexia learn better by seeing and doing than by decoding text. I was interested to compare Dr. Singh's experience with my own. Clearly dyslexia is no bar to achievement. Many of the world's most original scientists, inventors, and artists have had dyslexia. We see things differently, but also more creatively.

Dr. Singh is living proof that hard work, persistence, and grit can overcome the most discouraging obstacles. His stories are engaging. His views on life and the future of health care deserve our attention. *Your Heart, My Hands* will be an inspiration to all who read it.

Delos M. Cosgrove, MD
Former CEO and president, Cleveland Clinic

Introduction

The patient will not survive.

I realize this, and yet I cannot stop. I continue to slice my way through ribbons of tissue and plateaus of fat. The scalpel and retractor are like extensions of my hands as I probe and advance to the aortic valve—the gatekeeper of the heart, which allows blood to flow efficiently, unless it becomes narrow and calcified like a clogged-up oil filter.

That's where I come in. I am removing that valve and replacing it with an artificial one. Made of titanium and designed to last a lifetime, this simple object will keep the blood flowing, but inserting it is a meticulous and time-consuming, if routine, operation.

Carefully I lower the valve into the aorta; its slow, graceful descent and capsular shape remind me of the lunar module. It's as if the *Eagle* is landing, except this time on a flesh-and-blood surface. I carefully begin the threading of the stitches, typically about fifteen to twenty-two, used to secure the valve in position.

In a normal procedure of this type there would be a moment of high-tech genesis when the patient's heart, having been stopped for the operation in order to give the surgeon a clear, blood-free view, is restarted like a computer. The flat line on the electrocardiogram begins to spasm, slowly signaling a return to life. And then a miraculous moment: on the echocardiogram monitor, part of the assemblage of monitors and imaging devices set in the modern operating room, there is a flicker of movement as the two crescent-shaped flaps of the mechanical valve begin to flutter. It has come to life, and in turn will now restore a human being to life, to walking, to talking, and to breathing for the remainder of his or her days.

All thanks to a device no bigger than a quarter.

But that is not happening here in my surgery today, because I am not in the OR and this is not a human being. I am operating on the heart of a pig—purchased this morning from a local butcher—for the express purpose of demonstrating the procedure to a group of students.

It is the summer of 2016, and I am a guest lecturer at Bryant University in Smithfield, Rhode Island, not far from my home in Providence. Clad in scrubs, the students, all of them training to be physician assistants, huddle around or watch me on a screen at the front of the conference room as I work on the pig's heart, uncannily similar in structure to our own, on a long table. And while it is a demonstration, I have been drawn into it, my focus intense, my movements almost automatic as I do what I have done so many times before.

"Dr. Singh."

Lost in my work, I am suddenly conscious someone is addressing me. I look up.

"Dr. Singh... would you like to sit down?"

A polite offer, and yet I stare at the poor fellow who made it, dumbfounded by what I am hearing. In the OR, you might as well ask the surgeon if you could sneeze into an open incision.

"Sit?" I say, incredulously. "No, no. The surgeon always stands."

That is true both in fact and metaphorically.

My name is Arun Singh, and I have stood in the OR since the 1970s, first assisting in and then personally performing thousands of open heart procedures. According to hospital records, I have done more than fifteen thousand open heart surgeries during my forty-one-year career. Aside from the pioneering surgical duo of Michael DeBakey and Denton Cooley in Houston, Delos Cosgrove of Cleveland Clinic, and a handful of others, I have probably done more open heart procedures on both children and adults than any cardiac surgeon in America.

Believe me, I have the arthritic hips and creaky knees to prove it. As the standing surgeon, I have remained on my feet for ten hours straight at some points, working and watching my patients come back to life. I once performed four complex operations in thirty-six hours. Aside from short breaks between procedures, I was standing the whole time.

I have tried to stand for something else, too: compassion for my patients—sensitivity to the emotions they experience when it becomes clear that the only way they will stay alive is for me and my team to crack open their chests and descend upon their vital organs with an assortment of strange-looking instruments. Some look like the products of an advanced robotics lab, others of a nineteenth-century sewing circle.

In my opinion, the families of my patients are the real heroes. They entrusted me with an enormous responsibility and on the day of the operation could do little but sit in a waiting room and pray that I would be successful. Usually I was. But no matter how routine surgery becomes to those of us who've done it, I tried never to lose sight of how terrifying it all must appear from the patient's point of view.

I have also stood for—or should I say *as*—a symbol of something very different from surgical prowess. Call me the surgical patron saint of those who were once referred to as wayward boys or troubled youths. I was such a boy, in a far-off place and a culture vastly removed from the one I live in now. I grew up in Deoghar, a city in northeastern India. When I was born, in 1944, it was a nation poised for partition into two states—today's India and Pakistan. It was a violent time, a time of upheaval, when society was divided not only between Hindus and Muslims. There were those who had adopted British ways and views during the recently concluded Raj or Indian Empire period and wanted to keep India as English as high tea. On the other side of the divide were the nationalists who were fighting for independence, self-rule, and a return to our original culture and languages.

I embodied the tumult of the times. Mine was the quintessential misspent youth, one that hardly presaged *any* respectable career, much less a career in medicine. In two separate childhood incidents, partly due to the mischief I caused at the time, both of my hands were crippled, and for a time my right hand was paralyzed. I went through months of painful treatments, and finally, because of what we might today call the "tough love" of my strong-willed mother, I was able to regain full use of both hands.

Imagine that—a surgeon whose life began with crippled hands! Not only my hands; it was also my head that wasn't quite working back then. While the term didn't exist in India in those days, had I been growing up in America in that same period, the 1950s, they would have labeled me a juvenile delinquent. I ran with a bad crowd; I got into trouble; I flouted authority and skipped school. Although we didn't have pool halls or drag racing in India, I took to what was then (strange as it may sound to Westerners) a pastime popular with young rebels like me: kite flying. Not the passive kind you may know. This was competitive kite flying, a battle in the skies that I engaged in as fiercely as if it were fought with fists (and a few times it did come to that). Add to this the fact that I had dyslexia, a condition that was poorly understood at the time but that in retrospect helps to explain why I struggled to write and read at an early age.

Eventually I straightened out, and, to the absolute shock of most who knew me, I ended up getting accepted to medical school. While my debut was inauspicious—I fainted the first time I watched an operation—I applied myself and ended up doing well in my studies. To complete my training, I came to the United States.

I arrived in 1967 at the Massachusetts city of Worcester—at the only hospital that would accept me at that point—with exactly five dollars in my pocket. I had come to the United States at a time when people from my country were still a curiosity. Many Americans thought of people from India as snake charmers, half-naked Gandhi-like ascetics, or characters from *The Jungle Book*. Few of my colleagues and neighbors in Worcester, or even New York, where I went on to complete my training, had ever met anyone from India—much less heard the kind of accent that would become much parodied in movies and sitcoms in years to come and that some of my friends still find amusing today.

Indeed, my country of 1.3 billion people was most identified here not with any single person, but with an animal (the elephant) and a building (the Taj Mahal). It was assumed that I'd ridden around on an elephant as a child and grown up in the shadow of this famous landmark, or perhaps even in its basement. (The truth is, the Taj Mahal is 575 miles west of where I grew up.)

A lot of this was simply cross-cultural ignorance. But although I arrived in the US in the late sixties, a culturally vibrant and exciting time, there were other, more malevolent forces at play. I was painfully aware of the fact that as a nonwhite, I was under suspicion and unwelcome in some quarters, and that I was hated by some simply because I was of a darker complexion than most around me.

Of course, not everyone was averse to befriending a young man from India. A pretty nurse took pity on me during my first day as a resident at Columbia University's Francis Delafield Hospital. I was wandering the corridors of that now-long-defunct hospital, trying to find out where I was supposed to report. Barbara Schachter, a recent graduate of Queens College's nursing program, was happy to get me oriented. She was stunning, and I know some of the other young docs had their eyes on her. But for some reason, she picked me.

We began dating, and after eight months, when I rotated on to Presbyterian Hospital, we continued to see each other. After our shifts, Barbara and I would go out to a famous local eatery called King Arthur's Restaurant, where I enjoyed what seemed like an exotic meal to a guy from India: veal and red cabbage. Afterward we'd go for coffee at Chock Full o'Nuts. We fell in love during those wonderful New York nights, and on November 20, 1970, Barbara and I were married. The color of my skin didn't matter to her parents. Nor did Barbara's to mine. My father knew what it was like to be ostracized, because he'd had the temerity to marry for love, as opposed to caste or rank, and he wouldn't do the same to his son. He welcomed Barbara as his new daughter-in-law.

Meanwhile, my career was beginning to take shape. After completing my surgical residency at Columbia University College of Physicians and Surgeons in 1972, I did my cardiac surgical training at Rhode Island Hospital–Brown University Program in Medicine (now called Warren Alpert Medical School). A year of advanced training at London's prestigious Hospital for Sick Children (now Great Ormond Street Hospital) followed. It was there that I learned the delicate science of surgery on young hearts.

I was then hired back at Rhode Island Hospital, the third-largest hospital in New England and still the main teaching hospital for Brown University. There, in 1975, I embarked on the forty-one-year journey that forms a large part of this book. I was a cardiac surgeon, and my hands—my once-crippled hands—would both save lives and provide my livelihood. I have been well rewarded for my work, and not just monetarily. I was named a Hero at Heart by the American Heart Association, was recently named to the Rhode Island Heritage Hall of Fame, and have received many other honors.

Still, if you ask surgeons why they chose this branch of medicine, it's usually not because of the money or the prestige. It's because they feel that what they do has a positive and often decisive impact on a patient's life. Surgery is invasive, yes, but it is neither inconclusive nor ineffective. While we certainly want to avoid it when it's not absolutely necessary, for most of my patients the choice was clear: surgery or death.

Sadly, a few patients were beyond my skill to save. But the overwhelming majority have gone on to survive and enjoy long and healthy lives—or at least more quality years. Yet as much as I helped effect changes in their lives, so have they changed me. My patients have taught me about every aspect of life. Sometimes the lessons are cautionary. Others have been a source of inspiration. Their stories, as well as mine, will be told in this memoir. Also, I offer my thoughts on the state of surgery today, the issues confronting us, and the current challenges to the practice of medicine, some demographic, some social, and some political. I also relate the sobering, if eventually satisfactory, circumstances related to my so-called retirement in April 2016.

Oh, and by the way, it didn't last long—only a few months. And now I find myself before this late porcine patient, surrounded by an audience with an average age of twenty-seven, younger than my own two children! They are taking notes on their laptops, seemingly hanging on my every word as I continue to cut, splice, and sew.

The students seem awestruck by both this artificial valve and my ability to install it. I don't want them to be. "These can certainly prolong life, and they are effective," I say as I complete the job of sewing up the artificial valve that this particular patient will never need. "But remember that your own God-given valve is the best."

I also remind them that what I do is usually the last option. "Surgery should be done only when you have to do it," I say.

As someone who has done it for almost half a century, I know this full well. But because some of them may end up doing this procedure someday, or assisting in it, I want them to know that the surgeon must think on his feet. While I can't demonstrate this on a pig's heart, I tell them that there are many ways to insert a catheter, that when the conventional routes are blocked, one must open the chest and insert it right into a chamber of the heart.

"The surgeon will go anywhere!" I declare.

Like the point of honor about never sitting, this strikes me as having a broader meaning than a mere statement of surgical bravado; as a heart surgeon, I have followed pathways beyond the arterial. I have gone to some amazing places, tested emotional and physical limits—both mine and those of my patients— and I've experienced harrowing and awe-inspiring trauma and triumph.

I invite you now to come with me as I revisit them, as I tell

you the story of how the boy with the crippled hands and undiagnosed dyslexia, growing up in an impoverished society, went
on to perform over fifteen thousand open heart surgeries and
became one of America's most preeminent cardiac surgeons. I'll
introduce you to some of the people whose hearts were entrusted
to my hands.

YOUR
HEART,
MY HANDS

— *Chapter One* —

If Only They Knew

Late one night in the fall of 2014, I found myself on my porch, looking at the stars. Just as it had when I was a child in India, taking in the night sky led me to ponder life and the weird ways of the universe.

I had special cause for reflection that evening. A few hours earlier I'd been the guest of honor in a hotel ballroom filled with more than six hundred people. I'd received the President's Pursuit of Excellence Lifetime Champion Award from Rhode Island Hospital in Providence, where, for the previous four decades, I'd been a cardiac surgeon. I was the first physician to receive this award.

As I looked at the sky, I thought about the people who'd been at that evening's ceremony, and I thought about myself. They knew my professional highlights. They knew I'd performed more than fifteen thousand open heart surgeries. They knew I wasn't being recognized simply for being prolific. I'd been the driving force behind the heart surgery program's reputation for excellence and quality. While we might not have had the cachet of some of the big-name hospitals in New York, Los Angeles, Cleveland, or Houston, Rhode Island Hospital's cardiac center was consistently ranked among the top in the nation. A key reason for our high marks, I was reminded that evening, was my work there over four decades—my dedication to patient care and teaching, and my commitment to making the hospital a premier heart center.

But, I wondered, did the people who had filled that ballroom know how implausible it was that we'd all just spent the night celebrating my career? If they had imagined the time when I started out and pictured the trajectory of someone who could become a leading surgeon, my journey wouldn't be the proto-type. While it's true that both my grandfathers were medical men, by the time I came along, the circumstances of my parents and the realities of our life were as distant from theirs as Denver is from Deoghar.

To end up where I have, they would have thought one would first need an excellent education and extracurricular experi-ence, good health, strong family and community support, and a nice, cushy trust fund to fall back on. A surgeon such as me would have grown up in an upscale suburb, say, in Westches-ter, Fairfield, or Marin County, and my life would have been a direct ascent to success from the time I was getting straight A's at an exclusive private school. When I was starting out, surgeons didn't look like me, either—shouldn't I have been a six-foot-tall Caucasian male with perfect teeth?

Instead my upbringing was a surprising set of circumstances from which a preeminent cardiac surgeon was produced. No one else I know of in my field suffered two separate crippling hand injuries in childhood in rural India, with minimal health care available. No one else in my class missed as much school due to such injuries; no one else had to rely on a regimen of physical therapy, improvised by a dedicated mother with minimal school-ing, to make it back to the classroom. And I imagine there are few physicians who can claim as their most notable talents in childhood hopping trains, flying kites, and generally getting into mischief.

Then there was my learning disability, although it wasn't recognized as such at the time. As with most of those who suffered from dyslexia back then, people assumed I couldn't read or write well because I didn't care to—because I was lazy or stupid. My condition went undiagnosed for years, and it forced me to work twice as long in order to grasp the already-imposing body of knowledge required of a medical student.

When I arrived here, there was the issue of skin color. For a young Indian man, fitting into a medical establishment that was then as white as a Maine snowfall was a daunting challenge, and I felt the sting of racism in my early years.

And yet despite all that, there I was that night in 2014, looking at the stars—deciphering the constellations and zodiac signs in the night skies—after having been feted as one of America's top surgeons. It made me think of my own fate and recalled for me a time when it could have been said that I was born under a bad sign.

If only they knew, I thought.

—ᕀ *Chapter Two* ᕀ—

Problem Child

I was born in 1944 in my maternal grandparents' home in Darbhanga, in northeast India. Much of my childhood was spent in Deoghar (pronounced *DEEYO-gar*), about 150 miles southeast of Darbhanga. The small town is home to the Baidyanath Temple, which is famous because Hindus believe Lord Shiva—the first guru of Hinduism—visited it. My father, Avadh Bihari Singh, was the headmaster of our local high school. We lived on the school grounds in housing provided by the school. My mother, Krishna, was more than occupied running the household and looking after me, my two younger brothers, and my younger sister.

I grew up during a tumultuous period in India's history. The partition of what had been the British Indian Empire into India and Pakistan occurred in 1947, when I was just three years old. Part of that seismic change on the subcontinent was the division of Bengal Province, near Deoghar, into West Bengal and East Pakistan (which later became Bangladesh).

It was a dangerous time. "Nearly seventy years later," writes historian Nisid Hajari in his 2015 book *Midnight's Furies*, "partition has become a byword for horror. Instead of joining hands at their twinned births, India and Pakistan would be engulfed by some of the worst sectarian massacres the modern world has ever seen."

Thankfully, Deoghar was spared much of the violence. But when I think back, I'm struck by how the social climate of the time underscored the unsettled nature of my childhood. People had more on their minds than the upbringing of a stubborn child. Indeed, some of the divisions that roiled Indian society in that day were played out within my own family.

My maternal grandfather, Bhagwan Prasad Singh, was a London-educated physician. Although a native Indian, he wore a bow tie and a suit that looked as if it might have been tailored on Savile Row. He drank scotch, loved cricket, and called his colleagues "chaps." Although they were not blood relations, my paternal grandfather, Ram Ratan Singh, shared that common surname and was also a physician—a successful surgeon, in fact. There the similarities between the two men ended. My paternal grandfather was staunchly anti-British and pro-independence. Inspired by Gandhi, he wore handmade clothes and rode a bike to work. Despite his humble appearance, my paternal grandfather's family came from a higher caste than my mother's. When my father had the temerity to marry the daughter of an Anglicized, pro-Empire Indian—and from a lower social stratum, to boot—he was disowned by that branch of the family. That's why I never met Ram Ratan Singh, the grandfather with whom I would have had much in common, given that I ended up in the same profession. The day he died, my father came into my room, where I was playing with my younger brother Dilip.

"We're going," he said gruffly.

"Where?" I wanted to know.

"To pray for the soul of your grandfather."

"Nana died?" I asked tearfully, using the term for my mother's father, whom we knew well.

"No, no—your other grandfather."

I was puzzled. "We have another?"

"Yes, and we must pray for him," said my father crossly.

So my family and I climbed into a rickshaw that took us to the Hindu temple (we didn't own a car at that point). There we met the pundit, or *pandit* in Hindi, meaning "wise, learned man." He ushered us in and we knelt down and prayed, although I'm sure my father's prayers were uttered through clenched teeth for Ram Ratan Singh, a man who had disowned his son for marrying "beneath" him.

By contrast, I spent many hours watching Bhagwan Prasad Singh, my maternal, pro-British grandfather, treat patients at the clinic adjacent to his property mostly in the evenings. Nana, as we called him, was an eye, ear, nose, and throat specialist. In India at that time, ophthalmologists were also otolaryngologists, or ENT doctors. Although I took a great interest in Nana's work, early in my life it seemed more likely I'd become a chronic patient than a member of the medical profession. As a child I was often sick with asthma, allergies, and the like. One day when I was five, while walking in my grandfather's backyard, I tripped over my feet, fell down, and broke my right collarbone. I was in a sling for many months and missed some school and lots of normal childhood playtime. The accident had no lasting effect, but it was viewed as a sign of my frailty and an omen of what was to come.

I would be labeled a problem child, a troublemaker, and someone who could be counted on to cause mischief. I was rambunctious, yes. But I think the source of my alleged miscreant ways was simple curiosity. I was an inquisitive kid who liked to experience things firsthand. I was drawn to the natural world and always preferred exploring it over being told about it.

There was much to explore in the exotic land of my youth. Deoghar is surrounded by small mountains. Our backyard afforded a view of these rocky slopes, and held guava, mango, and blackberry trees. Wild animals—rabbits, monkeys, and, soaring above them, hawks—were frequent visitors. How could a restless little boy ignore such natural wonders in his own back-yard? One afternoon when I was seven, while my parents were sleeping, I climbed a guava tree. Doing so was nothing new—I loved fresh fruit, and it was my nature to obtain it myself, rather than wait for it to show up in our house thanks to someone else's labor. So I climbed to the top of the guava tree, ten to twelve feet off the ground, to pick some of the delicious fruit.

Unfortunately, some Hanuman langur monkeys had the same idea. I was there atop the tree when I heard Dilip yelling below.

"Look out! The monkeys are coming."

I turned and saw a monkey clambering deftly out on the branch toward me.

If you are envisioning an amusing chimpanzee or the chat-tering monkey you saw swinging from branches on your last visit to the zoo, forget it: there is nothing cute about a langur monkey about to strike. With an average weight of forty pounds, they aren't tiny, and they can leap twelve feet in a single bound. This particular monkey was quite literally in my face in a split sec-ond. He shrieked at me, and I found myself staring into a mouth framed by sharp fang-like teeth.

Startled and scared, I let go of the tree limb I'd been hanging on and crashed to the ground. I landed on a rock. Part of it lac-erated six inches of my forehead, very close to my left eye, caus-ing profuse bleeding. And that wasn't the worst part. My right elbow and hand had taken the brunt of the fall on the rock; my right elbow was shattered.

Dilip screamed for help. My parents came and we raced off to the local dispensary, which was more a simple emergency room than a sophisticated care center. The doctor sewed up my forehead with big, rope-like sutures, put a temporary cast on my arm to immobilize it, and told my parents I needed to go to a good hospital to get the treatment I really needed for my arm. The pain was unbearable, and I was scared. Mom spent all night with me, trying to calm me down.

The next day we went by train to Darbhanga, 150 miles away, where my grandfather had arranged for me to meet a bone specialist at the local hospital. He removed my plaster cast and saw that my elbow was mangled and that there was nerve damage. He said he would reset the arm while I was under general anesthesia. At that time in India, anesthesia was administered via a gauze mask over the face. Chloroform was poured over the mask while I inhaled deeply. I can still picture the mask descending, the woozy breathing, and the room spinning and humming as I slipped into unconsciousness. I had no way of knowing that there were much worse surgical procedures in my future.

After a few days, poor circulation in the extreme heat and humidity caused my arm to swell under the cast. The cast was removed, and it was discovered my hand had been set the wrong way. I was again put under general anesthesia while my arm was reset. I again experienced swelling and, eventually, bloody blisters under the cast. In an inauspicious start to my surgical career, I would slide sharp pieces of plastic between the cast and my arm to try to pop the blisters.

This cast came off after six weeks. The broken bone had healed, but my right arm and hand (I'm right-handed) were a mess. I couldn't bend my elbow. My hand was in a fixed extended position called frozen joint. I couldn't pick things up, I couldn't write, I couldn't even feed myself.

The obvious thing to do was to break my arm yet again and

hope that it reset properly. But things weren't that simple. While I'd had the cast on, I'd developed pneumonia, and I was still recovering from that. Because of the poor sanitary conditions of the time, I also had a severe case of hepatitis and had become jaundiced.

We returned to the surgeon, who, after examining me, explained to my parents that, with my liver in such a bad state, general anesthesia wasn't an option, because I could experience permanent damage or even die. But we still had a decision to make: leave the arm as it was or fracture it yet again.

This time, however, I would be wide awake the entire time.

I can still remember my father's explosive reaction to this news as we sat in the doctor's cramped, book-lined office.

"You are telling me that my oldest son will be a cripple!" he thundered.

The orthopedic surgeon, trained in London and one of the best in that part of India, began to politely protest that this was *not* what he was telling us. My father, in full rage, cut him off.

"You are telling me he will never be able to care for himself, that he will have no future... that he will end up a beggar on the streets!" He looked back at me, wild-eyed. I had never seen him like this. "You have shamed me with your foolish behavior, and you have shamed this family!"

I was taken aback.

"I...I'm sorry, Babuji...," I stuttered as I began to cry, using an Indian honorific for one's father. I had seen the frail, pathetic beggars on the fringes of the marketplace in Deoghar, and in my mind's eye I now saw myself among them, wearing rags and holding out a chipped, dirty bowl to passersby.

I began to cry harder.

"Stop this!" my mother said firmly, standing up to address

my father. "Your tantrum isn't going to change anything, and it's not going to bring your first son back."

Even in that tiny, airless room, the temperature seemed to drop several degrees. My father stiffened and went pale. Ignoring me and the doctor, who looked down at his notes at that point, embarrassed, he stormed out of the room.

Finally the truth was out. A truth that explained my father's distance and the anger that always seemed to simmer below the surface. Although well educated and a schoolteacher himself, he felt cursed, haunted—and perhaps with good reason. Avadh Bihari Singh had been wed once before. It was an arranged marriage, common in India. The union had produced a daughter and son. They'd lived in Lahore, in what is now Pakistan, where my father taught mathematics at the local university. When his children were young—the daughter three and the son just a year old—his wife took them on a trip to visit her parents. The train derailed and all three were killed.

My father left Lahore and never returned. Nor did he ever speak about his first family, his marriage, his wife, or his children. He subsequently lost more of his family when his father had disinherited him for marrying a second time beneath his caste. Now, with the oldest son quite obviously a failure, he felt that he was about to lose his family for a third time.

I was shocked at the revelation about my father's past, but even more traumatized by what he had said about my future. Was my life already over at age seven?

As I hunched over weeping, my mother stepped in to try to console me. She told me, "Get up, look up, and don't give up. We will do everything together to get you better."

Mom stood only five feet tall but had an outsize and profound influence on my life, even if I sometimes disappointed her.

She was the rock of the family: extremely intelligent, practical, but also sociable, and in contrast to my often-brooding father she had a quick wit and an engaging personality. I'm sure that the thought of what her miscreant son would have to endure the next day hurt her nearly as much as it did me, but she already had a plan to fix everything.

She prayed for a half hour every morning to the gods, chief among them Vishnu, the supreme being in Hinduism. She'd burn incense and place flowers in front of pictures and statues of the deities set up in a small space of worship in a corner of the bedroom. My father prayed daily, as well. But their devotions demonstrated their differences. Dad, somber and serious, prayed for an hour, and no one could disturb him. If the house was burning down during his time of worship, he didn't want to know. Mom's pious practices were more cheerful and efficient. She would devote about thirty minutes to the higher powers before getting on promptly with the business of life. And with a young family to raise and a particularly troublesome oldest son to contend with—me—business was brisk. Even the gods could be allotted only so much time in such a busy life.

On the night before I was to return to the doctor, I think I have a good idea of what their prayers might have been. My father probably beseeched the deities to make passersby generous with their coins to the street-corner beggar he was certain his son would now become. Mom, on the other hand, asked for strength. Strength in the arm that she was certain could be salvaged. She wasn't going to settle for leaving my hand as it was. She was going to do whatever it took to help me heal and work toward a good life.

The next morning, I was back at the hospital to have my arm reset. I was crying and screaming; I knew what was coming, and it was an even worse prospect than becoming a beggar. Anesthesia was out of the question because of the hepatitis I had developed. Instead of painkillers, I had four strong adults holding me down—one on each leg, one on my left arm, one on my head and chest. The surgeon and his assistant grabbed my hand. For the third time now, he would need to break my right elbow joint. This time, the break would need to be made at precisely the point where three bones—the humerus, the radius, and the ulna—converge. I saw the doctor position his hands carefully in order to break the joint cleanly. He looked up at his assistants, nodded, and they redoubled their grip on me. Then...

Snap!

I heard my bones break like a bamboo stick, and the scream I let out rumbled through those hospital halls and rolled up the mountain slopes, seeming as though it could be heard 792 miles away in Lahore.

Chapter Three

Progressive Resistance

The memory of that procedure—the sense of helplessness as I was held motionless, the dread of what was to come, the sounds of my bones snapping, and, of course, the pain itself—would torture my dreams for years to come. I'd wake up, soaked in sweat, just as the surgeon was breaking my elbow.

When the plaster cast was removed eight weeks later, my hand was flexed at a ninety-degree angle. The muscles of my hand were severely shortened and contracted. I couldn't extend my fingers. The only signs of hope were that I still retained some motor function (I could sometimes get my hand to do what my brain told it) and I had some feeling in my fingers. Still, I couldn't hold a pencil very well or feed myself with what was supposed to be my dominant hand.

To help with this, my mom bought me a *carrom* game. Sometimes described as "finger pool," carrom, popular in South Asia, is typically played on a twenty-nine-inch square board with corner pockets. The object of play is to use a flick of the finger to send a weighted striker disk—about the size of a large poker chip—into contact with lighter disks called carrom men, moving them into one of four corner pockets. The goal is to pocket the opponent's nine carrom men and the queen before they pocket yours.

I took to it and played for hours each day, which I'd continue to do for a few years, and the repetitive flicking improved the strength and dexterity of my fingers.

Although I enjoyed carrom, I still needed serious physical therapy and rehabilitation if I was going to be self-sufficient later in life.

In small-town India in 1951, such care didn't exist. Nor did schools that could accommodate someone with special needs. If I was going to get better, and if I was going to get educated, those things would have to happen at home.

Today, when you think of physical therapy, you might envision a facility that looks like a cross between an upscale gym and a doctor's office. In a typical PT center today, in either India or America, you will find patients young and old rehabbing from knee replacements, torn ACLs, or tennis elbow, reclining on clean, comfortable tables, watching high-definition TV, while ice is applied to their injuries or ultrasound—high-frequency sound waves that promote deep tissue healing—is administered painlessly through the affected area. Others perform strength exercises using colorful elastic tubing or on snazzy-looking resistance training machines, while being carefully watched and supervised by qualified professional physical therapists.

I assure you that this bears no resemblance to the physical therapy I endured in India in 1951. There was no TV. The only ice in Darbhanga was used to keep bodies in the morgue from decomposing. I didn't have ultrasound; I had anguish.

And it started not with a scheduled appointment at a facility, but in our house, with my mother dragging me out of bed.

"Wake up, Arun," she said. "Today we begin to heal."

I groggily followed her outside. My mother held out a brick, a bag, and a rope. She put the brick in the bag and attached the rope. She then tied the rope around the wrist of my right hand.

"Mama," I said, as my arm jerked down from the weight of the bag, "what are you doing?"

"*I* am not doing anything here," she said. "You, Arun…you are going to start to get stronger. Today. Now walk…"

I staggered down the street like an inmate in a penal colony, dragging my brick behind me. My mother accompanied me the first day, urging me on, as we covered two blocks from my house and back. I sobbed, I whined, I suffered, but I did it. I continued to drag my little burden twice a day for the next several weeks. Each day my mother would increase the weight slightly.

Toting the bricks was very painful and frustrating, both physically and emotionally. I was aware of people watching me and whispering that this must be some kind of punishment. I was also aware that this wasn't how other kids my age spent their time. They were off at school or outside playing. I wasn't part of their world.

But as I was feeling sorry for myself, something was happening: I began to get stronger.

With suggestions from the orthopedic surgeon in Darbhanga, my mother had devised what we call today a DIY (do-it-yourself) at-home rehab program for me. And if the idea of having your child drag a brick around sounds harsh, in principle it was really no different from what physical therapists of today do with much fancier equipment. It was progressive resistance, the same principle behind weight training in a gym; the idea is that as the weight steadily increases, the muscles respond by producing more fibers. Thus they grow larger and stronger.

In a gym or rehab setting, the stimulus is measured by the number of plates on the barbell, the level of resistance of the machine, the thickness of the tubing. For me it was the number of bricks in a sack. (I think I got up to four.)

Gradually the strength and range of motion in my elbow improved. But my wrist remained very weak; I still had great difficulty grasping and holding on to items. So my mother had me start the next phase of my rehab. This one, if witnessed in twenty-first-century America, would likely prompt an emergency call to Child Protective Services. But this was rural India in the early 1950s. Though the sight of a child hanging by his arm from a window might have seemed a bit odd, it was certainly nothing to get concerned about. The neighbors, who knew what a handful I was, probably assumed it was some novel but well-deserved punishment devised by my parents.

The windows in our home were higher on the wall than those in a typical American house and had vertical and horizontal bars across them to keep intruders out. My mother would lift me up to one of the higher bars, and there I would hang three feet off the ground. This was even more painful than pulling the weighted bag—it strains the muscles, which in my case were weak to start with. I was also afraid of falling and reinjuring myself. I was forced to do this for fifteen minutes twice a day. How I dreaded those sessions! But I knew I had no choice but to hang from the window every morning and every evening, and then to do it again the next day, and the next day, and on and on.

We were on our way to healing my nearly ruined hand. But healing the rift with my father was a different story. Despite the progress I was making thanks to my mother, he was very angry and frustrated with me, and was still convinced I was going to become a beggar. It was up to my mother to help with my education during the long stretches I wasn't in school. Unlike my father, the school headmaster, she hadn't graduated high school. But whatever she read, she knew well, so she taught me the basics—the alphabet, math, English, and reading.

I struggled with literature, because I'd never had basic education in grammar, and also, although the term and diagnosis didn't exist at the time, I was dyslexic. Even today, when I read a book I don't always go smoothly from line to line. I go from one section to another, starting at the top but sometimes moving around the page. Then I read the page again because I'm sure I've missed something.

Yet with her pushing and cajoling me, I applied myself—and surprised everyone, except maybe my mother. As it turned out, I graduated from high school at age fourteen, two or three years younger than the average student in India at the time. I think this was possible in part because of my homeschooling during times of recovery. Because my injuries hampered my ability to write, I memorized as much material as possible. When I was back in school, I did OK because I could memorize all the answers. Did I understand the answers? Not really. It wasn't until much later that I could do the second, more important part: really comprehend the underlying meaning of what I'd read.

The stubborn curiosity that put me in a guava tree occupied by monkeys played out in other ways when I was a kid. Although I managed to stay clear of situations serious enough to involve the police, I was forever getting into trouble.

For example, I used to hop trains. The train station in our town was the end of the line. The next stop was about four miles away. In the afternoon, as the train pulled out of our station, I'd run alongside and then hop on for the twenty-minute ride to the next town, Jasidih Junction. The station there was the main one on the line, and I wanted to see what things were like in this busier town. I'd walk around the station, eat some peanuts, take in the sights, and then, unburdened by a ticket, jump on the train back to Deoghar. I'd be gone for two hours. This went on for some time, and my parents had no idea. Eventually Mom figured it out, and my train-hopping career came to a screeching halt.

A few years later, I thought I'd hit upon an ingenious way to get a little pocket money. It was our custom to nap during the hot summer afternoons. After waking, we'd enjoy ourselves with fresh fruit, especially watermelon. One day I saw a woman selling slices of watermelon for fifty paise, or about a dime. This gave me an idea. While the rest of my family was sleeping, I took our watermelon, cut it into slices, and sold them in a stand I set up not far from our home. I sold the entire watermelon in less than half an hour and had twice as much money as what a single watermelon cost. Now all I needed to do was to buy a new watermelon and bring it home before the rest of my family woke.

One problem: When I went to the store to buy the new watermelon, the store was out of them. I went to another store and it was the same story. There were no watermelons to be had anywhere! I slunk back home, lay down, and acted as if I'd never been gone. When it came time for our post nap refreshments, my mother couldn't find the watermelon. She asked everybody where it was. My brothers and sister answered honestly that they didn't know. My mother knew me well enough to know that it was probably my fault. I knew her well enough to know there was no point in lying. I told her what I'd done and why. She got very upset with me, saying I'd stolen from the family. Mom then dragged me by the ear and, in front of my siblings (to keep them from getting any ideas), I was thoroughly belted on the buttocks.

— Chapter Four —

Heartless, Beautiful Sport

My injuries, illnesses, and antics took a toll on our family. My mother spent so much time on me that she couldn't give my siblings equal attention. Meanwhile, my aloof father, consumed by his own shame and losses, became increasingly withdrawn from all of us. He took his refuge in more hedonistic pursuits. Most evenings his friends, not his family, got his time. His buddies gathered in our home from eight p.m. to midnight to play cards, drink tea, and either smoke tobacco or chew *paan*, a stimulant that's a mixture of betel nut, tobacco, herbs, and spices.

My mother was not happy with this turn of events. She wanted us to move from Deoghar to Patna, which is an ancient city that sprawls along the south bank of the Ganges River in the state of Bihar, located in northeast India. The city's history spans three millennia, and it is known as one of the birthplaces of two ancient religions, Buddhism and Jainism.

The reasons for us moving, however, had nothing to do with antiquity. The hope was that there my father might get a better-paying job more in line with his credentials. Also the schooling and health care were better in Patna. And there young Arun would be separated from his troublemaking friends back in Deoghar.

As it turned out, my father's situation did improve: when I

was ten, he took a position as the head of the board of education for high schools in Patna. In his role he decided what textbooks would be used in schools. Many people in this position accepted bribes from publishers to select their books. While my father had his faults, corruptibility was not one of them. He refused to take the bribes. We remained a family of moderate means.

In Patna we lived in a yellow building owned by my maternal grandfather, Nana, who rented it out. He allowed us to stay there for free (something that I'm sure helped fuel my father's sense of shame and failure). While my mother kept a neat and tidy home, we lived in a squalid neighborhood. Drainage was poor, and filthy water often backed up onto the streets, which were generally littered with trash that was picked over by the many dogs that ran wild. Typhoid, malaria, and even smallpox were still common childhood diseases among our very poor neighbors.

Because we arrived in Patna after the new school year had started, I would again miss out on schooling and would have to continue my education at home. That independent, rapscallion streak of mine became more pronounced the more isolated I became from other children. I was often homebound due to injuries. I saw other kids living normal lives and got frustrated, angry, and jealous. Why couldn't I do what they were doing? Because I felt so constrained, I took advantage of every opportunity to explore, investigate, or otherwise pursue what interested me, regardless of whether I was supposed to do so.

Perhaps because I spent so much time wandering around outside, I became interested in gardens and flowers. I imagined a new career for myself, one that wouldn't require the inconvenience of attending school. I'd become a gardener! How pleasant, I thought, to spend one's time immersed in such beauty. An even better horticultural career path seemed to present itself to me when I was walking by a nearby park and saw a garden filled with peacock-blue roses. I thought that if I could plant and grow such roses and sell them in the market, I would be a rich man. Who needed school to do that?

I walked over to the gardener, who was tending the roses.

"Excuse me, sir," I said.

"What?" he replied grouchily.

"Could I possibly get one of these roses?" I asked in my most polite voice. "I'd be willing to pay for it."

"Kid," he said, "this is a city park. They don't sell these roses."

I grew indignant. "Fine," I said. "If you won't give me one, I'll just come back and steal it."

"Oh really?" said the gardener, who had now laid down his shears and put his hands on his hips. He towered over me. "You're going to come back and steal city property, eh? That's great. We'll be waiting for you, so that we can arrest you and throw you in jail."

I'm sure this gardener was hoping to intimidate me, but I was pugnacious. He wanted to escalate this? Game on. In my mind I'd made a perfectly reasonable request, and now he was just standing between me and something I wanted.

"You won't put me in jail, old man," I said. "Because you will never be able to catch me. I'm coming back, and I'm getting my roses. You'll see!"

He just laughed and turned away. He was treating me like a joke. I'd show him. Two days later, on a hot, sunny afternoon when most of Patna was taking a siesta, I took a shovel, went back to the city garden, hopped the fence, and started digging out a rosebush. When I was halfway through, somebody grabbed me from behind. It was the gardener. He hadn't been fooled for a minute.

"I told you that if you came back and tried to take these roses, you'd be in trouble," he said.

"I'm not afraid of you," I said, squirming as I tried to free myself from his grip. "I want one of those roses."

At that point I saw a twinkle in his eye. "Tough guy, are you?" he said. "OK, well, I'm going to do you a favor. I'm not going to tell your parents about this."

For once I was taken aback. "You...you're not?"

"No," he said, with a malicious grin. "But you're going to wish I had."

My heart skipped a beat. What was he going to do? Kill me? Instead he dragged me through the park and locked me into a dark, dingy toilet. This wasn't some municipal restroom with sinks, flush toilets, and a hand dryer, such as you'd find in an American park. This was essentially a rickety wooden outhouse—barely big enough for one adult—with a hole in the floor. It probably hadn't been cleaned in years. The stench was indescribable.

"Doesn't exactly smell like roses in there, does it?" the gardener said, chuckling, as he put the lock in place on the wooden door and walked off.

"Come back!" I cried. "You can't do this to me! I'll die in here!"

For a few frantic minutes, I thought I actually would. Desperately I looked around for a way to get out. There was only one—down through the hole and into what looked and smelled like a lake of excrement at the bottom. I contemplated it briefly, but the thought was too horrifying even for a rebel like me. With my back to the wall, as far away from the odious hole as possible, I slowly sank down to the sodden dirt floor, resigned to the fact that I was stuck here.

After what seemed like an eternity, the gardener returned

and unlocked the door. "If I ever see you in this park again, I'm calling the police," he said. "Get out."

I'd like to say this experience changed my life, and that I turned over a new leaf from that day on. But it would take more than the rough hands of a gardener to knock the chip off my shoulder. I continued to roam Patna, usually alone. I developed a bit of a tough-guy swagger, a streetwise mentality like some kind of Indian Artful Dodger. I prowled the markets, the station, and the squalid back alleys. I wasn't picking pockets like the fictional Dodger of Dickens's *Oliver Twist*, but I was clearly flouting authority, and I wore my reputation as a bad kid like a badge of honor.

While my mother's innate skill as a teacher ensured that I would not become an illiterate, the lack of structure in my daily schedule led to more mischief and, ultimately, another life-changing accident.

If you're familiar with the book or movie *The Kite Runner*, then you have some idea of the role of kite flying in the culture of Southeast Asia. It is not like kite flying in the West, where a parent and child might go to a field on a windy day and leisurely unspool a kite shaped like a cartoon character. The kite flying in Patna was aggressive and competitive. Tournaments were held in which the goal was to use your kite to cut the strings of other kites; the winner was the last one with a kite in the sky.

"The sole reason for kites is to fight them," wrote Kirk Semple in a 2007 *New York Times* story about the sport in Afghanistan. "A single kite aloft is nothing but an unspoken challenge to a neighbor: Bring it on!"

That's certainly the way it was in Patna. The goal wasn't to get your kite higher, or have the prettiest kite, or perform the most graceful aerial ballet with your kite. No, sir. This was a combat in the skies, and the sight of a swarm of kites, maneuvering like fighter planes in an aerial dogfight, was exciting. There was even a sound to them that I loved, the whistling and buzzing noise when you jerked the string to go faster.

I decided very quickly that this was something I wanted to excel in. I saved money to buy the equipment—efforts like my watermelon entrepreneurship would finance kite flying—and began to gain proficiency in this heartless but beautiful sport.

The objective was simple: slash through a competitor's line and send his kite plummeting to the ground. To learn the right tactics for doing this, and to avoid having my own line sliced, I sought the advice of a professional kite tactician. Yes, such an occupation—if you can call it that—existed in India at the time, and most of the young kite flyers like me hired these guys, mostly older men, to advise them.

I can still see the weather-beaten face of my coach, whose name was Lalo. He must have been in his fifties and was gray haired, with a few teeth missing. He worked for free, as I recall, and unlike some of the other coaches—who were Svengali-like in their control over their young charges—mine was calm and patient. He could sense that I was dedicated to doing well in this sport, and he taught me what I needed to know.

Starting with the "special sauce" of kite flying: *manja*. This is a thick, gooey concoction made of powdered glass that coats a kite's string and is then dried in the hot sun to make it crisp and sharp like a razor blade. Under my gap-toothed coach's tutelage, I learned how to mix powdered glass (which we got by grinding up old electric bulbs) into a gluey paste with soft rice and juice. You would then spool yards of thread through this. Once it dried, your line was stiff and as sharp as a hawk's talons.

My coach then taught me the ways of the wind. Kite flying

requires an intimate knowledge of wind dynamics, and particularly how they affect your ability to attack another kite. You have to decide whether to come from above or beneath; you need to learn how to position the tip of the kite before you start rolling the string, which is how you guide the kite as it swoops in for the kill. How fast you roll the string, which, given its sharpness, could cut your fingers, is also part of the art.

My skills are rusty now. But there was one lasting consequence that hardly seemed like a benefit at the time. A serious flier had to keep his eyes on his kite—often for hours, and while staring into the blazing Indian sun. You may laugh at this, but I contend that as a result, I developed ocular muscles of steel. I didn't require glasses until I was about Lalo's age, my mid-fifties, and at the time my optometrist commented on the strength of my eyes. When I told him that I suspected it was from staring for hours into the sky at a kite, he just stared back at me for a moment. Then he shrugged, nodded, and said, "You know, you might be right."

There was another long-lasting benefit from this. Kite flying—which demanded patience and concentration—helped me develop the focus to concentrate during six-hour surgeries. Am I saying kite flying should be a required part of surgical training, or that if you go outside now and stare at the sky you won't need glasses? No; perhaps somewhere in this seventy-two-year-old Arun is a need to justify the many hours my eleven-year-old self spent gazing up at the heavens.

At the time there was no doubt. Despite its seedy reputation, despite some of the unsavory adults on the fringes of the sport, I knew kite flying was a good thing for me. I'd felt so impaired and isolated for so much of my childhood. Now, suddenly, I had an outdoor activity to do with other kids my age. And it was something I had a talent for! Over my six months as a competitive kite flyer I became, if not quite a top gun, an experienced pilot. Kite flying gave me feelings of confidence, capability, and strength that'd been missing in my life.

My parents, of course, saw it differently. They were appalled by my kite flying, especially my father, who saw this as further proof that I was on the road to becoming an abject failure in life, only deepening his shame.

Alas, I suppose that view was given credence after my next accident.

Less than six months after taking up kite flying, I was in a tournament qualifying round. It was a beautiful spring day, and my spirit and equipment were set to soar. I flew a black-and-red kite very high in the sky. I was off to a great start, cutting many others' kites, catching them, and bringing them down.

Suddenly another boy's kite appeared out of nowhere. He was close to cutting my kite and knocking me out of the competition. I was so caught up in the moment that I wasn't minding my surroundings. I forgot that I was standing near a ditch with a fallen pole behind me. As I was working quickly to get my kite out of range, furiously pulling and spinning the string, I tripped on the pole and fell down five feet into the ditch. In a flash my kite was cut and my left arm was broken.

Another kid pulled me out of the ditch and got word to my parents. After all that had already happened to our family because of me, I knew my parents would be irate. Indeed, my father said I could stay there on the ground writhing in pain; he wasn't going to take me to the hospital. My mother arrived and pulled me up. We went to the hospital, where my hand and arm were put in a cast.

The fracture was the worst possible, with the two bones

of the forearm, the ulna and radius, broken in the same place. When just one of the bones breaks, the other can provide support. With both snapped like tree branches, recovery was going to be prolonged, and I would again be very limited in what I could do for myself. As had happened with my right arm, I had pain, swelling, and blisters.

When the cast came off after six weeks, the arm hadn't healed well. The two broken bones, the radius and ulna, were overlapping. The doctors decided to reset my arm and put my hand in a plaster cast. It stayed on for six months. I missed another year of school while I rehabbed the arm, using some of the techniques I'd done for my right arm. So more brick lugging. More window hanging. I was very familiar with the pain of those exercises by now. Even worse, I was familiar with the feeling of being excluded from normal activities of kids my age. That pain was even greater than before, as I missed the sense of freedom kite flying had brought. The day of the accident was the last time I ever flew a kite.

More than six decades later, those two childhood accidents are still with me. While my mother's primitive physical therapy regimen certainly helped, it couldn't totally undo the long-term damage. My left arm is an inch or so shorter than my right. Decades later, both my hands and arms are atrophied. While they never failed me when it came to wielding a scalpel, I often lack the strength necessary for simple daily activities like working a screwdriver or opening a jar. I couldn't tie my shoelaces or pajamas until adulthood.

Perhaps, I sometimes joke to my wife, Barbara, I ought to get back on the old exercise regimen. Maybe I should spend a little more time hanging with one arm from the window of our home in Providence. ("Don't expect me to catch you when you fall," she responds. *Touché!*)

In all seriousness, I can see a clear line from those accidents to my career as a cardiac surgeon, despite the physical toll they took on me. Because of the physicians in my family, and because of how doctors helped me, I was inspired to go into medicine. As unlikely as it may have sounded at the time, the boy with two crippled hands, the boy who could barely read or write because of dyslexia, the boy who ran with the wrong crowd, who besmirched the name of his family, and who seemed to get into trouble constantly was on the road to medical school.

But as with much of my early life, that road was pitted with obstacles, most of my own making.

Chapter Five

My Own World, My Own Rules

Most of the young surgeons I meet today have steadily ascended the academic ladder. These bright, dedicated men and women started early. Their trajectory is typically marked by science camps or volunteer work in hospitals while still in high school, by college summers spent in African missions or clinics in underprivileged communities, or by prestigious fellowships. They gain honor society invitations and have jaw-dropping SAT and MCAT scores.

It's all very impressive and bears very little resemblance to my academic career. Not only was I, at best, an average student, I was actively looking for ways to subvert, if not avoid, my education entirely.

My stumble toward medical school began at age fourteen with a flop on the most important exam of my young life. Every year, students in India must take a rigorous examination to graduate from high school. The exam is given in May, and when I took it the test included a lot of history, math, literature, and language arts. Students were required, quite reasonably, to demonstrate some understanding of our Indian culture and history and to show some proficiency in the Hindi and Sanskrit languages.

I cared not a fig about any of this. A rich, five-thousand-year-old culture? Boring. Epic heroes and villains? Yawn. The birthplace of modern religions? Give me a break.

I failed the test. Fortunately for me, those who didn't do well got a second chance in September. Because the alternative was to drop out of school and essentially fulfill my father's prophecy that I'd end up a beggar, I actually buckled down a little for the retest, and I got a middle-of-the-pack grade.

Still, an average grade on the exam meant you would go to an average college. Mine was in the very town of Patna, where I lived.

I wasn't going very far, in any sense.

Even by Indian standards, fourteen was a young age to start college. Most kids in India entered college at ages sixteen to eighteen (and that is still true today). Add to that my proclivity for finding trouble, and it is no surprise that my college years bore little resemblance to those of my sons or their friends, or most young Americans of today. Mine are not memories of leafy campuses, inspiring professors, or lifelong friendships forged in an environment of intellectual discovery.

I attended the College of Commerce, Patna. Not a bad school, but, as the name suggests, it was geared mostly toward getting students on some kind of career track. An elite institute of learning it was not.

At Commerce I was a boy in a young man's world. Most of my fellow students were three or four years older. Some of them sported beards and mustaches, making them look even older, whereas I looked younger than my already-tender age. It was as if a ten-year-old child had accidentally wandered onto a college campus. I saw the strange looks when I'd walk into class and heard the snickers and comments from my classmates. "Who let that kid in here?"

In an attempt to fit in, I tried to take up smoking, a popular habit among cool older kids at the time. After several attempts resulted in extended coughing fits, I gave up. At the time it seemed like another failure. I also tried to shave in the hopes that this would stimulate beard growth. It didn't. (I still can't grow a proper beard.)

One group of guys did seem to accept me. At least they allowed me to accompany them when they would go hang around in the local parks or at the movie theaters in Patna. They were a rough crowd, more or less a gang, who would ride by my house on their bikes and whistle. That was my signal to join them.

As soon as she saw them, my mom sensed that they were trouble. She was right—although I didn't realize exactly what kind of trouble. Most of these guys were of the hirsute, smoking type. But one of them, a guy named Amit, always seemed to be staring at me. It was a malevolent glare, and I was always afraid that he wanted to beat the hell out of me the first chance he could. That wasn't what he was after, I learned. One day, the group decided to catch a movie and asked if I wanted to come along. "Sure!" I said.

Immediately Amit, usually a man of limited vocabulary, spoke up. "The kid can ride with me."

His ride, like that of all of those guys, was a beat-up three-speed bike. So I sat on the handlebars and off we went, winding our way through the back streets of Patna. At one point Amit took a sharp turn, and we veered off from the rest of the group. I thought he was taking a shortcut. Then I noticed we were on the outskirts of town. He pulled into a field that was sheltered from view by a grove of mango trees. We stopped.

"What are we doing here, Amit?" I asked as I hopped off. He leaned the bike against a tree and approached me menacingly.

"Here's what *you're* doing," he growled. And with that he unbuckled his belt and unzipped his trousers.

It took me a few seconds to even process what was going on. I had no sexual experience at this point, and I suppose I had never really considered that sex with another man was even possible.

"On your knees," he demanded. He put his arm on my shoulder and tried to force me down to perform oral sex on him.

I imagine that with one well-placed kick at that moment I could have stopped this sexual predator for good. But I was too scared for that. Instead I pushed him away and ran as fast as I could through the trees and onto a nearby street where a bunch of laborers were taking a break from their work. I wanted to tell them what had happened to me and see what kind of street justice they might mete out on Amit, but I just kept running.

I never told anyone this story. Amit, of course, never spoke of it, either. The crowd of tough guys we hung around with would have been incensed at an attempted homosexual assault by one of their own on someone they knew, even someone like me who was on the periphery of their circle. But had I gone to them, it would have been my word against his. I opted to remain silent. Instead I spent the rest of my time at the college trying to avoid this guy. The few times I saw Amit, I immediately walked the other way, or moved to another corner of the room.

The incident with Amit ended my association with this unsavory crowd, and although my mother would never know the real reason, she was happy to see that. Homosexuality was such a taboo subject in Indian society at the time I decided not to tell my parents. Although I'm sure they would have understood that I was the victim, word of such a thing could have labeled even a victim as a sexual deviant—the last thing my family needed as we were trying to make our lives in a new city.

Cut off from the gang, I began to grow isolated again, and before long I was looking for opportunities to wander off on my own path, a path that inevitably led to trouble. I found it when my required history class at Commerce took a field trip to Nalanda, about sixty miles out of Patna.

Nalanda is truly a remarkable place. For over eight hundred years, starting in the third century BC, it has been a center of spiritual and religious learning. The site of a monastery and an ancient university, Nalanda is where many scholars believe Buddhism developed into an organized religion. Now a UNESCO World Heritage site, in the early 1960s it was a collection of towering, ancient stucco-and-stone buildings, long abandoned, but still imposing.

While our professor wanted to expose us to this seminal place of learning, I had something else in mind. While the class toured the main ruins, I sneaked off looking to find something I could sell. I suppose I still had this idea that by taking something of beauty and value—as I had attempted to do with the roses in the city park—I could make a quick buck without having to endure the drudgery of schooling.

Improbably, considering that it was a center for Buddhism, a religion that rejects material things, there were always rumors of golden icons, ancient coins, and artifacts left in the ruins of Nalanda. I began looking around and spotted what I thought would be just the spot for some treasure like that: a long fissure running along one of the stones at ground level. I took a long stick and probed the crack. In a flash, like the confetti tendrils fired from a Taser, a snake sprang out. In seconds it had wrapped itself around my feet. I managed to kick myself loose and ran for my life as the snake—which I had probably disturbed during a morning nap—slithered back to its lair.

I was shaken, of course. India is home to many venomous snakes, and to this day I have no idea which species I might have disturbed, whether cobra, viper, or krait. People ask me, "What color was it? Was it striped? Was its head shaped like a diamond?" I just know it was a snake, a long one, and an angry one, and I'm sure that if it had gotten its fangs into me, or constricted itself around my body, I would have been in serious trouble.

One of my classmates saw the whole thing happen. He had spotted me wandering off and decided to follow. He knew that baby-faced Arun was always up to something interesting. Worse, this guy was from Patna, and he knew my family. He reported the incident to my mother, who was furious. Not only over my stupidity in poking sticks into dark crevices, but for my continuing disobedience, my flouting of rules, my propensity for getting into trouble.

"What are you doing with your life?" she asked me. "What is wrong with you?"

I didn't have a good answer. I knew I wasn't really evil. I'd met some genuine bad guys by that point, and I realized that I was not like them. But I didn't like boundaries, I chafed at authority, and I was inquisitive. I was also rootless. While I was blessed to have had a strong and loving mother and a good family, I could count few friends. Because of my misadventures and the various injuries and accidents that had kept me out of school, I'd ended up spending much of my childhood alone.

I had created my own rules, my own world.

I continued to teeter along like that for three years at Commerce. While I managed to avoid any more serious danger, I followed my own path and kept my own counsel. In school I did the minimum possible amount of work to get by. And yet, somehow, my grades were good enough that when I graduated at age seventeen, I was accepted to Darbhanga Medical College, a state college with no tuition. Even more surprisingly, I was also offered admission to a much higher-rated medical school in my hometown. But when my mother heard that, she forbade me from accepting. She wanted me out of Patna. The ostensible reason was that she didn't want me mixing with the wrong sorts again. I would be living with her parents, and Mom thought that the formidable presence of my grandfather Nana would help keep me on the straight and narrow. But I think the real reason was that, as much as she loved me, she needed a break from her troublesome older son. And maybe, she hoped, a change would do me good.

Chapter Six

All In

Why did I even bother applying to medical school? Because as a child who was always getting injured or sick, I had had plenty of experience with doctors, and I admired their skills. I was also close with my Nana, and I loved hanging around the clinic attached to his home.

In a time and place when regulations about patient privacy were nonexistent, I was welcome to sit in on my grandfather's procedures. He enjoyed having me there. I saw him literally help the blind to see, as he did with a number of patients with cataracts. But the most memorable moment was when he treated a choking child.

When a local child had swallowed a large coin, and it stuck in his throat, he was rushed to Nana's office. I happened to be there visiting him when it happened. There was a clamor at the door, and in rushed a group of people. The child was blue and his mother was wailing. All was commotion. My grandfather gently nudged the others out of the way and calmly inserted a scope down the child's throat. As I watched, he then stuck a pair of forceps in, and, as smoothly as if he were flicking an ash from his cigar, plucked out the coin. Almost immediately the child turned pink again and started talking. Amid the tears of joy and thanks, Nana calmly walked over to the sink in his surgery room and washed off the coin—a silver one, as I recall. He held it up to the parents, smiled, and said, "This is my fee."

He then pocketed the coin.

That got my attention. So you could make people see…bring choking children back to life…*and* make money? Interesting. And, I had noted, Nana certainly made money. He wore the finest suits, drank the best scotch, and lived in a five-bedroom house that was a mansion compared to ours. Also, unheard of in India at that time, he owned *three* cars—a Ford Custom, a Chevrolet, and an Opel.

My father wanted me to be an engineer. But I wasn't good at math. Besides, I thought, what engineer owned three cars?

My grandfather encouraged me to pursue medicine, not just for the material rewards, but out of a sense of obligation. He knew how competent and skilled surgeons had helped me recover from my injuries as a child. Now, he suggested, it was my turn.

"Your doctors helped you when you were a kid, Arun," he said during one of my visits. "Now maybe you'll become a doctor and help other kids."

That stuck with me. For once I began thinking about something other than my own instant gratification, my next silly scheme for getting rich, or my next impulsive dive into trouble.

You might think that this was the point when I began to see the light and take my studies and my life a little more seriously.

Not quite. I still wasn't ready to shed my bad habits or to summon the inner resolve it takes to succeed.

In medical school I picked up right where I'd left off in college. We were ranked by our grades, and since I had done as little as possible at Commerce, I was in the lowest third of my medical school class.

At first I did my best to maintain my mediocre academic

standing. Part of the problem was, as usual, my attitude. While I liked the idea of owning three cars someday like my grandfather, I definitely didn't like the idea of studying three hours a night. But as I became lost in the increasingly challenging lectures and readings, I realized something else was at play. I'd always had problems with reading comprehension. It was one reason I'd done so poorly on the college exam. That continued in medical school. Somehow, whatever the instructor wrote on the board ended up garbled in my notes. I lost focus quickly. I couldn't concentrate and would often end up getting kicked out of class for talking when I should have been listening to the lecture.

In a day and age when the concept of learning disorders was barely understood by educational psychologists, my problem, which would not be diagnosed until much later, went unrecognized by me, my parents, and my teachers.

I was dyslexic.

Dyslexia is a complicated and in some ways still poorly understood cognitive disorder. The International Dyslexia Association defines it as a "language-based learning disability." Although it is often thought of as a problem specifically with reading, students with dyslexia experience difficulty with both the spoken and the written word. They have trouble writing, spelling, and even pronouncing words.

These were—and, to some extent, remain—challenges for me. Back then it was mystifying. Here's an example of how it would affect me: In Physiology 101, one of the first and most fundamental classes in any program of medical instruction, the professor would say something like this, explaining the human circulatory system: "The blood pushes out when the heart contracts. We call it output."

Simple enough, right? He would then go on to explain in

detail how that output was regulated—by the blood pressure, by the heart rate, by the force of the heart's contractions.

And by that point I'd be lost, because the words would enter my head in some garbled fashion. As if my brain possessed its own malfunctioning editing system, it would come out grossly oversimplified. I might hear "blood…heart…regulated…contraction."

It was like receiving a text or email with missing words and having to puzzle out the complete message based on incomplete information.

An early scholar of this condition referred to dyslexia as "congenital word blindness." That's exactly what it's like. I was blind and deaf to certain words—often they were the same words, but occasionally new ones presented problems, too. Even today I must carefully read and reread emails and articles to make sure I've retained everything.

As he relates in his memoir *My Dyslexia*, Philip Schultz— who grew up in Rochester, New York, in the 1950s—was consigned as a child to what was commonly referred to in his school as "The Dummy Class."

He later went on to win a Pulitzer Prize for poetry.

Many dyslexics have gone on to achieve remarkable things professionally: Pablo Picasso, Steven Spielberg, Sir Richard Branson, to name just a few. In my own field, my friend and colleague Dr. Delos "Toby" Cosgrove—an eminent cardiac surgeon who later became president and CEO of Cleveland Clinic—is an inspiring example of what those with dyslexia can achieve.

Like Toby and many of those other overachievers with dyslexia, I learned to manage it a little better as I got older. But as an eighteen-year-old with a brain that just seemed to work strangely and differently from everyone else's, it was frustrating, disheartening, and infuriating at times. Blind to my word blindness, I responded to my inhibited ability to learn in medical school with what seemed like a perfectly logical solution at the time: I played cricket.

While that may seem an odd strategy for getting through medical school or overcoming a learning disability, it made perfect sense to me then. Indians are mad about cricket. It's like American baseball, football, basketball, and NASCAR rolled into one. In India, cricketers are famous and feted like movie stars. I knew I wasn't good enough to be a pro, but I thought proficiency in the game would offset my obvious deficits as a student, make me more popular, and somehow improve my scholarly standing (I hadn't quite figured that part out).

Besides, swinging the cricket bat on a sunny morning at the college cricket pitch seemed far preferable to sitting in another class, wrestling with strange and fragmented medical terminology.

I became a pretty decent cricketer, despite a weak arm (the result of my injury) that kept me from being the bowler, the cricket equivalent of the pitcher in baseball. Meanwhile, my social life also expanded—slightly. I made my first real friend—a fellow of character, too, not like some of the lowlifes I had been associating with at Commerce College. Bijoy Mehta was an excellent student and an eloquent speaker; he was on the school's debate team. He had a deep command of literature—not just the medical literature, but great works in both Hindi and English. Listening to Bijoy was an education in itself. He talked to me about current affairs, of which I knew little. It was from Bijoy that I first learned about a brewing conflict in a place called Vietnam, and about how black Americans were fighting for their civil rights, using tactics borrowed from an Indian, whose name I recognized but whose significance had heretofore eluded me: Mohandas K. Gandhi. The world outside Patna and

Darbhanga was changing; young people everywhere were being roused to action against perceived injustices, and Bijoy was keeping up with all of it—while at the same time getting straight A's in medical school.

Bijoy (who later became a successful cardiologist in New York) was the first peer I could consider a role model. I wanted to be able to speak like him, to think like him. I wanted to be as tuned into the world as he was. I wasn't sure how I could. It began to dawn on me, however, that I would probably not achieve all this by simply playing cricket while also playing catch-up in all my classes because I didn't fully understand what was being said. Something had to change.

At the end of the first year of medical school, I headed home for the summer recess. It was early May, a Friday, and I was on the train from Darbhanga to Patna. I spotted a familiar face among the passengers who boarded at the first stop: my uncle Shivnandan. This was my mother's younger sister's husband. He was a physician and, like Nana, an ENT specialist. I liked him and was happy to see him appear amid the faces in the crowded car.

"Uncle Shiv!" I called.

He made his way over to me, a grave expression on his face. "Arun, I don't think you've heard the news, have you?"

"What news?" I asked.

He put his hand on my shoulder and said, "Your father is very ill."

"What?" I said. This was the first I'd heard.

"He had a stroke last night," my uncle continued. "I just got the telegram this morning, and I'm headed there now. I was hoping I might see you."

It's hard to imagine today, but in India at that time, many homes—including ours—still did not have telephones. Even in the year 1962, the most effective way to reach people quickly was through a nineteenth-century technology: the telegraph. People would send telegrams—or cables, as we called them—when they really needed to reach someone. But they were expensive, so you had to keep them as short as possible. I would learn later that my mother had thought of sending one to me at school, but worried that a terse message like, "Your father is sick, come home immediately" would throw me into a panic, and she knew that I was already scheduled to come home anyway.

That was Mom, always thinking about my well-being, even at a time of crisis.

Now, on the crowded, overheated train, my uncle told me what had happened. My dad had suffered a major stroke the day before. He had been up for his usual hour-long morning prayers, but right afterward, as he readied himself for work, he collapsed. He couldn't walk or talk.

As soon as I arrived in Patna, I went straight to the city hospital. It was not a pretty sight. Indian hospitals, particularly in provincial cities like Patna, were by and large miserable places. My father was in a common ward, a large open hall holding about thirty patients, all on rusty metal cots. It was India-hot and humid. Overhead a few rusty fans rotated wearily, providing little comfort to the patients, some of whom were surrounded by family members fanning them to keep the flies away. The place smelled of death.

My dad was lying in his fetid bed, paralyzed. His breathing was labored, his jaw slack, and tubes protruded from both his nose and his mouth. He couldn't speak, but he was alert. When I walked in he looked me right in the eye.

I immediately broke into tears. Part of it was his shame. He didn't need to speak to me: I knew from the look what he was thinking. "Here comes Arun, my disappointment, my burden, my problem child."

He had good reason to feel that way. I had let him down time and again. I had monopolized my mother's time, stolen the attention she should have been directing toward her other children, because I always needed her to help sort out my latest mess.

On the other hand, I saw my father as cold, distant, inflexible, and unloving. Yes, I'd gotten into trouble, but his response had never been constructive. He'd typically stormed off, exclaiming how I'd embarrassed the family yet again. He would then disappear into his daily prayers, asking the Gods what he had done to deserve such a miscreant son, while leaving my mom to work out a solution in the here and now.

As far as a so-called normal father-son relationship, we had none. We'd never shared any hobbies or interests. He'd never taken me to the park to play cricket or fly a kite, which plenty of other dads did with their boys. When I later got involved in those activities on my own, he saw them as sordid and beneath us.

I realize now that Dad lived with tremendous guilt. He had never been allowed by his parents to forget the shame and stigma of marrying out of his caste. He could probably never allow himself to forget the tragic death of his family from his first marriage. And his own career had been a disappointment.

I believe that today he would be diagnosed with clinical depression. We might have gone to some family counseling, perhaps, and he and I might have learned to coexist more amicably. But this was India more than half a century ago. Life had a harder edge. And no matter how much you prayed, the sodden beds of the local city hospital were never too far away.

The proof of that was right before my eyes. Here was my dad, just fifty-two years old and incapacitated.

For the first time in my life, I felt his pain, along with a wave of conflicting emotions: love, resentment, guilt, anger, despair, and frustration.

And that was why I wept.

It was my mother, of course, who was there to console me. "Arun," she said, taking me in her arms as my father looked on with his cold, paralyzed eyes. "I know it's upsetting, but you have responsibilities now. Remember, until your father gets well again, you are the guardian of our family."

This was not a bromide by Mom to snap me out of my grief. In our culture, particularly back then, this idea that the elder son became the head of the household in situations like this was not something to be taken lightly. Things did not look good for my father. Time went on, and the paralysis showed no signs of releasing him from its grip. He developed pneumonia. Who knew how many months, weeks, or days he would live? I had to step up. Now.

My sister, Ampali, was about to start college. I was expected to become her legal guardian. She would need me to accompany her and sign the paper saying that I was responsible for her fee and her education. And it wasn't just Ampali I would have to sign my life over to. My mom, my two younger brothers, and my father—if he survived—would all now be depending on me!

My first instinct was to get the hell out of there. To get back on the train to Darbhanga and pick up a cricket bat.

But I didn't. For perhaps the first time in my life, I rose to the occasion.

A few days later, I accompanied my sister to school and dutifully signed the papers that allowed her to attend classes. Ampali was sixteen. She was distraught about our dad and the upheaval in our lives. But she was determined to go to college, and she was grateful for my help.

"Bahia," she said, using a term of endearment for an older brother, "thank you for coming with me and taking care of the paperwork."

"I have no choice," I admitted. "This is what I'm supposed to do."

"Well, that may be so," she said with a smile. "But a lot of times in the past you haven't done what you were supposed to do. I'm glad you did this time."

She was right. And my responsibilities were just beginning. It was now mid-May, the primary and high schools were still in session, and my two younger brothers, Dilip and Ashesh, had to attend. There was no nice yellow bus to pick them up as we waved goodbye. It was up to me to get them to class on time. With Ashesh on my handlebars and Dilip sitting behind me on the seat, I pedaled them to school every day for over a month on our creaky old bike. It was a tough job in the sweltering Indian sun. I remember thinking that my dream of being a doctor, the dream of a big house and three cars like Nana, was vanishing as fast as ice on a steamy Patna sidewalk. Now I was no different from a rickshaw driver in the grimmest slum of an Indian city. Except at least they got paid!

Then again, I reflected, what had I really done to ensure that I would have a decent career? Poke sticks into crevices? Play cricket? Look for lots of ways to do as little as possible? I began to realize how foolish I was, and how errant and misguided my entire approach to school, to life, had been.

They say we have only a few of these moments of absolute clarity in our lives, moments when the path we must take is illuminated with dazzling, if sometimes dizzying, clarity. This was such a moment. I vowed then that if I was able to return to medical school, I would take it seriously. I would be, in the wonderful phrase that American professional athletes like to use, "all in."

Whether I'd even get the opportunity for redemption was still an open question at that point, however. After a month in the hospital, my father was able to return home. But there was no rehabilitation or follow-up care available. Just as my mom had supervised my physical therapy after my childhood accidents, she now had to take care of her husband, with my help. We would carry him in and out of bed, bathe him, and feed him. After several weeks, he began moving slowly on his own. He was also able to speak, although his words at first were slurred and he drooled uncontrollably.

But while my father's condition began to improve, our financial situation deteriorated. Everything for Mom now centered around the house and the family. Aside from being a mother and wife, she became a maid, a servant, and caretaker to an invalid. Because she couldn't work outside the house, we watched our meager savings dwindle.

We were also laboring under a harsh system. My father had a government job, which—unlike government jobs in the West—did not provide health insurance or disability benefits. On top of that, if he could not return to his post in six months, he would lose it. There was no safety net in India, no Social Security or Medicaid. Any major illness or death could be financially devastating to a family.

We survived the way people in most traditional cultures do in times of crisis. The extended family was expected to help, and, for the most part, ours did. Many relatives, including my uncle Shivnandan and Nana, contributed toward the cost of my father's medical care.

Remarkably, Dad would eventually recover to the point that he could return to work. But that wouldn't be for a year or so. As the summer drew to a close, my mother took me aside.

"Arun, I want you to return to medical school."

"But Mom," I said, "you need me here."

"I'll manage. What we really need is for you to finish school and become a doctor. That's how you can best help the family."

I hugged her. "If that's what you want, Mom, I'll do it."

I could see the financial stress my father's illness had put on our family. A doctor's salary would prevent that from happening in the future. Mom was right: finishing my medical education was what I needed to do. Even more important, it was what I *wanted* to do.

This was now my responsibility, my duty—concepts that I'd never really entertained before.

And this time there would be no bullshit, no half-assed measures.

I was finally going to start taking my life seriously.

⌒

When I got back to Darbhanga, a few days before my classes began, I visited Nana, who had recently retired from his practice.

As we sipped tea in his study, I updated him on my father's condition and also told him about my conversation with my mother. I was coming back to school with a new attitude. No more screwing around. He was pleased. I then told him something that I'd been mulling over on the train ride back from Patna.

"Nana, I've also been thinking about a direction in medicine. I think I'd like to become a surgeon. Maybe an orthopedic surgeon."

He froze, his teacup in midair. "A surgeon? What gave you that idea?"

Considering that he was a surgeon, I was surprised at this response.

"Well, Nana, I had some really good orthopedic surgeons who helped me when I got hurt. And now I want to do as you once suggested. I want to help other kids in return. Also, weren't you a surgeon, too?"

He took a deep breath. As he placed the cup back on the saucer, I noticed something I never had before. His hand was trembling.

"Arun," he said after a long silence. "I'm very happy that you are now going to take your medical studies seriously. It's hard work to become a doctor."

I nodded. "I'm ready to do it."

"Good," he said. "And I would be very happy if you would become a physician." He paused. "But I don't want you to become a surgeon."

"What? Why not?"

"It's time you learned some of the realities of the medical profession, Arun, not just the stuff they teach you in the classes and labs."

After only one year in medical school, I was still trying to learn the basics of anatomy and physiology. Outside of the fact that I knew doctors made money and seemed to have some control over their own schedules, I'd never really stopped to think about the realities, much less the politics, of the medical profession.

"When you're a surgeon you're on the top of the heap." Nana went on. "*The surgeon is God* is an old saying, and in our profession there's some truth to it. When you've developed those skills, and you can intervene and make a huge impact on people's lives... Well, it's a powerful feeling."

I was confused. "I realize that, Nana. I've seen what you've done. And I want to be able to do that, too."

He continued. "But like any kind of power, it has its limits. And like any powerful figure, you develop enemies."

"What kind of enemies?"

He chuckled. "Quite honestly, Arun, the main enemy is time. No matter how skilled a surgeon you become, you will get older. Like I did. Your eyesight may grow worse, as mine did. Your dexterity may become diminished. You may not be able to perform as well as you once did."

I looked down at his hand. Still trembling.

"People notice that," he said, perhaps aware I was looking at his hand. "You will have colleagues who are jealous of your success or who feel it's their time to become the top dog. There'll be whispers about how you can't do the job anymore. How your skills have diminished. Your reputation and eventually your practice will be affected."

I was stunned. Was this why my grandfather had retired? Because he had to?

"Nana, people said this about you? I'd like to know who they are."

He shook his head. "Arun, I'm just trying to tell you the way things are for a surgeon. Now, on the other hand, let's say you decide to become an internist, a general practitioner, a family doctor. It's a completely different picture. As you get older, your gray hair and your glasses will be seen as signs of your vast knowledge and experience. Instead of thinking you've lost your skills and going elsewhere, more patients will come to you, because they will see you as wise."

When he looked me in the eye, I noticed something I'd never seen before. He was pained. Hurt. It became clear even to me that he was talking about his own situation. "Arun," he said, almost as if pleading, "my advice to you is don't let them run you out of your practice when you're not ready. Don't let them dictate when it's time for you to retire. Which is exactly what will happen if you become a surgeon."

For the first time in my life, I remember feeling anger toward the dignified, successful old man who was my grandfather, my beloved Nana.

"I can't believe you're telling me this, Nana, just when I've decided to become serious about my career."

"I'm just trying to tell you—"

"No," I said. "Please don't tell me anything more. You've said enough. I have to go."

I was seething. I loved and respected Nana and would continue to. But I was angry about what he'd told me. I felt as if he didn't think I could make it as a surgeon. I thought what he had said about his situation was really a roundabout way of telling me I wasn't as good as he, and that he was steering me away from surgery because he felt I didn't have the brains or the abilities.

The conversation left me more determined than ever to become a surgeon. With youthful bravado I vowed to myself that I would exceed his achievements. I'd become a bigger and better surgeon. I'd own a bigger house. Maybe even more cars (although when I considered the impracticality of owning four cars, I amended that to more-expensive cars).

Nana didn't know it, but he helped me that day, by making me more determined than ever to succeed in medical school and to become a surgeon.

What I didn't realize, and wouldn't until a half century later, was that everything my grandfather had said and everything he'd predicted—about being a surgeon, about aging, about the profession—would prove to be true.

—⁕ *Chapter Seven* ⁕—

Life Out of Control

Driven by a desire to help my mother at home and prove my grandfather wrong, I plunged into my second year of medical school. But even as I began to diligently apply myself—no more talking in class, no more lackadaisical attitude, and no more blowing off studies for cricket—I realized I had a serious problem.

I was unable to learn.

As odd as that sounds, it was the truth. The material was getting more challenging, and as much as I was trying to absorb and process what was being presented to me, I couldn't. I'd read a chapter in a medical textbook, and when I finished, I'd barely have retained a thing. At best I recalled random fragments of what I'd just pored over. It was as if the pages I'd just read had been partially blank.

In class I'd listen to my professors as they filled the room with their knowledge, only to realize at the end of the lecture that much of that knowledge had gone right over, or in and out of, my head.

I didn't yet have a name for this problem. Years later, when I began to read about the symptoms, I spoke to some experts on dyslexia and put two and two together. At the time, however, I assumed the root cause of my learning difficulties was that I was mentally deficient—that, as some of my elementary school teachers had phrased it (in both Hindi and English), I was just plain stupid.

Perhaps my father had been right. If not begging on the streets of Patna, my future might more realistically lie in what we might today call a blue-collar occupation. Maybe I should forget medicine and go to a vocational school. At least then I'd make a respectable living and be able to support my family.

Throughout my life I had been insulted, mistaken for someone lacking intelligence, and bullied and laughed at. But at this point I wasn't looking for a diagnosis. I wasn't interested in *why* I had trouble reading, *why* I failed to comprehend much of what I could read, or *why* I couldn't properly pronounce words. Those answers would come later. What I needed was ways to work around these limitations in order to keep up with the workload of medical school.

And I needed them fast. During those first couple of weeks in the new semester, I was floundering. I had been lucky my first year, managing to get passing grades on a few key exams to avoid expulsion, but I knew I couldn't keep that up. Ironically, it seemed that now I'd gotten serious about a medical career, it was quickly receding out of reach.

I decided that the first thing I needed to do was expend a lot of effort. Simply put, I just had to work harder—maybe harder than anyone else in my class. If I couldn't retain all the information in the chapter through one reading, I'd simply have to go back and read it again and again until I could. Maybe, I reasoned, bombarding my brain with the same information over and over would enable some of it to stick.

Secondly, while I had trouble with comprehension and pronunciation, I knew that I did have a good memory, especially for the spoken word. My retention, in fact, was exceptional. As a small child, I'd once heard my father recite, during his worship, an ancient Sanskrit prayer. Roughly translated into English, it goes like this: "Lord, give me enough that I'm not hungry and that nobody ever walks out of my door hungry." My parents told me that I'd recited it word for word later that day—and in a language I neither spoke nor understood.

This ability to memorize had helped me in some ways: I knew the history and statistics of every top cricketer in India, for example, something that had impressed some of my fellow students. But oddly, like the Sanskrit prayer, I could also retain information on subjects that I knew little or nothing about. I might not be able to explain what it meant, but, like a parrot, I could play back what you said almost verbatim.

That happened in school, however, only when I made a conscious effort. Sitting in a class like most other students, taking notes, experiencing the satisfaction of intellectual discovery, of *learning*, didn't work for me. My listening had to be different. I needed to be more like a court stenographer reproducing, word for word, every utterance in a trial—not like the prosecuting and defense attorneys, who listen to the same testimony but must process and work with that information.

I realized it wasn't an ideal learning strategy, but I was desperate, and my memory seemed one of the few tools I had at my disposal. Today I might have tutors who could instruct me in some of the various techniques used to help students with dyslexia better recognize words, such as the now-popular Orton-Gillingham Approach, which teaches you how to decode words, or break them down into their component syllables and sounds in order to be able to read them. But there were no such specialists and no proven methods or strategies in Darbhanga in the 1960s. I was left to my own devices. When a professor talked about the digestive process, I'd memorize what he said. I'd repeat it and repeat it to myself after class, and during my marathon study sessions at night. And then, if asked to explain it in class the next day, as we often were, I'd play it back. I'd talk about bowels, and enzymes, and absorption into the blood. Even if I didn't grasp it the way my fellow students did, I certainly sounded as if I did.

I also employed a technique that many people use to study, but that I became especially reliant on: I would come up with code words and acronyms to remember strings of facts or terminology. In anatomy class, for example, we'd learn about veins, arteries, and nerves, in that order, because that is the way they lie in the groin. The vein will be closer to the groin, the arteries in the middle, and the nerve on the lateral side, and we needed to know the order because to be able to operate you have to know what you're cutting and what you want to avoid cutting!

I would remember this as V-A-N, using the first letter of each of the three words in sequence. Before class I'd write the codes on my hand in ballpoint pen, like a quarterback in the NFL who writes the plays on his sleeve before taking the field. I'd walk into class looking as if my hands had been tattooed as part of some bizarre cult ritual. There would be eight to ten combinations of letters penned across my knuckles, wrists, and palms. It looked weird, but it worked. When I was asked questions, I would glance down at them, and again, through rote memory and repetition, recite the terminology I'd written down in an abbreviated fashion.

All this additional studying and eccentric preparation made for a regimented, monkish existence. We were in school all day. At six p.m. I'd eat dinner and then go back to my room in my grandfather's house and work until the early hours of the morning. There was no TV in Darbhanga at this point, and, while the movies were popular, I just didn't feel I had time for them. There were assigned chapters and papers to be read and reread ad nauseam. There were lectures to memorize, words to practice saying aloud, acronyms to fashion.

My nighttime studies would go like this: First I'd read the chapters we had been assigned three or four times, underlining the important points with a pencil. After this I would read the underlined sections over and over. I would then create the code or shorthand by which to remember the information. I'd rehearse this code, repeating it and what it stood for, over and over again. Around two or three a.m., I would fall asleep, often with a desktop full of highlighted readings and strange scribblings in front of me.

The next morning at seven a.m. it would start all over again. I generally rehearsed the material a couple more times in the morning before heading to class. I knew I'd be expected to have mastered it overnight, because the instructors moved fast—we would be on to new subject matter in each class almost immediately.

Many people afflicted with dyslexia have difficulty spelling and enunciating words. I am no exception. It's hard to explain, but essentially, when I hear a word and try to pronounce it, what comes out of my mouth sounds garbled. It's still a challenge for me now. I know what some people say about me: "That Dr. Singh mumbles a lot." It's embarrassing. Sometimes when I hear these whispers I want to shout, "It's not mumbling, I'm not tongue-tied, I'm not shy, and I *am* fluent in English!" The problem is not my intelligence; it's essentially a congenital malfunction in my brain.

In her book *Overcoming Dyslexia*, Dr. Sally Shaywitz describes the cause of dyslexia as a "glitch within the language system." Most humans can almost instinctively and effortlessly articulate the building blocks of words, called phonemes. But for those of us with dyslexia, the phonemes are less sharply defined, so we are not able to properly construct and articulate words (an example would be confusing the word *cat* with *scat*).

The problem persists to this day. When I was elected into the Rhode Island Heritage Hall of Fame and had to give my acceptance speech in front of hundreds of people, I didn't read from my prepared text. I couldn't take the risk that suddenly my word blindness would crop up and I'd miss individual words, or even complete sentences. Instead I memorized my six-minute speech, just as I had memorized the salient points of my medical school lectures fifty years earlier.

I also knew that because of my impaired speech mechanism, it was possible a word or two would escape me during the speech, and the best way to deal with it would be to slow down and give my brain time to process. That's why at the beginning of my 2017 Rhode Island Heritage Hall of Fame speech, you might have thought I had just been roused from a nap. I took the podium and looked with heavy eyes out at the room as I gathered my thoughts—not about *what* I was going to say (I knew that), but *how* or even *if* I could actually find the words (I never know for sure).

I spoke slowly.

"I want to thank you all"—a long pause—"for being here." Probably few outside my family noticed the pause. But at that instant, alarm bells rang in my brain. Even granted a few seconds of extra processing time, I could not articulate the words I'd originally written for my opening sentence, something about the "distinguished group of other inductees" that night and all the "commitment and dedication" demonstrated by them. Hence the pause, followed by a weak ad lib.

Luckily, once I got past that phrase, the rest of the speech went smoothly.

This is what I've been dealing with my whole life. And if fairly common words like *distinguished* and *inductees* won't come to mind at command, imagine how it was for me with medical terminology such as *choledocholithiasis* (stones in the gallbladder or common bile duct) and *borborygmus* (the sound of your stomach growling, when gas moves in the intestine).

The pronunciation issue became particularly important as we approached the end of the term. The second year of medical school in India culminates in two days of grueling examinations, which are given in written and oral form. Both presented distinct challenges for me. The questions in both formats would be long and complex. I might be asked, for example, to describe the blood supply to the heart. They'd want all the details. This was a tall order. Comprehension was hard, writing was hard, spelling was hard, and clear speaking was (and, as noted, remains) hard for me.

But I redoubled my efforts and went into the exams as prepared as I could be. And the sixty-four-dollar medical words managed to roll off my tongue without a problem.

At the conclusion of the second day of exams, I went back to my room and prayed to any and all Indian deities that my efforts had paid off.

A few days later, the grades were posted. This was always a flourish of academic theater on the part of the medical college. At an unspecified time soon after the exams—you never knew exactly when—the grades would magically appear on the wall outside the office of the principal of the medical school.

I still remember the morning in May 1963, the end of my second year, when the grades were posted. The word went around the dining halls, student lounge, and classrooms. "The grades are up! The grades are up!"

A group of us decided to go see them. There was trepidation, of course. Bad grades meant bad career prospects. The previous year I'd been among the last names on that piece of paper. I'd shrugged it off then. Now it was different. It really mattered, because my standing in class this year would determine what kind of clinical rotation I'd get, which in turn would influence where and in what specialty I'd ultimately work.

With my friend Bijoy leading the way, a group of us approached the posted grades as if they were Martin Luther's Ninety-Five Theses nailed to the church door. Bijoy, big man on campus and stellar student, strode right up to the wall confidently and without hesitation. He knew he'd done well.

I stayed back, almost afraid to look.

When Bijoy began studying the list taped on the wall, I saw surprise register on his face.

"What's the matter?" I asked.

"Arun, come here, look at this," he said.

"I'm afraid to," I said, and meant it.

"No, really, come here and look."

The other students, who had gathered around and were also studying the list, parted to allow me to get right up to the wall. I noticed that some of them were looking at me strangely.

"You finished in the top ten, Arun," Bijoy said. "Right up there with me." He smiled and clapped me on the back. "Way to go, my friend!"

I couldn't believe it. I knew my grades had been improving, that my slow, laborious study methods had been paying off to some degree. But I still had problems comprehending a lot of the material, and occasionally my acronym system would fail. I really had had no idea how I'd done on my finals, especially the written essays. But there I was. I also saw that alongside my name in the class rankings was an asterisk. It meant that in addition to having finished in the top ten of a class of 150, I was one of the top *five* students in physiology—a core class for second-year medical students. Me, a guy who the previous year couldn't tell a vein from an artery, a bowel from a bunion—*I* was one of the best students in the school, and in one of the most important subjects an aspiring physician must master.

"I'm proud of you, Arun," Bijoy said. "I know you worked hard for this."

He didn't know the half of it, but I appreciated his kind words. I *had* worked harder than I'd ever worked before. And for once in my life, I felt a swell of pride. Arun Singh, who had finished near the bottom of his class his first year, was now in the top 10 percent. I was like a baseball team that goes from last place one season to making the playoffs the next. I think a lot of people were surprised, not the least of them me!

Maybe, I allowed myself to believe, I'd amount to something after all. Maybe I *could* be a doctor, even a surgeon.

Chapter Eight

"Dr. Singh"

The third year in medical school in India is when students begin their clinical rotations—meaning that they actually get to work in a hospital setting, with exposure to real patients. I was looking forward to this. I'd enjoyed my practicums and labs, the classes where we weren't asked to read or learn about the workings of the body. This was where I could actually *do* things besides memorize and repeat. Here my brain cooperated as we attempted to solve a different kind of puzzle.

Consider: A patient comes to you. He or she is not feeling well. As the doctor you are the investigator—trying to figure out what's wrong based on an examination. Outside of plain X-rays, there was no other imaging available at this point in rural India. No CT scans or MRIs we could order up. We had to decipher what the symptoms were telling us. Could it be an infection? A serious disease? Or just an upset stomach or stress? We would listen to the heart and the breathing. Look at the patient's eyes or complexion. Examine the body for swelling, apply pressure here or there.

I loved this. The body could often hint at what was wrong if you knew where and how to look. You'd use your senses here, not your speech-processing ability. Maybe I couldn't clearly pronounce *bronchitis* or *hepatitis*, but I could hear congestion. I could see bloodshot eyes or yellowed skin. I could feel a swollen liver.

And that's how we'd come up with a diagnosis. By using our senses and skills to figure it out, by process of elimination, and by asking questions and listening to the patient.

"Inhale...Exhale."

"Take a deep breath and hold it."

"Does this hurt? Does that hurt?"

Then, once you had a diagnosis, you would have to figure out the appropriate treatment: Rest? Certain kinds of medication? Surgery?

I was eager to start my rotation at our hospital. In India, unlike in the United States, the state-run medical schools operated the local hospital. It was at the hospital of my school, Darbhanga Medical College, that I was introduced to the challenges and joys of being a physician. But it was also an underfunded institution in an impoverished country.

All of that was evident before you even entered the building.

Just outside the hospital doors garbage was piled high, and stray dogs and pigs could often be seen gnawing on discarded bandages. The place had all the charm of a POW camp; the building was painted a sickly yellow, and there were blacked-out windows, a corrugated tin roof, and what looked like a guard tower nearby (it was actually a water tower). Inside, it was even worse. A dedicated staff struggled to care for an indigent population living in unsanitary, crowded conditions and afflicted with diseases that had already been eradicated in the West. We had cases of tuberculosis, leprosy, polio, and rabies—ghastly ailments that swept through the city slums and deposited their victims into our casualty room, which was what we called our emergency room. Along a lengthy corridor flanked by two walk-ways, patients, often accompanied by their families, lay on filthy cots or on the floors, which ran with human effluent. The very air reeked of sickness and misery.

Disgusting? Yes. Shocking? Not to someone who had grown up in India. This was the world we lived in; even those of us whose families had managed to stay just above the poverty line were still in close proximity to homelessness, disease, and filth. That these were juxtaposed with India's natural beauty, its mag-nificent culture and heritage, didn't change the reality of what I'd seen every day of my life.

I was, quite frankly, used to it.

At the hospital, what upset me most was not the squalor, but the injustice of it—a rude lesson that was driven home to me in my first days on the job.

I was assigned to work with one of our professors, Dr. Desai, whom I knew as a competent physician and a good teacher. We students would accompany him on his rounds to observe and learn as he examined patients. My first morning, I watched him make his way through the casualty room. There were people with infectious diseases, there were people with broken limbs or burns, and there were people with common colds and cancer. He asked every single one of them, regardless of age or gender, the same initial questions:

"When did you eat last…and *what* did you eat?"

He would carefully write down their answers.

At first I assumed he was asking these questions to help for-mulate a diagnosis. But when he asked them of a man whose arm had been broken in a construction accident, I was puzzled. What did his diet have to do with treatment of a broken limb?

After several hours we took a break in the crowded staff

room. "So," he asked the group of us, "do you have any questions for me?"

I raised my hand. "My question is about your question. You ask everyone about when and what they ate. Clearly, for some of these patients, that has nothing to do with their illness or treatment."

"Ah, you noticed. Do you know *why* I ask everyone that question?"

"No."

"Well, Arun, you've learned a lot in your two years of training about the practice of medicine and the science behind it. But you don't know much about the business of it, do you?"

I thought back to my grandfather keeping the silver coin he had extracted from the child's throat as payment for his services.

"Well...not really."

"Let me explain. We're a poor hospital in a poor city, operating on a shoestring budget. That much is apparent, yes?"

I nodded as yet another patient, this one elderly and unconscious, was dumped unceremoniously on the floor just outside the door by a couple of attendants. He looked, I thought, like Gandhi.

"Many of these people simply can't afford medical care. You know that. They have nothing. But some of them have a little. And a few of the people who come here are actually well off enough to own a car."

My eyes widened. You had to have some dough to afford an automobile in India in those days. Again I thought of Nana and his three cars. Amazing.

"So," Dr. Desai continued, snapping me back from my daydream of driving a Porsche. "How do you think we're able to tell who is genuinely poor and who could probably afford to pay for at least part of their treatment? Do you think they tell us their occupations and volunteer their annual income as they arrive?"

I shrugged. "Their clothes...?" And then I looked at the elderly figure lying next to us. Like the real Gandhi, he wore nearly nothing. And the real Gandhi was a lawyer. No, it couldn't be that. Then it dawned on me. "You mean...?"

"Right. Whether they could afford to have a nutritious meal. The poor in our city barely get by with a meal a day. And that's normally the evening meal. They wouldn't have eaten this morning. And if they did, and they were really poor, they would have likely eaten rice and lentils, the cheapest food you could find."

I stood staring at him. His logic was inescapable. But the morality of it left me cold. This was how we triaged patients? By their ability to pay? Apparently, on the basis of Dr. Desai's notes, the family of each patient who appeared as if they could afford some kind of payment—meaning each patient who admitted to having had a decent meal in the prior twenty-four hours—would then be asked to contribute to the cost of their care.

This was the brutal reality of health care in India in the 1960s. And as I learned over the subsequent days and weeks, it was not because Dr. Desai and his colleagues were penny-pinching or coldhearted. Far from it. I saw some of the most compassionate care I've witnessed in my career given by the doctors and nurses at Darbhanga Medical College Hospital. But when the hospital couldn't afford to stock sufficient intravenous saline, iodine, bandages, antibiotics, or needles—the basics—and yet was obliged to treat everyone who came in, regardless of economic background, *somebody* had to pony up the money. What had developed was a version of a "pay as you go" system. Essentially, you paid what you could afford—even if it was only for a few liters of saline to help keep your child or parent alive.

Or you could go back out into the streets.

Still, while it made financial sense, the harshness of this system was infuriating. It instilled in me a belief that I still hold today, that basic health care is a right every person should have regardless of whether they can afford to pay for it. Later this attitude would bring me into conflict with hospital administrations in places I had barely heard of at that point in my life, and would also put me on the opposite side of the fence from some of my friends in what would become my adopted country.

But that was still years away. In my third year of medical school, I had been taught a valuable lesson about the reality of the profession I was aspiring to: Doctors do save lives. Doctors do care. But we do so while laboring under a system that is often cold and unyielding.

One morning I reported to the hospital and, instead of following Dr. Desai during his rounds, I was assigned a patient, a man in his mid-forties, and simply by laying eyes on him I could tell he was quite sick. He was ashen, his eyes sunken, and his mouth was a rictus of pain and fear. His clothes were dirty and stained with vomit. I made a point of not asking him what he had eaten. Instead I had him immediately put on a stretcher and taken from the floor of the casualty room to an examination room. There his filthy clothing was removed, and right away I could see that his stomach was distended, as if he were nine months pregnant. I asked him when he'd last had a bowel movement. "Three days," he whispered hoarsely. I took his pulse: elevated. I stuck a thermometer in his mouth: low-grade fever. I pressed my right hand on his belly: he moaned. I looked at him again, closely: his skin looked as dry as parchment.

I ran through the symptoms in my mind. It seemed to me this man had some kind of bowel obstruction.

Diet was likely part of the problem. Although they were often undernourished because of their poverty, many Indians ate a diet that was heavy in roughage. That was good in some ways—I barely heard of colitis until I came to America with its rich diet—but too much roughage or fiber, like too much of almost anything, can cause problems. In his case I suspected volvulus, a condition in which part of the colon becomes twisted on itself. Left uncorrected, this obstruction can lead to perforation of the colon, spread of infection, and death.

The man, whose family stood around him, looked terrified and miserable. Why was he so scared of a fresh-faced medical student? "He has never seen a doctor before," admitted one of his siblings, a bearded man in shabby clothes. *Never visited a physician? Ever?* Today this would be almost unheard of. But amid the grinding poverty of our backwater province in 1963, poor people avoided physicians and hospitals. They were afraid they would have to pay. There was also ignorance about modern medicine. When illness struck, many of the poor sought out homeopathic or herbal remedies. Sometimes these worked. But the concoction of herbs this guy may have been given was likely to have only added to his medical problems.

I reported to Dr. Desai after the conclusion of my exam.

He listened and nodded. "Very good, Arun. I think you're probably right. It's probably sigmoid volvulus. What should we do now?"

"First of all, we've got to get some fluids in him right away, no? He's severely dehydrated."

"Correct. Let's get to it."

With Dr. Desai and a senior resident guiding me, I slid the

needle through the skin and into a vein of his left arm. But there was a problem. We didn't have an intracatheter—the thin plastic tubing that is threaded into the vein for intravenous infusions of fluid and stays in the vein despite the movement of the hand or arm. Without that, the needle I'd just slid into the patient's arm would simply dislodge itself the minute he moved.

Dr. Desai seemed to read my mind.

"What do we do here, Dr. Singh? How do we keep it from dislodging?"

It was one of the first times he or anyone had addressed me with that honorific. I straightened up with pride, determined to come up with an answer worthy of a man addressed as *Doctor*. But my solution was obvious and basic: I saw the family standing there, watching. "Excuse me," I said to them, in my most authoritative voice. "Someone is going to have to hold his arm and keep his hand still, to make sure the fluid he needs gets into his vein."

A woman in a faded sari, presumably his wife, immediately stepped forward. I showed her how to hold the intravenous tube and the position in which her husband's arm and hand needed to remain. Then I stood back. She, and by turns other members of the family, held his arm in precisely the position I had indicated for the next twenty-four hours. The family never left as we began to prepare for the surgery the man needed if we were going to save him.

But before we could, there was a problem: After a few liters of fluids were pumped into the patient, he had improved. But he was going to need more, and I was told the hospital had only so much fluid available. He had reached his limit.

"Well, what are we supposed to do?" I asked the fellow in charge of supplies.

"Young doctor," he said, smiling, "you need to tell his family that they have to buy more fluid."

It was outrageous, and yet this was the system. When I explained to the man's family that they would have to come up with one hundred rupees to buy more saline fluid if they wanted to keep their loved one alive, they didn't respond as you or I might, with anger over the monstrosity of such a request. (A hundred rupees—that could have been a month's earnings for this family!) Instead of blowing up they immediately huddled and began an earnest discussion. I tried not to eavesdrop, but at one point I discerned the hissing of a woman's voice as she softly but emphatically spoke to one of the men: "This is your brother, Rohit. Do you want him to die?"

The haggling went on for a few minutes. Finally the knot of relatives disengaged from each other and stepped back, and the wife turned and walked up to me. "Here," she said, handing me some crumpled notes and coins. "And thank you for what you're doing, Doctor."

I almost didn't have the heart to tell her that she would have to go out and buy the saline fluid herself. We didn't have the manpower to do it. I gave her back the money, wrote down the address of the local dispensary, and told her exactly what to purchase. Back to the family circle she went. Within a minute I saw a man I presumed to be another one of the patient's brothers go walking quickly toward the exit. The precious rupees in his hand were literally the price of his brother's life.

But the patient was still weak, his belly distended and tender. Without the removal of the obstruction, his bowel would eventually perforate and he would develop a serious infection. After an attempt to clear the obstruction by passing a tube through from below had failed, surgery was the only option.

Now that he was hydrated and stable, the man was deemed ready to withstand the procedure, which would involve removing the blockage and carefully untwisting the colon. While delicate, this was a common procedure. Dr. Desai would perform the operation with one of the residents assisting, while I would observe from nearby.

This was my first time watching a major surgery. I'd seen my grandfather perform delicate eye procedures, but removing a cataract, while technically demanding, is very different from cutting open a man's belly. Like the posting of our grades at school, the whole thing had an air of theater to it. This was high drama: The patient was placed in the operating room as we all watched. Then...house lights up! The operating theater was suddenly and brilliantly illuminated.

An anesthesiologist put a mask over the patient's face and poured a trickle of liquid ether onto the mask. He was asleep in seconds.

Now the lead actors made their appearances. Eventually I'd learn my part in this drama, but the first time seeing it was quite impressive. The surgeons took center stage, and after ceremonially washing their hands, they raised their arms high like potentates about to invoke a curse or make a grand pronouncement. From behind the nurses appeared and draped these mighty beings in their white gowns, and then laid their instruments neatly along the table at the foot of the slab upon which the unconscious man lay. He was wrapped in sheets, with just his stomach (now only slightly distended) exposed like a hillock on a broad flat plain.

It was all done so flawlessly, everyone so confident in their parts that I almost felt like applauding, and yet the play had not even really begun.

With what seemed to me a great flourish Dr. Desai picked up the scalpel. He appeared cool and confident—almost omnipotent. This was what my grandfather had meant about the surgeon as God, I thought.

After a quick look at the lump of human anatomy in front of him, he smoothly and confidently sliced into the hillock. The minute he did, a bright red geyser of blood spurted from the man's swollen stomach and splashed on his mask. Dr. Desai seemed unperturbed, almost as if he'd expected it, and kept right on working.

I, on the other hand, was aghast. I had never seen an explosion of blood like that during Nana's eye surgeries. Suddenly a wave of nausea swept through me. I became dizzy and tried to catch my breath. Before I could even find a nearby wall to steady myself against, I collapsed onto the floor.

I was carried by some OR techs into a nearby room.

Dr. Desai apparently continued without a pause. Does a great actor onstage notice if someone in the audience takes ill? The operation, like the play, must go on.

The next day, I learned that the operation had been a success; the patient was expected to make a full recovery. I, on the other hand, thought I was going to die from embarrassment and shame. Nervously I approached the staff room, where Dr. Desai sat going through some reports. Surely this was a black mark on my record. What kind of surgeon faints at the sight of blood?

"Dr. Singh, how do you feel this morning?" he asked cheerily when he saw me hovering at the door.

I told him that, while I was fine, I wished to apologize for what had happened. He laughed.

"You're hardly the first medical student to pass out at the sight of blood, Arun," he said, reverting to my first name. "Listen," he said. "That's a common reaction. I bet half the surgeons in India felt sick the first time they were in the OR." He put his hand on my shoulder, a rare gesture of affection in the rigid hierarchy of Indian medical schools at the time. "Dr. Singh," he said, reverting to the honorific. "Your diagnosis and your quick treatment helped save his life."

I felt as if I floated through the dingy corridors of Darbhanga Medical College Hospital for the rest of my shift. The day that registers in my mind as the first time I really felt like a physician ended on another magical note. As I was finishing up my rounds, I heard a soft voice in the corner of the casualty room call my name. It was the wife of the man who had had the surgery.

She handed me a small box of what I'm sure were expensive Indian sweets. "From our family, Doctor," she said in Hindi, bowing her head as she made the offering. "*Bhagavaan aapaka bhala kare.*" *God bless you.*

For once my sense of anger and despair over the unjust system that this woman, her husband, and all of us labored under was put aside.

On that day the former juvenile delinquent, the former ne'er-do-well of the Singh family, the student who couldn't learn but had managed to succeed, felt blessed indeed.

Chapter Nine

Betrayal in the Family

Over time I had grudgingly forgiven Nana for what I felt was his lack of faith in my ability to become a surgeon. I still did not realize he had attempted to steer me away from the very real humiliation he had felt when he had been forced out of his hospital position.

Part of it had been his age. Part of it had been his pro-Western, pro-British inclinations, which put him at odds with the Indian authorities of the time. He had left his practice with a bitter taste in his mouth.

As I was living in a back room in his house during medical school, I usually bumped into Nana daily. One morning I saw him standing in his garden in the backyard, puffing on his pipe and staring at the sky, lost in thought.

"Nana," I asked, "what are you looking for up there?"

He smiled. "Good morning, Arun," he said. "Another day at the factory, eh?"

I smiled. "You know what life is like for a medical student in a city hospital," I said. "But what about you? What are you doing?"

He sighed and looked perplexed. It was a countenance I rarely saw. Although he had a wry sense of humor, Nana's face and bearing were often impassive, as befitted his status. His broad forehead, high cheekbones, and white hair added to his air of eminence.

But on this morning, he looked more like a confused old man.

"I'm bored, Arun," he said.

"Sorry, Nana," I joked. "I'm working twelve-hour days. I have no sympathy. Invite some of your friends over and talk about the state of the world."

I was referring to the salons he used to hold, in which various prominent citizens of Darbhanga would join him to drink, smoke, and gossip about politics. He raised his eyebrows and grinned at me as I waved goodbye.

"Maybe that's not a bad idea," he said.

A few days later, he announced that he had accepted a part-time position at a clinic in the city of Purnea, about two hundred miles from Darbhanga. He had worked there in the past as a consultant. Now, he said, he would be going there about ten days a month. He'd see some patients, advise younger physicians, and generally get treated like the grand man he was. This was a good thing, in my mind. Whether he admitted it or not, he missed being a doctor, missed being the hero who could pluck a coin from a child's throat and save his life.

I'm not sure my grandmother was ever consulted about Nana's consulting. I doubt it. Theirs was a "traditional" relationship, a nice way of saying that all the decisions were made by the husband. It had been an arranged marriage, and while Nana had gone on to medical school and a successful career, my grandmother—whose name was Saraswati—had stayed in the home, exactly where she was supposed to stay according to the customs of the day.

The couple had produced six children—one son and five daughters, including my mom. I would later learn that a seventh, my uncle Prem, had been adopted. This was a bombshell, because adoption—particularly by parents who had children of their own—was taboo in India at that time. And yet my grandparents had taken that risk to help an infant they'd found abandoned. It revealed two things about them: my grandmother's compassion and my grandfather's complexity.

Here was a man who would put his much-valued reputation on the line to take in an orphan child and raise it as his own, and who later did so much for his grandchildren, particularly me. Yet this was the same man who, as I had witnessed, had insisted on exacting his insignificant fee from the family of the child who had swallowed the coin.

Saraswati's life had been devoted to the care of their seven children, and later to that of her ever-growing flock of grandchildren. Unlike her husband, Saraswati had little education. Whereas Nana spoke both English and Hindi fluently, and read newspapers and books in both languages, my grandmother spoke the traditional language, Hindi. She knew only a few words of English, a source of embarrassment to her—and to her husband. I noticed that she was never present at the salons.

For my part, I remember Saraswati as a warm and loving grandmother who was always there with a hot cup of tea, a freshly washed set of linens, or a hug for the grandson who had become a resident of her house. And she made it clear that I was always welcome there for as long as I wanted.

I loved her, and I revered him. But the odd conversation in the garden that morning had left me with an uncomfortable feeling. Nana seemed as if he was girding himself for a major transition. Was he ill and not telling anyone? But then why would he have gone back to work? In India in the early 1960s, people didn't have midlife crises—you would be more likely to have a midlife celebration, as you'd consider yourself lucky even to have survived into your fifties. But I remember wondering if Nana was beginning to come to terms with his own mortality.

Or was there something else?

At first, I thought the new job was the answer. Maybe he was, as he'd said, simply bored. The position seemed to agree with him. When he returned after his first ten-day stint he was in an exceptionally fine mood. I ran into him in the hall of his house. He was reading the *Times of India*, the English-language national paper, smoking his pipe, and sipping a glass of scotch. "Arun!" he said. "Have they promoted you to chief of surgery yet?"

"Not yet," I said. "How's the clinic? Good to be back at work?"

"Brilliant!" he said, sounding like the English aristocrat that I think he always fancied himself as being.

I didn't see him after that for a few days. Our next encounter was not as pleasant. I was reviewing some patient notes before bed, and I heard raised voices. I walked out in the hall. The sounds were muffled, but I could tell it was Nana and Saraswati fighting upstairs. I heard her sobbing as he clomped down the stairs. I walked through the hall to see what was happening, in time to hear him mutter to himself, "Stupid woman," as he poured himself a scotch. He then saw me and froze.

"Arun," he said. "A piece of advice for you. Never get married."

And he marched back down the hall to his study, shutting the door behind him.

The next day he was scheduled to return to his clinic. I had a rare few days off from the hospital. I had gone over to the college to use the library, and on the way back home I impulsively decided to follow him to the train station and give him a surprise visit. I wanted to see for myself how he was doing there. I wanted to share quality time with him and thought I also might pick up a few words of his wisdom. I saw him emerge from a cab with his suitcases. He wished the driver a good day, slipped him a tip, and walked onto the platform, a coolie hauling his baggage behind him. He was smiling.

Now, I realize a good night's sleep can help people see things differently in the morning, but it seemed to me he'd undergone quite a mood swing from the sullenness and anger of the previous night. I heard the "all aboard" call for the train and did something more characteristic of my mischievous ten-year-old delinquent self than of a serious twenty-one-year-old medical student. I sprinted across the platform and hopped on the last car of the train.

As we rolled out of Darbhanga, I stood in the back, panting from the exertion and shaking my head in bewilderment over my impulsive move. *What have you just done . . . and why?* I asked myself. I didn't have an answer. Nana had boarded the first-class car farther ahead. If he spotted me I would have no good explanation for why I was on the train. Luckily, he didn't see me. When the train stopped, I jumped off onto the platform. It was crowded. Indian train stations were routinely chaotic; thousands of people jammed the platforms as vendors hawked tea, newspapers, religious trinkets, and garlands.

I knew I had a few minutes before the train pulled out again. Threading my way along the platform, through the crowds of people rushing, haggling, hawking, I got to the first-class car. I peeked in the window and could see what appeared to be Nana's mane of white hair. I moved up a bit so I could get a better view.

There he was.

And there *she* was.

The glamorous young woman I had met a few times at Nana's house during one of his salons. That night he had paraded me out of my room and into the midst of his study, where his guests sat. "This is my grandson, the next doctor in the family."

This woman had turned around from her overstuffed chair in Nana's study and looked me up and down. She had skin the color of light chocolate, intense dark eyes, and lustrous hair.

"What a handsome young man," she said, her eyelashes fluttering.

I stuttered some form of thanks in return. Her name was Devi, and she held a government post, thanks to which she was well connected to the political elite of Darbhanga. She had, as they used to say, brains and beauty, not to mention a flirtatious nature. I must admit that I was impressed.

Obviously not as impressed as my grandfather, who was easily twenty-five years older.

Later, I would hear that rumors of their affair had been floating around for some time. But now I'd caught them together. Still I thought, *Could it be innocent? Could this be something platonic?*

At that very moment I saw a waiter arrive with tea. Nana poured Devi a glass, and as he did he stroked her back. Even I, a complete neophyte in the ways of love, knew an intimate gesture when I saw one. They were more than friends.

I heard the "all aboard" and backed away from the moving train. I had no desire to see anything further. I would cross the platform and catch a train back. I was, as the Brits say, gobsmacked. So this was what Nana was doing for ten days every month. And this was why he seemed so happy after he'd returned home and so eager to go back.

The idea of seeing one's grandparents in any intimate situation is, as my grandkids would say, yucky. But this was worse: this was catching Nana—the man I had revered for much of my life, the man who had essentially bankrolled my family and who now put a roof over my head—in a terrible betrayal of my grandmother.

What was I supposed to do? As my train rolled through the hot Indian afternoon, I wrestled with the right approach. Confront him when he came home? Say nothing? Wait?

I made my decision. The next morning before school, I walked into the kitchen where my grandmother was preparing breakfast.

"Arun, you were gone all day," she said, giving me a hug.

"Grandmother," I said, "I have something to tell you."

I related to her what I had done, and what I had seen. She stared at me in disbelief for a moment, and then collapsed into my arms, crying.

"What can I do?" she said aloud. "I can't leave him. I can't leave this home, and I can't survive on my own."

This was the reality in India in those days. Divorce was out of the question. The man—especially a powerful, respected man like Nana—held all the cards. Saraswati was barely literate. She had no profession or trade outside the home. Outside of the money Nana gave her each week to keep up the house, she probably had no financial resources of her own, either. She was trapped and she knew it. Maybe she was just as unhappy with their marriage as Nana was. I felt terrible for her and wondered aloud whether I should have told her.

"No, you were right to tell me," she said, composing herself. "And I'm sorry you had to see it. But come, have your tea."

I had little appetite, but as I sipped my tea, my grandmother talked to me about things she'd never told me before. How earlier in their life, when their children were young, Nana had gone off for four years of advanced medical training in England. When World War II broke out, it was difficult for him to return, so he remained overseas. "Who knows what he was doing for four years while he was in London?" she said angrily.

My grandmother was left alone to raise seven children as a war raged. One time, she told me, Nana had written that he was coming back. She and others had flocked to the port in Bombay, eager to be there when the ship arrived. But at the last minute, as Nana's ship was approaching—my grandmother could see it on the horizon—they were turned around because of a concern that Japanese warplanes were in the area. It turned out to be a false alarm, but the ship did not return. Saraswati was left wailing on the dock. Nana would arrive home ten days later. But, she claimed, her husband came home a different man. Angry, resentful, and selfish. What had happened to him while he was gone? She dared not ask. It was not her place to question.

I listened, wide-eyed. I'd had no idea of this. What had happened to my grandfather in wartime London? I wondered. Had he become bitter, having experienced the humiliation of racism? Entirely possible in that time and place. On the other hand, maybe he hadn't wanted to leave England? Was there another woman there, as well? That, too, couldn't be ruled out.

I shook off my speculations about him to focus on her: my poor grandmother! I hadn't known any of this, hadn't understood anything of her frustrations and fears. Despite all of it, she had never seemed to lose her good cheer and warmth, at least toward her grandchildren.

Perhaps embarrassed by this rare admission of her deepest feelings, she gave me a hug and changed the subject.

"I'm sorry," she said, over my protests that she had nothing to be sorry about, "we'll talk no more about it until he gets home."

Nine days later Nana returned, while I was home. I had been hoping he'd show up while I was in class or doing my rounds at the hospital, but there he was, walking in the door, whistling his happy tune—I could understand why now but tried to keep the image out of my head. When he went to give Saraswati a peck on the cheek, she pushed him away.

"You've been cheating on me," she cried. "You've betrayed me and this family."

I had never seen my grandmother so angry, and apparently neither had Nana. He looked guilty as sin.

"How do you know?" he asked.

She pointed at me. "Here is my witness. Arun saw you with your whore."

The look of seething hatred Nana shot my way is seared in my memory. "My own grandson," he snarled. His eyes were bloodshot; I could see that he was shaking. "Your father was right. You have never been anything but trouble. God help your patients and colleagues. I never want to speak to you again."

He turned his back and, my grandmother following him, demanding that he speak to her, they left the room. I stood there alone, shaking. What would he do to me? Throw me out of the house? Use his influence in the medical profession to have me blackballed?

I paced the floor, conflicted and confused. Upstairs I heard their voices. Occasionally I would discern my grandfather's raised voice. But this was one argument he was not going to win. After several minutes I distinctly heard my grandmother's voice, louder than I'd ever heard her. It had the ring of an ultimatum to it. "My grandson will stay in the house until he has finished school," she said. "As long as I am alive, he isn't going anywhere."

This was one time when Nana was overruled. I would remain in his house for the rest of my time at medical school.

—◦ *Chapter Ten* ◦—

From Pipe Dream to Possibility

In my last year of medical school, I did a rotation under a cardiologist named Anrudh Singh. Dr. Singh had been trained in cardiology in England and the United States. He was a well-respected professor and clinician, and a kindly, low-key man who became my mentor. He knew my background and told me that my best chance for success lay in America. There were more opportunities and better hands-on training for surgeons there, he said. He talked to me about his time at the University of Chicago and about how advanced the US was.

"Night and day," is what he'd say about the Chicago hospitals in which he'd done his clinical rotations, compared to the grim institution we worked in. "You'd be amazed at the stuff the Americans have."

It got me thinking. So did two books that Nana had given me, before our falling out. Not medical textbooks—Lord knows I had enough of them! These were interesting stories about young medical students like me who had gone on to change the world.

One of them was a biography of the Mayo brothers. It was fascinating to read about how two young siblings from Minnesota—a place I'd never heard of—had created one of the foremost medical facilities in the world.

The other was a book that I read over and over. It was about Dr. William Halsted, a name that, unlike the Mayos', is not well recognized today. His story, which began when he was a boy during America's Civil War, captivated me. Maybe it was because he, too, had had a stern and difficult-to-please father; or perhaps it was because at various points in his life, he had felt like an outsider. But through hard work and persistence, Halsted did nothing less than invent modern surgery, particularly through his advocacy of sterilization as a way to stop infection and reduce mortality rates—a then-new theory that many American surgeons refused to accept. Halsted later became chief of surgery at Johns Hopkins Hospital, where he influenced and educated the twentieth century's first generation of surgeons.

I related to the young Dr. Halsted, and also envied him. I wanted a new frontier to explore, too—one in which I could practice surgery in new lifesaving ways.

It so happened that such a new field of surgery was just emerging. The first open heart surgery had been performed in the 1950s. In 1967, René Favaloro, an immigrant from Argentina working at Cleveland Clinic, introduced the coronary artery bypass surgery for relief of angina and to prolong the life of patients with blockage of the coronary arteries. This breakthrough procedure would provide new hope to millions of people. My mentor, Dr. Singh, saw the implications of these new developments.

"This is an exciting new field, Arun," he said. "It's going to change medicine. It will be young doctors like you who will be part of this revolution."

It sounded exciting, all right, but I was still learning the basics of medicine, still practicing general surgery at the crowded, dirty hospital in Darbhanga. Once in a while, I'd let the dispiriting reality of this get me down. *A surgeon in America? Who are you kidding? You're just a poor Indian kid in a poor Indian hospital. You'll probably end up working in a dump like this the rest of your life.*

In truth, I was not much better off economically than some of the patients I was treating. Yes, I had a wealthy grandfather, but he'd more or less disowned me. Thanks to Saraswati's insistence, I was still living in the back room at his house, but my inventory of possessions is almost embarrassing: While I was in medical school, I owned three pairs of pants, four shirts, and one pair of shoes. Most of these clothes were baggy hand-me-downs from my father or uncles that barely fit me. My grandfather had given me a watch during my clinical rotation so that I could take a patient's pulse. To get around campus and to the hospital, I rode an old bike one of my uncles had thrown away. I took it from the trash.

Dr. Singh continued to encourage me, though, and finally, at his behest, I took the test administered by the Educational Commission for Foreign Medical Graduates, commonly known as the ECFMG exam. This assesses whether physicians from international medical colleges are ready to enter graduate medical education programs in the United States.

Using the same study and memorization skills that had gotten me through medical school, I passed the exam and did very well. The prospect of being a resident at a teaching hospital in the US no longer seemed like a pipe dream. I began to allow myself to imagine being in America. One of my fellow students, who had visited this magical land on the other side of the world, told me wondrous stories. "Arun, the streets are paved with gold," he said.

"Come on, Ravi," I said. "Do you think I was born yesterday? That's probably a story every immigrant tells the folks back home."

"You don't believe me?" he said. "Look at this." He produced a photo of a street that he said was in New York. Running down the middle of the road, and clearly visible, was a broad golden line.

I was taken aback. "Really?" I said. Maybe there was something to this!

There was certainly no gold in the streets of Darbhanga, a point that was made eminently clear that summer when one of India's periodic floods sent torrents of water coursing down its crowded, narrow byways. Power was out, the hospital temporarily ground to a halt—and the commencement exercises at Darbhanga Medical College were canceled. By the time they were rescheduled, many weeks later, I was gone. Several months after that, I received my diploma by mail.

The boy who had barely passed his first year, the boy with the paralyzed hand and learning disabilities, had graduated second overall in his class. Although the only public recognition I'd get was on that list of grades posted outside the school's main office, I was proud. Not as proud, however, as my mother, who welcomed me back home to Patna and wasted no time in providing encouragement of her own.

"Babul," she said, using my nickname. "I'm so excited that you're going to study and practice medicine in America."

"Mom, hold on," I protested. "I took the exam, but I haven't been accepted yet. And even if I do get accepted, I don't know if I can afford to go."

This was a real concern. In the last several years the family's financial condition had essentially stayed the same. My father was still recovering from his stroke, and while he had begun to transition back into his job, he was earning less than a full salary. Given this, I was still responsible for my siblings.

My sister, Ampali, had graduated from college, and my family wanted her to be married and secure before I left the country. As a matter of pride and according to our culture, we'd need to pay for the wedding and provide the groom with a respectable dowry—traditionally given as security should something ever render a husband unable to provide for his family. This would deplete our savings, making the prospect of my going to America seem all the more impossible.

About 85 percent of marriages in India are arranged even today, and perhaps one of the main reasons for this practice is that many Indian families feel the responsibility to protect and care for their daughters until that responsibility is passed to their husbands. But I wanted Ampali to be happy in her marriage and would proceed only with an arrangement between her and someone she wanted to be with. She decided to marry a long-time friend of the family and one of my high school classmates, Anil, who had become an engineer, and to whom she's still happily married today. As per Indian custom, we held a beautiful wedding, combining religious ceremony and celebrations that spanned three days, to properly honor Ampali and our family. I will never forget how moved I felt to see my only sister a beautiful bride, and to be relieved of my duty to her and our family.

That happy occasion aside, I was still in knots over the fact that we had no savings left to draw from—no money for America, and no money to keep the family going if I should be accepted into a medical program there.

My mother remained optimistic and wouldn't hear of it. "Somewhere, somehow, we'll get the money for you to travel to America," she said.

"OK, but what then? How are you going to get by?"

"We'll manage. Nana will continue to help us," she said,

looking at me knowingly. She of course had heard about my role in exposing his infidelity. "Your grandmother will make sure of that."

I wasn't convinced, and I pressed my mother on how the family would endure financially.

"Arun, don't worry. Something will come up."

Something eventually did happen. Unfortunately for me, it happened three years after I started scraping and scrounging for a way to afford my ticket to America, but it was still miraculous news for our family. In 1970 my younger brother Dilip bought a lottery ticket, and by the grace of God, he was the sole winner of 1.5 million rupees. It was one of the biggest payoffs in the history of the national lottery to that point. The big win didn't come without drama: Dilip had left the winning ticket in a shirt that had gone to the laundry. When it came back, it was still neatly folded in his shirt pocket. That was pure luck—or divine intervention! It was the first time we'd really gotten a break as a family, and my brother was very generous. He used the money for two things: a motorcycle for himself and a house for my parents. It also freed me from the responsibility of sending most of my paycheck back home.

In the years since, I have joked with Dilip about why he didn't buy that lottery ticket in 1967. It would have saved me a lot of agita!

Thanks to my performance on the ECFMG exam, I got accepted into a graduate medical program and received offers from hospitals in New Jersey and Massachusetts. I chose Worcester City Hospital in Massachusetts because they promised me room and board and said they would also pay for my plane fare. Since no one else had made such a generous offer, I took theirs. I was going to Worcester—wherever that was—as a surgical intern, where I would be paid the princely sum of $4,383 a year.

All arrangements were made for me to leave—and then, in early June, a bombshell. I received a letter from the hospital telling me that while the job was still there for me, they could no longer pay my airfare, which was about $500.

This was a disaster. Five hundred dollars was a small fortune to an Indian family like mine. We didn't own property or a house. At one point, while we were trying to figure out how to pay for my ticket, I noticed that during dinner, my mom wouldn't eat. "I'm not hungry," was her explanation. "Besides, there's more for you." It took me a while to realize that she was doing this intentionally; it was a desperate strategy to ensure that her family was fed while spending as little as possible on food.

We tried our best to raise the money. My mother pawned some jewelry; I sold some of my medical textbooks. But we still weren't close to $500. There was only one recourse, and I almost would rather not go to America than resort to this. I took a train back to Darbhanga to ask Nana for the money.

We had barely spoken since the night I had told my grandmother of his infidelity. When I arrived he sat stonily in his study, avoiding eye contact, as I explained to him the situation and said I had no other option than to ask him for the money.

"Sorry," he replied, after my long speech. "I can't do it."

He refused to talk further.

On the train home, I was furious. I began second-guessing myself for having done what I thought was the right thing after I followed him that day. I should have just kept my mouth shut about what I saw on the train to Purnea. So what if he had a woman on the side? Plenty of men did. What good had it done me?

The situation deteriorated. I had written to Worcester asking for more time; perhaps they could allow me to start in September, which would give me time to raise the money for the flight?

In July, the hospital wrote saying that if I could not arrive in early August as agreed upon, they would have to give my job to someone else.

At a loss for practical ways to raise the money, I sought spiritual help. I went to every temple, mosque, and church in town for prayer and blessing, even in religions and languages I was unfamiliar with! At this point, I thought... *Why not?*

Finally my prayers were heard. Someone stepped in—a person whose role was usually to keep *out* of affairs involving money or careers or almost anything outside of caregiving and housekeeping. My grandmother, Saraswati, apparently went to Nana and shamed—or maybe threatened—him into helping me.

Whatever she'd said to him worked; Nana wired us the money, and we immediately made the plane reservations. My flight was set for August 11, 1967. I'd fly to Calcutta, then to London, then to New York, and finally to Worcester, which, I had learned, was located in a place with another strange-sounding name: Massachusetts.

The entire family—aunts, uncles, cousins—were going to assemble at the airport to see me off. But the night before, as I was packing my meager possessions, we got an unexpected visitor: Nana, with Saraswati at his side.

While he hugged my brothers and sister, and greeted my mother warmly, Nana studiously avoided any contact with me. Except to whisper, "I want to talk to you later."

Great. He's going to give me another lecture on the proper behavior of grandchildren or try to tell me that what I saw on the train wasn't what I thought I saw. Or worse, he'll attach conditions to the money he gave me—or take it back altogether!

After dinner I went out into the scruffy backyard of our building to find Nana sitting there, smoking and scanning the evening sky. It was that rare thing in India, a cool summer night. I sat down wordlessly next to him. Without acknowledging me, without even looking at me, he spoke.

"I love your grandmother," he said.

"I know you do, Nana," I said, although to be honest I had wondered.

"While you may have learned a lot about anatomy, there is one thing they don't teach you in medical school. The heart. You know nothing of the heart."

"I...Well...," I stuttered.

He turned and looked at me. His face was hard, but his eyes were red, as if he had been crying. I had never seen Nana cry.

"I was eighteen when I was married," he said. "Younger than you are now. She was fourteen—a child! We knew nothing of each other. It was our families who arranged everything, and we had no say." He paused and turned his gaze up at the night sky. "I was lucky. She is a wonderful mother. A good person. A caring person. But..."

He turned back to look at me. "You know nothing about what marriage is. You will learn. It's not just sex."

I shuddered at the mention of this word. My grandfather talking about *sex*? Please, no details!

"It's also about common interests," he continued. "It's about intellectual stimulation, about being able to have conversations about things other than the house or diapers."

He paused again, as if listening to some invisible accuser.

"It's not her fault. And what I did was wrong, I admit it. But people shouldn't judge me. Especially people who don't know what it was like growing up when we did."

He sighed deeply. I was beginning to wonder if I should just leave this old man to his guilty conscience and ramblings when he turned and looked at me again with his great patrician's face.

"Don't judge me, Arun. And I won't judge you for what you did."

I began to protest that in my view there was no moral equivalency here but thought better of it.

"Enough about that," he said. "Here is what I want to tell you. I am sorry that I said some of the things I did to you. The truth is that I am very, very proud of what you have achieved. I know medical school wasn't easy for you, and I know what it's like working in that excuse for a hospital we have in Darbhanga. You did very well, and I believe you will continue to do well in America. In fact, you might even end up surpassing your old Nana in your career." He winked. "Although considering what a damn fine surgeon I was, that's going to take some doing!"

He stuck his hand out, as if we had reached some unspoken agreement. I took it warmly.

"Oh, and one last thing."

"Yes, Nana?"

"The five hundred dollars for your plane ticket? It's a loan. I expect you will pay me back in full."

The next day was cloudy and muggy as my family gathered at the Patna airport. Everyone was there—uncles, aunts, cousins, and some old neighbors and friends. It wasn't every day that someone from our circle traveled to the next province, much less to America—and to work as a doctor, no less. I think a lot of those who showed up figured they would never see me again.

They were right.

While I would return to India periodically, I would never

again reside in the country of my birth. I think my mother, too, realized this, because after having been so supportive of my efforts to take the job in Worcester, she was now weeping. "Am I wrong to be letting my oldest son leave?" she said. "What will we do without you?"

"Mom," I said, choking up. "If you want me to come back, just tell me, and I will."

"No, no," she said, wiping her tears. "You've worked your whole life to get to this point. When I think of you as a child and your"—she looked at me, and grinned when she carefully chose the right word—"*mishaps*, it makes me smile. I always knew you would come out OK, but I never dreamed you'd end up a doctor. In America! I can't tell you how this makes me feel."

A few minutes before it was time to board the plane, the pundit—essentially a Hindu priest—gave his good-luck blessing. He was dressed in a white gown, his head shaved, and he bore the traditional tilak, the white clay mark running from the root of his nose to the forehead marking him as a servant of Lord Krishna. The pundit prayed and chanted and waved incense around me. Everyone bowed their heads. Then he put a garland of marigolds around my neck for good luck. While I wasn't especially observant, I prayed right along. I figured I was going to need all the help I could get.

It had been my father's wish that we have the pundit present for my send-off. Dad had hobbled to the airport that day, though he was still recovering from his stroke, and prayed fervently along during the ceremony. He and I had settled into a polite, if cool, relationship since he had been hospitalized. I'd long since stopped trying to please him, and I think he finally realized his troublesome son had mended his ways and would no longer bring shame or trouble on his family and good name. And if he did get in trouble, it would be in America, and it would be their problem now, not his.

Still, I was surprised when he hugged me and wished me the best. "We're going to miss you," he said.

It was time to go. There was little airport security in those days, so the whole crowd just followed me out onto the tarmac. As I boarded the propeller-driven plane, I stopped and waved one last time. I caught Nana's eye, and I thought I saw a glint of a smile as he raised his hand in a dignified farewell salute.

In the next few months, I would repay his loan of the airfare from my first couple of American paychecks. I received a note acknowledging the repayment and reiterating the pride he felt in me. I responded that I would look forward to seeing him on my first visit home, and told him about my experience working as a surgeon in an American hospital. A few years later I found out that he had donated the payment to a charity in my name.

That conversation never took place. Nana, the grand old patrician of our family, the man I had both emulated and exposed, died of a massive heart attack eight months after I departed. He was sixty-seven years old. Saraswati would pass away a year after her husband.

What other secrets had died with Nana? About his years in London? About his true feelings toward Devi and my grandmother? I still think about this brilliant but complex man half a century later. As much as he had influenced me, guided me, and, yes, loved me, to the end my Nana would remain a man of mystery.

ᕙ

The day after I left for America, a small item appeared in a local edition of the newspaper *Indian Nation*. Underneath a black-and-white headshot of a very young Dr. Arun Singh, a caption informed readers that I was "flying to Massachusetts, USA for higher studies and fellowship in Cardiovascular and Thoracic Surgery." The announcement had been placed by my mother, who had probably walked over to the paper's offices, armed with the headshot of me, and persuaded the local editor that my departure was of immense newsworthiness to the citizens of Patna.

As it appeared the day after I departed, I never saw the piece until years later, when my brother fished it out of an old scrapbook. It was strange to see it a half century later. The really odd thing about it is that, at the time I left, I was leaning toward becoming an orthopedic surgeon. While I had discussed cardiology with Dr. Singh in medical school, we'd never seriously talked about my becoming a cardiac surgeon; the specialty barely existed. And I had certainly not spoken of it with my mom. And yet she had insisted to the newspaper that this was what I was going to be studying in America, as if she'd divined my destiny.

~ *Chapter Eleven* ~

Immigrant's Journey

Seven thousand, nine hundred miles in thirty-six hours. That was the length and duration of my journey to America in the summer of 1967.

Because I'd booked the cheapest ticket possible, my itinerary read more like a rock band's world tour than the solo journey of a young medical student. It involved three different airlines, with stops in Calcutta, Karachi, Beirut, Athens, Istanbul, Amsterdam, London, New York, and finally Worcester, Massachusetts.

Yet the distance I traveled was greater than even those numbers suggest.

It was as if I were in a *Twilight Zone* episode in which a jet wanders into some unusual atmospheric disturbance and is transported far into the future. Literally overnight, I had left an ancient, tradition-bound, and impoverished society for one that was gleaming with possibility and innovation.

My initial KLM flight from Calcutta had delivered me to a new world of unimaginable technological wonders whose pleasures I tasted well before reaching the US. For someone whose primary modes of transportation had been a secondhand bicycle, rickshaws, and slow-moving, crowded railroad trains, flying in a modern jet aircraft at thirty thousand feet—while being served refreshments—was itself a revelation. But then, after six stops and several plane changes, there was London.

It was a rainy, cool evening as I dragged my suitcase onto a double-decker bus from Heathrow to the hotel. Nana had shown me pictures of London from his time during the war, but seeing it firsthand was something else. By contrast to the cities of India that I knew, London was clean, efficient. Traffic flowed smoothly, gardens grew lush in the moist climate, and a sense of order seemed to pervade this great metropolis.

Even my dingy little hotel room near Victoria Station—courtesy of KLM Airlines—was a revelation. And not just because of the private bathroom—a rarity in India in those days. It was that magical box—all twelve inches or so—with the long antennae sprouting from its head that greeted me when I checked into my room.

Television.

I knew such marvels existed, but so rare a thing was this in India that the only time I had seen a television set back home was from fifty feet away, as it was guarded by ropes in a museum in Patna. Even such a prosperous man as Nana did not own one. But here it was, in all its black-and-white glory.

I watched a live cricket match and was in heaven.

The next morning—or was it the next decade?—I was on a Qantas flight bound for New York's Kennedy Airport, which I'd find to be a glittering, modern palace of air travel.

But as we roared over the Atlantic, I began to worry.

I'd left India with only eight dollars. That this was the maximum amount allowed by the government due to a shortage of foreign currency in the country at the time was almost irrelevant; we probably couldn't have raised any more money anyway!

I had already spent three dollars for bus fare to my hotel in

London. While I carefully folded and placed my precious five-dollar bill in my pocket, the unfamiliar face of Abraham Lincoln had stared up at me with his inscrutable smile, seemingly amused that someone like me would have the audacity, the gall, to think that he could come to the country Lincoln had helped build and practice medicine on its citizens.

Throughout the flight I would reach into my pocket periodically to make sure Lincoln had not escaped.

The friendly Qantas stewardess must have noticed my consternation. "Do you need anything?"

Her accent was hard to understand—was it English, American, Australian? I couldn't yet discern the distinctions. I smiled weakly and shook my head. I wanted to ask her for more peanuts, but I was already on my second bag—peanuts and cashews were about the only thing I ate during the entire trip. The airline meals of pork and beef—foods that we eschewed in India—had seemed hearty but unappetizing.

"No thank you," I croaked.

The truth was that I desperately needed many things. I needed food I could stomach and people whose language I could understand. I needed my family; I needed advice from Nana and a hug from my mother. Heck, I would have even settled for the cramped but collegial staff room at Darbhanga Medical College Hospital at that moment.

Soon our plane was descending into the great swath of New York. I gasped when I discerned the giant buildings and bridges in the distance.

"Welcome to John F. Kennedy International Airport," our flight attendant intoned cheerfully as the other passengers—most of them seasoned travelers—rubbed their eyes and stretched their arms after a long transoceanic nap. I hadn't slept a wink.

"We hope you have a pleasant stay in the New York area or wherever your final destination is."

And just where was my final destination? That was part of what had kept me from getting any rest. While I knew that I still had one last leg of my journey before me—from New York to my new hospital in Worcester, Massachusetts—where I would ultimately end up was still an open question. I assumed I would return to India to live at some point. Certainly there was no way I could possibly become a permanent resident of this unfamiliar, futuristic society, was there?

Fifty years later, on a 2017 layover at Kennedy during an overseas trip with my wife, I would find myself reminiscing about that afternoon my flight arrived in 1967. The famous saucer-shaped international terminal where I deplaned that day is long gone, but one can still see overseas passengers as they spill out into the arrivals area for the various airline terminals. As I watched them, I imagined what I must have looked like on that day long ago.

I had emerged, blinking in the bright lights of the terminal, in a rumpled suit—the same one I'd worn through medical school— and wondering what had happened to my suitcase. An airline official in a crisp blue uniform, probably trained to spot clueless arriving passengers, was immediately at my side offering help.

"Good afternoon," he said. "Do you need help? Do you know where you're going?"

I shook my head. I most certainly didn't.

"Then let me help you."

He guided me through customs and passport control, and then over to the baggage claim area. I think even he must have had to stifle a laugh when he saw the old, battered suitcase I fished off the conveyor belt. It was another hand-me-down, and the handle had broken somewhere between Karachi and

London; I had used my belt to hold it together. As a result my beltless suit pants were sagging as I dragged my suitcase through the terminal by its jury-rigged handle.

As disoriented as some of them appeared, I don't think any of the passengers arriving at JFK Terminal 4 in 2017 looked as utterly ridiculous as I looked, or at least felt, in 1967.

To board my flight to Worcester I would need to go to another terminal. The fellow from the airline guided me outside and showed me where to wait for the airport shuttle bus. "Good luck, young man," he said. I'm sure he thought I was going to need it.

Further proof of my naivete was now in front of my very eyes. As I waited for the bus, hugging the wall of the terminal while cars and baggage carts and taxis and people zipped past me at New York warp speed, I glanced out at the road abutting the terminal. I noticed a yellow median stripe, and in front of where I was waiting for the bus, the words painted in that same color on the ground: "No Parking."

I sighed. Somewhere my medical school chum Ravi was laughing his head off. This was the gold in America's streets that he had told me about and that I had seen in the picture. Yellow paint. I managed a smile. He'd pulled one over on me for sure.

The shuttle bus followed the yellow stripe to the terminal where I would board my Yellowbird. Named for their distinctive yellow-and-white exteriors, these planes were then part of the fleet of the now-defunct airline Northeast. There was something soothing about the very sound of a Yellowbird flying me to the final stop on my trip. My tranquility was short lived, however. The flight was about an hour, and almost as soon as we'd taken off, I began worrying again. How was I going to get from the airport to the hospital? I hadn't considered this. I had only five dollars. Would that be sufficient?

We landed in what was then a very small airport, located on a prominence known as Tatnuck Hill and surrounded by woods. Even today the Worcester Regional Airport, while modern and spacious, is a lonely place. "Like a big dinner party attended by just a handful of guests," is how the *Boston Globe* described it in a 2016 article, and I agree.

It was especially empty on a languid summer night in August 1967. I asked a woman at the information desk for directions to the city hospital. I explained to her my situation, and even though she had to ask me to repeat myself a few times—my Indian accent was very thick—she handed me a map and patiently went through the directions with me.

When she was done, I was thoroughly bewildered, but still determined. "May I ask one more question?" I asked.

"Of course," she said.

"How long do you think it would take to walk there?"

She was taken aback. "Walk?" she said. "I assumed you were going to drive or take a cab. I don't think you can walk it."

"How far is it?"

She raised her eyebrows apologetically. "I'm not sure, but around five miles," she said.

People walked farther than that in India, I thought. Not because they were exercise buffs, but because they had no choice. Moreover, we never used maps. With these unfamiliar-sounding American street names, there was no way I could find my destination.

By this time most of the crowd had left from my flight. I was the last passenger wandering around. Dragging my sad little suitcase along, I grew more and more despondent. How should I proceed? At that point I noticed a taxicab parked on the curb. The window was open and I saw the driver sitting behind the wheel, puffing on a cigarette. He had dark skin and wore thick glasses—the first non-Caucasian I had seen since leaving Kennedy Airport.

Finally, I thought. *Someone who looks like me.*

I approached him. "Hello, sir," I said, and I saw him do a double take when he saw my color, as if he needed to adjust his glasses, such a rare sight was I to behold. "I've just arrived from India," I said, "and I need to get to Worcester City Hospital."

He smiled. "Welcome, brother," he said. "Hop in."

I hesitated. "I'm afraid I must first ask, How much will this cost me?"

"It's about twenty minutes," he said. "So I figure three dollars and fifty cents."

Imagining Lincoln glaring at me from inside my pocket, I opened the door. "Let's go!" I said.

The man was from Iraq, then a place few Americans had even heard of. "Everyone assumes I'm Indian," he laughed. "They ask me about the Taj Mahal. I tell them, 'Wrong country!'"

The driver had emigrated here a few years earlier and now had two children. He had obviously learned the roads of his adopted city well. He pointed out some of the sights as we drove through what was then a largely rural landscape on the edge of the city. I saw farms, hills, and streams. I saw stone fences, erected with boulders by the early settlers, and attractive, spacious houses. "This is a beautiful place," I remarked.

He laughed. "Yes, the country is nice. The city…" He shrugged dismissively. "It has its good parts and bad parts."

I couldn't tell. Once we got downtown there were tall, new buildings and others that had clearly seen better days, which I'd later learn were from when this city had been a hub of the textile industry. Regardless, the entire city was an improvement over what I was used to. I was impressed that the roads were paved and relatively clean and that there were no pigs or other large animals roaming around. Also the traffic here, sparse as it was on a weekday evening, seemed to flow in some kind of order, as opposed to the chaotic scrum of vehicles that India is infamous for.

We arrived at the hospital. There was a newer building surrounded by several quaint-looking Victorian-era buildings. My driver was uncertain. "It's a big place," he said. "Do you know exactly where you're supposed to go?"

I didn't.

He let me off at the main entrance, where we figured someone would be able to direct me. I handed him my five-dollar bill and he gave me back a dollar and two quarters—all the money I had left. As he departed, my driver raised his hand in a solemn farewell. "Good luck in America, my brother," he said.

The main entrance to the hospital was quiet and almost empty. Again, completely unlike any Indian hospital I'd ever been in, which would have been packed with people moaning or sobbing.

I approached the telephone operator, seated at her switchboard around the corner from the empty front desk. I told her my name and that I was the new surgical intern from India. "Oh yes, Dr. Singh," she said. "We were told to expect you, we just weren't sure when."

I breathed a sigh of relief. I think there was still a part of me that had half expected to arrive and learn it was all a mistake or a hoax, or that Nana's check had bounced or that they had confused me with another Dr. Singh.

I had finally arrived.

The receptionist handed me a key to my room. Before I even

unpacked, I needed to let my family know that I had reached my destination. A three-minute call to London from New York in those days cost twelve dollars. India from Worcester might have been double that. And besides, only Nana in Darbhanga had a phone. Instead I had the helpful hospital operator connect me with Western Union. Sending the most concise possible telegraph to India, I was told, would cost me a dollar and twenty-five cents.

I gulped. That would be almost all the money I had. But I didn't want my family worrying.

"Arrived safely" was my short and thrifty message to my mother. I would have liked to add, "but broke."

I picked up my suitcase and walked the empty halls of the hospital to the residence area and my room. There was a bed, a wooden desk, a table lamp, and a ceiling fan. I would share a bathroom in the hall with others. While tiny by American standards, the room was big enough for me. I admit to being mildly disappointed at the absence of a TV—my brief exposure to this amazing new technology in London had whetted my appetite. I put my battered suitcase on the desk and sat down for a moment to let my new reality sink in.

For a second I thought about my family and was gripped by a wave of homesickness so strong I considered taking my belted bag and leaving. But then I recalled my long nights in the room in Nana's house, memorizing yet another chapter from my medical textbooks. I thought about my long days at the hospital in Darbhanga. I thought about taking the exams, about all the effort it had taken to win this position and raise the money to get here.

This was what I had worked toward: the opportunity to study with the best, to become a great surgeon, and to perhaps even eclipse my Nana's achievements.

Finally I unpacked my suitcase and laid out my precious belongings carefully: few clothes; Bailey's textbook of surgery; one of the holy books of Hinduism, the Bhagavad Gita; a bag of peanuts; and lastly the picture of Saraswati, the goddess of knowledge, music, arts, wisdom, and learning (after whom my grandmother had been named). I knelt down before her and prayed for strength and courage.

As I got ready for bed, I emptied the contents of my suit pockets. I was down to my last twenty-five cents. I carefully laid the coin on the desk and fell asleep in the New World.

Born July 6, 1944, I was around six months old here.

Paternal and maternal grandfathers, (*l to r*) Ram atan Singh and Bhagwan Prasad Singh (Nana).

Me with my parents and siblings, (*l to r*) Ampali, Ashesh, and Dilip in 1950.

Me visiting my childhood home and neighborhood in Patna, India.

Me as a freshman in college, having just become a national junior champion in carrom (1958).

Mr. Cool: Here I was a senior in college (1960).

With my favorite style of a red-and-black kite in Patna (2016).

Darbhanga Medical College and hospital campus (1960)

Hospital.

Medical ward.

Medical school.

Me at age seventeen during my
first year of medical school (1961).

Medical school graduation (1966).

Medical school cricket team photo (1963).

Nana's house in Darbhanga (1964).

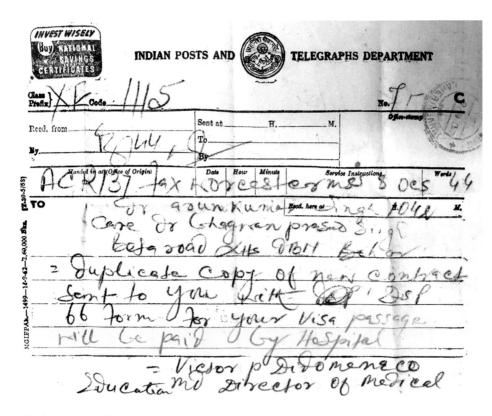

A telegram from Worcester City Hospital shows the hospital will pay for my passage (1967).

As I left for the USA, Mom put a garland around my neck for good luck as Nana and my sister looked on (1967).

Nana and my grandma Saraswati receiving my last loan payment (1968).

Mom put a notice in the local newspaper at my departure—proclaiming her son a future heart surgeon.

Dr. Arun Kumar Singh M.B.B.S. (Hons) of Patna is flying for Massachusetts, USA, on August 12 for higher studies and fellowship in Cardiovascular and Thoracic Surgery.

Here I was a Columbia University surgical resident (1970).

Me as a heart surgeon with Dr. Kenneth Forde in New York City (2016).

Barbara and me at our wedding in New York (1970).

Here with my in-laws.

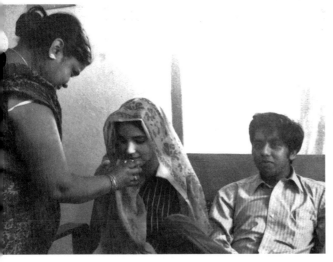

On my first visit to India
with Barbara; Mom offered
a blessing to us (1971).

At Great Ormond Street Hospital. Top row: (*l to r*) Me and Dr. Marc Deleval. Bottom row: Dr. Richard Bonham Carter and Dr. David Waterston (1975). *(Courtesy of Archive Service, Great Ormond Street Hospital for Children NHS Foundation Trust)*

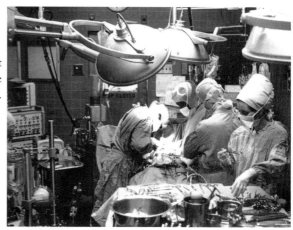

Performing the first open heart surgery on an infant at Rhode Island Hospital (1975).

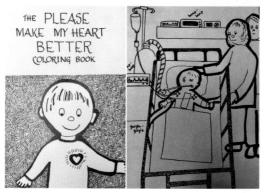

Coloring book from my patient Shawn (1977).

Family picture with my sons, Ari and Mike, and my wife, Barbara (1978).

Dad, at left, praying, and, at right, on a morning walk around the courtyard of his new home in Patna (1980).

Me with my parents and siblings (1980).

My parents with Ari, Mike, and Barbara during the Holi festival of color in Patna (1980).

My last visit with Mom in India (2006).

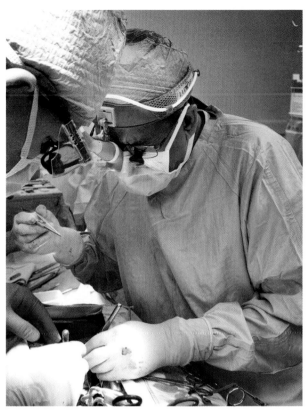

In action.

Presented to me by operating room staff after completing 10,000 open heart surgeries (1997).
(Courtesy of Lydia Rodrigues)

After thirty-six hours of a heart surgery "marathon" for patients pictured (*l to r*) who received a third heart valve replacement, an emergency David procedure, a fourth-time aortic surgery, and a David procedure with CABG.

My heart team (partial) in 2016.

The Lifespan Health System and Rhode Island Hospital thank *Arun Singh, MD*, for more than 40 years of commitment to the hospital, to his patients, and to the field of cardiothoracic surgery.

With nearly 20,000 open heart surgeries on adults and children, Dr. Singh has been a true force in cardiac care. He has saved countless lives, and his name is synonymous with open heart surgery. He is known for his passion and dedication and has made Rhode Island a better place not only to live and work, but to receive life-saving medical care.

Dr. Singh's leadership has been instrumental in shaping Rhode Island Hospital's award-winning cardiac program. We are grateful to him for his steadfast commitment, and above all, for sharing his genius with Lifespan and the people of Rhode Island for so many years.

Dr. Singh will remain as an honorary member of the medical staff but has decided to stop performing surgery in early April.

An announcement by Rhode Island Hospital and Lifespan Health System (2016). *(Courtesy of Lifespan Corporation)*

At my induction into the Rhode Island Heritage Hall of Fame, (*l to r*) Dr. Connelly, Mr. Visconti, Esq., me, and Mr. Molloy. *(Courtesy of the Rhode Island Heritage Hall of Fame)*

Deepak offering made in honor of my parents' souls at the Ganges River in Varanasi, India (2017).

My entire family (2018).

Unless otherwise noted all photographs are from the author's personal collection.

—⟶ *Chapter Twelve* ⟵—

Cheap Labor

The next morning, I met the chief of surgery and was given an orientation and a tour of the hospital.

Worcester City Hospital, located on Queen Street, had been established in the nineteenth century to care for the indigent. A century later, it was still fulfilling its mission. But while most of its patients were old and poor—many of them beneficiaries of a then-new federal program called Medicare—the hospital seemed to me an amazing, state-of-the-art facility compared to where I had come from. The corridors were clean, wide, and well lit. Instead of being lined up on the floor, or in a vast common area—like my father when he'd suffered his stroke—the patients, two apiece, were in rooms. Some even had private rooms—and with TV sets, no less! The beds, the sheets, and the bathrooms were spic-and-span. I also noticed a small but telling detail—the nurses and physicians alike wore gloves while examining patients as well as during any procedures. In India we wore gloves only for surgery. We couldn't afford to have pairs that were constantly being disposed of.

I saw also that patients were served proper meals on trays. And during visiting hours, family members would sit on chairs, not on the bed with the patient, as was the case in India. And there was something else the patients here had, something most

Americans expected and took for granted—privacy. Each patient was separated by a screen, one that could be closed to encircle the patient's bed while they were undergoing some kind of procedure, or even just performing basic bodily functions. There was no privacy in India. Especially in Indian hospitals in the sixties.

That morning, I was also introduced to my fellow residents. To my surprise, out of about forty people only one was an American. The rest were from India, Pakistan, Korea, Taiwan, Thailand, Iran, and Iraq. These guys, along with one woman (a senior resident from India), welcomed me. I was told not to worry. They would help me. And they did, which I appreciated, although I didn't do much socializing. My goal was to succeed. To that end, I spent my whole life in the hospital. One of the perks for the interns and residents was free meals in the cafeteria. I ate nothing but hospital food for the first two months. When I wasn't working, I would spend time in the hospital library reading medical journals, eager to glean the latest knowledge in my rapidly changing new profession.

I didn't have time for much else. My day started with rounds at five a.m., and I generally worked until six p.m.—except when I was on call, which meant that one workday could extend to the next. On average we were working around 110 hours a week. (Today, residents are limited by law to about eighty hours.)

My duty was to see the patients, prepare them for their surgeries, do a history and physical, and draw the blood for the lab tests. I also assisted in the operating room, although to my surprise I was mostly used just to hold retractors. These are the long-handled, curved-headed instruments used to pull back underlying organs or tissues during surgery, so that the doctor performing the surgery can clearly see what he's working on. It's an important part of the procedure, for sure, but holding the retractor is more or less a passive job, like that of the squire who holds the knight's horse while he charges into battle, waving his sword over his head.

That was fine with me, at first. I was there to watch and learn. But after a few of these procedures I noticed that the American surgeons performing them would barely talk to us foreign residents. In India the senior men explained to the residents what they were doing and why. I was puzzled as to why no one was doing the same for me here.

It took me a few weeks, and a few guarded discussions in the cafeteria with some of the other residents, but I eventually figured out what was going on. We weren't learning because they weren't interested in teaching us. Unlike the great university hospitals of America or Great Britain, this wasn't a place where the next generation of surgeons came for their training. The residents here were simply a form of cheap labor. Like foreigners everywhere, we were used to doing the work that the natives—in this case the American surgeons—didn't want to do, the kinds of things that in most hospitals today are done by physician assistants or nurse practitioners. I hasten to say that these professionals play a vital role in the modern hospital, and I respect their skills and compassion. (Indeed, I am on the faculty of Bryant University's Physician Assistant Program, so I know full well how bright and competent many of these young men and women are.) But in the 1960s I was young, hungry, and chasing a different goal: I wanted to become a surgeon. I didn't want to spend my entire time giving enemas to patients, taking blood, or holding retractors. Once I realized what the hospital was doing, I was angry.

I was incensed further when after a month or so I began to notice turnover among my colleagues. Suddenly the friendly fellow from Iran with the big smile and the quiet, polite young man from Thailand were gone. Last I had heard they were supposed to take their boards. What had happened? I inquired. They had failed the exams and were now going back home, ignominiously, I was told.

This seemed to happen to a lot of the guys who were there when I arrived. These residents were failing in large part because they hadn't been taught anything!

Of course, I had no power. What was I going to do about this? March into the chief of surgery's office and accuse him of exploiting foreign workers? Go over to the offices of the local newspaper, the *Worcester Telegram*, and tell them that their local hospital was really the medical version of a sweatshop? I didn't even know where the *Telegram*'s offices were and could barely have found my way there if I had!

As it turned out, the chief of surgery wanted to see me. I got a call one morning from his secretary. *Uh-oh*, I thought. *He must have heard that I was asking around.* Now I'd be branded as a troublemaker and punished or expelled.

I entered his office prepared for the worst.

"Dr. Singh," he said, barely looking up from a pile of papers. "How long have you been with us now?"

"About three months, sir."

"Well, you've done a good job here. We're impressed with your skills and your attitude. The patients like you, too. And so do the senior men."

On what basis? I wondered. *Because I could hold a retractor steady for two hours and keep my mouth shut?*

"That's why we want to keep you around," he said. "How would you like to join us? You could finish your surgical training here in four years."

He thrust a paper in front of me and offered me a pen. He wanted me to sign on the spot! I told him I was flattered, but politely declined.

"Sir," I said, "I must speak frankly with you. I have traveled nearly ten thousand miles to be here and to learn. And in the time I've been here, I'm sorry to say that the only place I'm learning is in your library. Not in the OR."

I explained to him that my plan was to leave here after a year and seek admission to an American university hospital.

He laughed. "Dr. Singh," he said, "the residents in American university hospitals are Americans. That's why those institutions exist. To educate our own residents, not foreigners. Look, we're offering you a four-year surgical residency. You'd be one of only two surgical residents here. And the odds of you getting a residency at one of those teaching hospitals...well, no offense, but they're pretty slim."

I *was* offended. The chief of surgery was confirming what I had suspected. He looked at us foreign doctors as inferior—as cheap, interchangeable parts he could use to keep his hospital running. While on one level I was glad he had singled me out, there was no way I was going to stay here.

"Sorry," I said. "While I appreciate your confidence in me, I can't accept this position."

He looked at me darkly. "You're making a mistake, Doctor."

I walked out of his office that day overwhelmed by the reality of my situation. Worcester was essentially a dead end, but after all my family and I had been through to get me here, there was no way I could return home and again be labeled a failure. I was only months into my training, and in order to become a surgeon I needed five to seven years. Not to mention that the J-1 visa I had arrived on was good for only a year and needed to be renewed in just a few short months. This visa was granted to those seeking medical or business training. I didn't have a new program to sponsor a visa renewal, and the clock was ticking for me. I agonized over every day and sleepless night that passed as I wrestled with the uncertainty of my future.

I knew that I was going to have to make some changes, fast. What could I do? Some of the residents who had left Worcester had gone into pathology. The thinking of many back then was that this was an area of medicine "acceptable" for foreigners. They rarely dealt with patients, so language and bedside manner were not issues. While I found pathology an interesting branch of medicine, it wasn't what I had come here to do. Besides, I liked interacting with the patients and thought it was an important aspect of practicing medicine.

Then I got a fortuitous call from a medical school classmate of mine. His name was Mohan, and I had not heard from him in a year or so.

"Where are you, Mohan?" I asked when he called out of the blue.

"I'm in Chicago now," he said. "But I'm heading to Columbia University Medical Center in New York for a surgical residency. I heard you're working at that sweatshop in Worcester." Interesting, I thought, how everyone seemed to know about this place's reputation except me. "Arun. You know you're not going to learn a thing at that place."

"You're right," I said. "But what am I going to do?"

"Mohan is the man with the answer, my friend," he said. "It just so happens they're looking for a few residents here to start this summer."

"Surgical residents? At Columbia? But don't they want Americans?"

"They do, but they can't find them."

The Vietnam War, which had intensified in that past year, had created a demand for physicians in the armed forces, Mohan explained. Rather than get drafted, many US medical students had enlisted. No doubt they would learn a lot in difficult situations and then return to the US, where many would complete their training and go on to successful careers in medicine. However, the shortage of residents had left the hospitals in a difficult position: Vietnam War or no, they could not function without a full complement of staff.

I was on a Greyhound bus to New York two days later.

This was a gamble. I had pretty much burned my bridges at Worcester, and while Columbia seemed to be in a hurry to interview me when I called the office of the residency program, I had no idea what kind of competition I was up against, or whether the surgical residencies would be filled by the time I arrived.

When we pulled out of the tunnel and into midtown Manhattan, I was overwhelmed. I'd gotten a tantalizing glimpse of the city from the air a few months earlier, but now I was in the heart of it. Yes, it was scary, but there was also something about the energy there: you got a sense that everything was in forward motion and everyone was on a mission, all heading toward something—a goal. Which was exactly what I was doing. Maybe, I allowed myself to hope, maybe I actually belonged here?

I arrived in the late afternoon. My interview was the next morning at Harlem Hospital, one of three teaching hospitals then affiliated with Columbia University College of Physicians and Surgeons. Following directions given to me, I took a city bus uptown. I had booked a room at the YMCA on 135th Street and Lenox Avenue in Harlem. It was the cheapest place I could find in the area: for three dollars they gave you a clean metal cot with a bedsheet, a blanket, a towel, and access to a common bathroom with a shower. Despite such luxuries, I couldn't sleep that night. It wasn't just because of nerves, it was also because of noise—sirens blaring and people outside talking and laughing. I heard what sounded like a gang fight around midnight—it turned out to be a vigorously contested basketball game.

I had arrived in May 1968—a very hot time to be in America. The Tet Offensive that had begun earlier that year had rocked American confidence; antiwar protesters now filled the streets. The riots in reaction to the assassination of Martin Luther King Jr. that April were still a fresh memory.

This country, I was learning, while far more advanced than mine, had its problems, too. One of them was clearly racism. I didn't know that Harlem was a largely African American area. I had seen a few people of African descent in India, but this seemed to be an entire community. The thing that was most striking to me, in Harlem and in Worcester, was the size of these Americans, whether white or black—especially the young males. Here I was, five feet, eight inches and 120 pounds, dwarfed by these strapping guys at six feet two and 200 pounds and with powerful upper bodies. I felt like a child.

The next morning I walked into the office of the chief of surgery, Dr. Jose Ferrer. Dr. Ferrer's brother, Mel, was an actor and director who was perhaps most famous for being Audrey Hepburn's first husband. Despite his glamorous Hollywood connections, Dr. Ferrer was unaffected and well mannered. There was none of the condescension I had felt from his counterpart in Worcester. He quizzed me to see how much I knew, asking me how I'd prep a patient for a particular kind of procedure and what kind of operation a patient would require if he had this or that condition.

I answered to the best of my ability. At the end of my informal oral exam, he explained the Columbia residency program. If I took the position, I would have to spend four years of training among three hospitals: Harlem, Francis Delafield (now defunct), and Presbyterian Hospital.

I knew that Columbia was an elite American university. And I figured that these hospitals—none of which I'd heard of—must be top notch. So I nodded to signal that I understood the terms.

"Is that a yes, Dr. Singh?" Dr. Ferrer asked.

"Excuse me, sir?"

"I'm offering you the position."

I blinked. *This must be how they do things in America*, I thought. Everything was fast, now, immediate. None of this "OK, we'll get back to you in a few days," or even "Think about it and let us know." There were things to do, operations to be performed, lives to be saved...and much to be learned!

I was ready to be a part of it.

"Yes, Dr. Ferrer," I said, smiling. "Thank you. I accept."

Chapter Thirteen

The Greatest City in the World

My first night on call as a surgical resident, all hell broke loose.

It was July 1968, just a month after my interview. My battered suitcase and I had arrived the day before; I was staying in a dorm while I found an apartment.

Suddenly here I was, in the emergency room of Harlem Hospital, taking care of every patient who came in. That first night we had intoxicated people, people who'd been in car crashes, and stabbing and gunshot wound victims, including one guy who had taken a bullet to his head. Apparently he had been with his girlfriend when they heard a knock on the door. He looked through the peephole and his ex-wife was there with a gun. She fired, dislodging the peephole into his head. To my amazement and everybody else's, he was awake and talking. As I recall, he survived.

Another patient came in accompanied by two NYPD officers. He had apparently been in the process of stealing a television set when the owner came back to the apartment. The thief attempted to get away with the TV by lowering himself out of a fifth-floor window on a bedsheet. But the sheet tore and he plummeted to the ground and was brought into our emergency room with a broken leg and pelvis. (The status of the TV I never did learn.)

That night I also saw a stab wound to the heart. I had to help crack open the chest in the emergency room, and then I cradled the heart so a senior resident could suture the wound to stop the bleeding. This was first time I held a beating heart in my hands. What an amazing feeling. I would love to say that I had an epiphany that night and decided then and there to become a heart surgeon; the truth is that we were way too busy for me to stop and entertain such thoughts. It was on to the next patient.

This was nothing like Darbhanga. The casualty room there was a grim, crowded, dirty place. But in my six years there we had never treated a gunshot wound. Nor had I seen police officers or patients who had to be handcuffed to beds, or gurneys and beds spattered with as much blood as I saw here.

Indians, it appeared to me, died slowly and often quietly, from malnutrition or nasty, infectious diseases. Americans, based on what I saw those first few weeks, tended to go out in a more spectacular fashion, in a blaze of gunfire or through other acts of violence.

Of course, most of the patients at Harlem Hospital's emergency room didn't die. They survived. That was thanks in large part to the facility itself. The support system was super: the lights, the equipment, the medications, the instruments—all better than I'd known in India. Still, the disparity was too much for my friend Mohan. After treating trauma victims night after night that summer, he left. "I can't handle this," he said. He got a residency at a prestigious hospital in Detroit, and I was sad to be parted from another familiar face. He went on to a successful surgical career, albeit in a slightly less hectic environment.

I, on the other hand, was determined to make this work. Columbia and Dr. Ferrer had put their faith in me when I was going nowhere at Worcester City Hospital. I was ready to stick it out, no matter what.

My third night on call, I got a call from the pediatric intensive care unit. A newborn baby was very sick and dehydrated, and the nurses could not get an IV started. I was needed to do a *cut down*, meaning that I had to cut deep into her skin to find a vein so a catheter could be inserted directly.

The baby weighed only three and a half pounds. She was thrashing around, and her respiratory rate was high. While routine, this was a delicate procedure. One slip and I could have seriously harmed this infant. I'd never worked on a human being so small. I'd never done a procedure like this. I looked around for help—there was no senior resident available.

The senior nurse sensed my fear. While this might have been my first time doing a cut down on an infant, it certainly wasn't hers. "Don't worry, Doctor," she said reassuringly. "We'll hold her arm. Make the cut right here." She pointed to a spot just about an inch above the elbow crease, the antecubital fossa.

A procedure that normally took five minutes took me a half hour. It wasn't the last time an experienced nurse would come to my rescue.

A couple of days later, I heard, the child was back home. I felt a sense of relief—and, I must admit, a little pride that I'd come through under pressure.

The morning after that emergency, I was exhausted. We were doing our rounds, when all the residents would get together and talk about our patients. This was an excellent opportunity to learn together, and while normally I looked forward to sharing our patient notes, this time I couldn't focus. As one of my colleagues was explaining how he'd dealt with an acute appendicitis, I yawned.

"Dr. Singh!" Startled, I looked up. It was our chief resident, Dr. Mohammed Parsa, an Iranian and a super physician—not to mention one of the hardest workers I've ever known.

"Excuse me, Dr. Parsa," I said apologetically.

"Please come see me when you're done today."

Oh great, I thought. *Now I'm in trouble.* The surgical training at Columbia was a competitive and pyramidal system. I was one of twelve first-year residents; the next year they would narrow that number down to four. The remainder would either go on to different branches of medicine or, if they lucked out, find training somewhere else. If not, their surgical careers were done.

It was survival of the fittest, and a puny first-year resident who could barely stay awake didn't inspire much confidence in the fitness department. That evening, around seven p.m., when I had completed my last rounds, I went to see Dr. Parsa. I had worked continuously for thirty-six hours, and even strong black coffee wasn't helping at this point. All I wanted to do was lie down. Stifling yet another yawn, I tried to look alert as I sat down for our meeting.

"Arun," he said earnestly, calling me by my first name. "I know you really want to be a surgeon, but just wanting to do it isn't enough. You're competing for only four spots in training next year. Some of them are American graduates, and they'll be the preferred candidates, unless you can prove that you are better than they are. I've watched you. I think you really have what it takes. But it's up to you. How much do you want this?"

He handed me a copy of an advanced anatomy text. The message was clear. Start doing your homework. Put in the extra time. Outwork everyone else.

This was not the first time I'd been faced with such a challenge. I thought back to how I'd turned things around in my second year of medical school despite my dyslexia.

I'd succeeded then, I could succeed again. But this time it was going to take more than memorization. My experiences with the baby and a few other patients had revealed to me that this time I had not a cognitive shortcoming, but a physical one: the lack of strength in my hands. The carrom playing and homegrown rehab methods my mom had forced me into as a boy had enabled me to regain the use of those hands after my childhood mishaps. But through most of my early adult life, I still suffered from agonizing, burning pain, tingling, and numbness in my right hand due to nerve damage. I didn't have the grip strength or dexterity to handle the scalpel or tie the sutures with the control and assurance that I would need—no pun intended—to make the cut in the Columbia residency program.

I had watched some of the top surgeons, including Dr. Ferrer, at work. They cut and sewed smoothly and with precision. Their hands were both strong and delicate. To be in their league, I had to get better. What could I do to train and strengthen my hands while improving my dexterity? What would be, to use a modern exercise physiology term, cross-training for surgery? Who, I wondered, needed nimble and strong fingers besides those wielding scalpels?

Suddenly I had a mental picture of my mother sewing. Like many women in India, she was a seamstress. My father, in fact, could sew, as well. I recalled how as a child I had watched them as they sat side by side, darning and stitching the old clothes we couldn't afford to replace.

That's it! I thought. For the next few months, while my fellow residents explored the great New York metropolis during our rare nights off, I stayed alone in my Spartan apartment and created my own little sewing circle.

I would practice every night for an hour, tying knots and suturing on a pillow. It ended up looking embroidered, with tiny, precise knots running up and down its side. I found others and eventually had more embroidered pillows on my couch than a posh hotel.

No one ever saw this. And although I had been challenged to make this kind of extra effort by Dr. Parsa, I didn't even tell him. I decided to let my hands do the talking. And over the course of weeks of daily sewing at home, they did, as I saw the work pay off. I could feel that my hands were stronger and more dexterous. When I was asked to make an incision on a patient, my cuts were cleaner and more precise.

And there was an added bonus—when I got a hole in one of my socks, I could now mend it myself.

After a time, I was able to find a two-bedroom apartment with a kitchen in the neighborhood known as Spanish Harlem. At 163rd Street and Amsterdam Avenue, I was centrally located among all three of Columbia's hospitals.

I shared the apartment with another resident, named Kundu, and our rent was sixty-three dollars a month. Even then that was a bargain, but I soon learned why. The first night, when I walked into the new apartment, I heard a crunching noise under my shoes. I turned the light on and couldn't believe what I saw. There must have been thousands of cockroaches crawling around the floor. I had seen a few lizards and mice in the house in India, but they were usually outliers. I'd never seen anything like this— an army of roaches. I stood there, horrified, not sure what to do. Then I noticed that all the roaches began disappearing through cracks in the wall and along the floorboards. They lived there, and came out only at night, when it was dark in the apartment. This was their routine. Who was I to question it? Besides, the roaches may have been ugly, but they didn't bite. I shrugged. "Live and let live," I remember saying to my roommate. Which was what we did, sharing the apartment with the local roaches for three years.

Today, Harlem is a pricey, stylish neighborhood in Manhattan. In the late 1960s it was, like many parts of the city, poor, dangerous, and crime-ridden. It was also predominantly African American and Latino. When people heard I lived in Harlem, their eyes widened. "Be careful," they'd say. That, I soon realized, was code for, "Watch out for the blacks and Puerto Ricans." Being dark skinned myself, perhaps I looked at people of color in a different way. Regardless, I never had a problem in the time I lived in the neighborhood. And I was frequently walking home at three or four in the morning, alone, after a long shift at the hospital, conspicuous in my white physician's coat.

It wasn't just me. None of the other residents and hospital staff who had chosen to live in that neighborhood seemed to have problems, regardless of the color of their skin. I think the reason for our immunity was simple. The residents of those neighborhoods knew who we were, knew where we worked. They understood that we performed an essential service and that it might be one of their friends or loved ones we'd help if they got sick, or whose life we might save in an emergency.

By that point in my residency, I needed to decide what kind of surgery I'd specialize in. I had done my rotation of neurosurgery and orthopedics, and it had confirmed what I'd suspected back in India: I just couldn't physically handle the demands of orthopedic surgery. I lacked the strength needed to lift and manipulate the heavy limbs of American patients. No amount of sewing would help this problem. Perhaps today I might have hired a personal trainer and worked out diligently at a gym to get stronger. But gyms were few and far between in those days—especially in my neighborhood. And the concept of a personal trainer didn't even really exist.

Reluctantly I abandoned my dream of becoming an orthopedic surgeon, like the doctors who had helped me as a child in India. However, I did become very interested in neurosurgery. The brain was fascinating, and I liked the challenge of making a diagnosis. But I became disappointed once I started working in neurosurgery at Harlem Hospital. Although it was a top unit, the outcome of the operations was often ambiguous. One of the great rewards of being a surgeon is to know that you achieved something decisive through your actions—to see a tumor removed or a leaky heart valve repaired or replaced. That wasn't the case in brain surgery in those days. Recovery was slow. It took a long time to determine if the patient had benefited from the procedure, and results were often unclear.

I wanted my surgery to have an immediate and positive impact on my patients. Neurosurgery was not the avenue for me.

After ten months, my second rotation was at Francis Delafield Hospital, which was behind the Presbyterian Hospital on 168th Street and Broadway. It was a city hospital for terminally ill cancer patients.

This alone was an unusual concept for me. Going to a hospital to die was not something one did in India. Unless they were indigent, most people died at home. Here our patients were in the final stages of life. They were suffering. None of the skills I was developing, none of the medical knowledge I had begun to amass, could help them.

My first day on the floor, I went to see a patient with cancer. She had an ulcerated tumor the size of an orange on her left breast. It had metastasized, and at that point she had only a few months to live. She was in agony, moaning, when I walked into her room. I had read her chart. I could see the tumor and hear her cries. And I knew her prognosis. She wasn't even old. In her forties. And yet there was nothing I could do!

Just then, I felt the presence of someone next to me. It was one of the nurses, and it was as if she had read my mind. "I know you can't save her," she said softly, "but we *can* make her more comfortable."

She showed me how to change the patient's dressing and administer her medication. And maybe most importantly, she showed me how to treat that woman and the other terminally ill patients—with kindness and compassion.

"How are you today?" the nurse asked, bending down to talk to the dying woman.

"It hurts," she said in a groggy voice, without specifying where. "Can you do anything for the pain?"

"We can," said the nurse reassuringly, as she reached out and took the woman's hand. "This is Dr. Singh. He's going to give you something to make you feel better."

"Thank you, dear," said the woman.

I was humbled and deeply moved. As we stepped out of the patient's room, I thanked the nurse, whose name was Barbara. She was young and had big brown eyes and long, dark-brown hair.

"I really didn't know what to say," I admitted. "What can you tell someone who is dying?"

"Not much," acknowledged Barbara. "But you can show them kindness, show them you're here, and that you care."

"You did all that in there," I said. "You're in the right profession."

"I hope so," Barbara said. "I just got out of Queens College six months ago."

"I'm impressed!" I said.

And indeed I was. Not only with how well she comported herself and how kind and loving she was. She was also very attractive.

I saw Barbara again on my next shift. And again, she taught me by example how to interact with the terminally ill patients of our hospital. Of course, she wasn't the only one. The entire nursing staff was first-rate. But Barbara intrigued me: She was tender, but not soft. She had grown up in a housing project in Queens, and as a nursing student had worked in a psychiatric unit at Creedmoor, one of the city's large mental hospitals. She could be tough, too. But funny—and direct in the way New Yorkers often are.

"Do you like hot dogs?" she asked me one day.

"Uh…yeah, I think," I said. The truth was, I had steered away from many unfamiliar American foods.

Her eyes narrowed. "Have you even *had* a hot dog since you've been in New York?" she asked suspiciously.

I admitted that this particular pleasure had eluded me.

She sighed in exasperation. "How can you live in New York without ever having a hot dog? Next thing you'll tell me is that you haven't been to a Broadway play or that you never went to the top of the Empire State Building."

"Uh…well, I've been pretty busy…"

"OK, that does it. Come with me."

"Where?"

She looked at her watch. It was lunchtime.

"We're going to the hot dog stand in front of the hospital."

And so we did. She ordered two frankfurters, both with mustard, relish, and sauerkraut, or, as she told the vendor behind the Sabrett sign, "the works."

I must admit it was delicious. Even when the relish dripped onto my chin, and Barbara and I laughed and laughed.

I'm not sure if I fell in love at the hot dog stand that day, but it certainly wasn't long after. Barbara, whose last name was Schachter, was a revelation to me. I'd had no real girlfriends up to that point; I'd been too focused on my work and helping my family. She was devoted to her work and family, too, but unlike me, she also knew how to have fun in what she reminded me was "the greatest city in the world."

Together we explored that city during the hours I could break away from studies, sewing, and surgery. We went to the Metropolitan Museum of Art. The American Wing was Barbara's favorite, and it became mine, as well, as there, for the first time, I developed an appreciation for painting and sculpture. We went to the Statue of Liberty. We strolled in Central Park. I was fascinated by this vibrant metropolis, so different from the cities I knew in India. Besides hot dogs, Barbara introduced me to other New York delicacies, such as salted pretzels, bagels and lox, and hamburgers, not to mention the fuel that kept the city running in the pre-Starbucks era, Chock Full o'Nuts coffee.

Every time we got together, Barbara had a great idea for a new place, a new part of the city, a new museum to visit or a movie to see. Afterward we'd end up discussing what we'd seen over dinner at our favorite haunt, King Arthur's, a diner in the Bronx that was well-known for its veal cutlet and red cabbage.

After a while I decided that Barbara shouldn't have to plan everything, and that I should take the initiative for once. I had seen an ad in the *New York Times* for a new Broadway show called *Oh! Calcutta! Perfect*, I thought, *a play about a city from my home country. Maybe we can go over to Chock Full o'Nuts for coffee after the play, and I can tell her a little more about India, just as she's told me so much about her city.*

That night, we took our seats in the Belasco Theatre. It was sold out. "Wow," I told Barbara. "I had no idea people in New York were so interested in Calcutta."

The lights went out. The curtain rose, the cast began dancing. And then, to the tune of a song called "Taking Off the Robe," everyone on stage took off their clothes.

I was mortified!

It turned out that *Oh! Calcutta!* had nothing to do with India, but lots to do with indecency. There was full frontal nudity, by both male and female actors, there were implied copulation and masturbation, and there were silly sex jokes. It was a scandalous musical of its time, essentially an avant-garde sex romp, and it was a huge hit.

I was embarrassed beyond belief. While neither of us thought the show was very good—critic Clive Barnes called it "sophomoric and soporific," and I agreed—Barbara got a big laugh out of the whole situation. Especially later, when we found out that the Calcutta of the play's title had nothing to do with the city, but was supposedly a play on a French phrase, *o quel cul t'as*, which loosely translates to "what an ass you have."

Which also described how I felt.

Chapter Fourteen

What Racism Looks Like

Pomonok Houses, the fifty-two-acre Queens development that had been Barbara's home growing up, was an exemplar of what we now call "diversity." Built in 1951 on the site of a former country club in south Flushing, Pomonok Houses had been designed for lower- and middle-income families. While most of the residents were white, there were also African Americans living there. As a child, Barbara had had friends and neighbors of every race and ethnicity.

For her, color—the fact that her skin is white and mine is brown—was never an issue. Sadly, that was not the attitude everywhere.

I certainly felt the sting of racism, even in a profession supposedly filled with by highly educated people who should have known better. Part of it, I realize now, was simply ignorance; people of Indian descent were less common in the US than they are now, and I think there were some who never could quite figure out what I was: black, Caribbean, Cuban?

At the hospitals, resentment toward the foreign residents was overt. Several times I had to bite my tongue when I'd hear someone complain loudly about "foreigners" coming here to "steal" resident positions from American medical school graduates. We were accused of other questionable motives and nefarious behaviors, as well. One day I was having lunch with colleagues when one American guy started railing against immigrants. "They come here and get married just to get the benefits of US citizenship," he assured his listeners. "They never go back. They come here to work the system." He noticed me and added a perfunctory "no offense"-type caveat: "Present company excluded, Arun."

This blowhard had no idea that I was dating a nice Jewish girl from Queens. While I nodded politely in return, as if to say, "No offense taken," I really wanted to shove a hot dog, with the works, right in his face.

By this time I had moved on to Presbyterian, the third hospital in my residency. This was rarefied air—the top surgeons practiced here. But, as I learned, even that air could be polluted by prejudice. One day our chief resident, Daniel, invited a few of the junior residents for dinner at his house in a posh suburb of New Jersey, just across the George Washington Bridge. We felt it was very nice of him to invite us and give us an opportunity to spend an evening together with fellow residents.

I drove over with another junior resident, Mitch, who had a car. We sat in the living room of Daniel's beautiful split-level home, sipping drinks and listening to soft jazz. At one point Daniel introduced us to his daughter. She was a cute little five-year-old, blond haired and blue eyed. When he led her out to say hello, she took one look at us and ran behind her father.

"Don't be shy," he said gently. "Let me introduce you to my friends."

She peered out from behind his legs.

"That's Mitch," he said, pointing to one of my colleagues. "He's Jewish, and that's how Jews look. Next to him is Wally; he's Afro American, and that's how Afro Americans look. And this is Arun; he's from India. And that's how Indians look."

Shortly afterward he escorted his daughter back to her room. At that point Wally turned to Mitch and me and whispered, "And that's Daniel. He's a racist, and that's what racism looks like."

I laughed, but I couldn't believe what I'd just heard.

There was nothing funny about being discriminated against, but even I had to laugh at one incident. The Department of Surgery held a black-tie event near the newly built World Trade Center. I elected to go. I rented the cheapest tuxedo I could find; it was the first time I'd ever donned formal wear. The setting was magnificent. We were in lower Manhattan, right on the water near Battery Park, surrounded by enormous yachts and even more enormous buildings. There was a band playing and lots of food and drink. All the hospital brass was there, from administrators to senior doctors. Many of their names I recognized from internal memos or employee publications, but I had never actually seen them in person.

At one point I needed to use the men's room. There an older surgeon stood washing his hands at the sink next to me. I was closer to the stack of white towels neatly laid out on the sink counter. So out of courtesy, I handed him one.

Without even looking at me, he put a five-dollar bill in my hand.

The old doctor thought I was the washroom attendant! Why? Because in those days, it was easier for him to assume that someone with dark skin would be doing that job than that he would be a fellow doctor. For a moment I thought to myself, *Maybe I should stay here and pick up a little extra money*. But then one of my friends came in to tell me that the food was being served.

That was the nature of prejudice as I experienced it; even if it was not always mean-spirited or intentional, I felt it. People looked at me a little bit differently. While I could occasionally laugh it off, it made me angry and sometimes made me feel humiliated. Still, as I saw it, there was only one response: to show all these white guys that the brown guy, the immigrant with the funny accent, was not only just as good as they were—but maybe better.

—ᴗ *Chapter Fifteen* ᴗ—

New Family, New Friends, New World

By this point I was fully immersed in my life in New York and in my relationship with Barbara. But I still had a family in India, and one member of that family—my youngest brother, Ashesh— now wrote and told me that he wanted to come to the United States and study medicine. He had the academic credentials, but no means of supporting himself (my other brother had not yet struck it rich in the Indian lottery). Could I give him the plane fare? he asked.

Clearly he didn't understand my situation. I was making only $19,000 a year, and much of that was going home to our mother. But then I thought back to what I'd gone through for my plane fare two years earlier, how I'd had to grovel before Nana, and how my mother and I had sold old clothes to get a little extra cash. Did I really want Ashesh to have to endure the same humiliation and hardships? I wrote him back and said that I would pay for his flight.

A few months later, using the money I'd sent to him, he flew to Chicago to study cytology, a branch of pathology that involves studying diseases on the cellular level. But Ashesh suffered greatly in the cold Midwest winter and also felt homesick.

He called me and said he wanted to move to New York. He had an opportunity for a scholarship in a cytology program affiliated with New York University.

How could I deny my younger brother?

"Sure," I told him. "Come to New York and stay with me."

Meanwhile, I was spending every free hour I had with Barbara. I had met her family in Queens. Her father, Oscar, worked in real estate, and because it was not always the lucrative profession in New York that it would later become, he supplemented his earnings by driving a cab. Oscar had come to this country at a young age from Romania. He spoke fluent German, and during World War II had served in the US Army as an interpreter. But the Holocaust had claimed most of his extended family. That loss and the horror of war haunted him for the rest of his life.

Barbara's mother, Frieda, had been born in the US of Polish descent. When I met her, I saw where Barbara had gotten her caregiving instincts. Frieda was a warm, compassionate, and lovely person. She made me feel comfortable and welcome from the first time I visited Pomonok.

Barbara's parents never questioned their daughter's relationship with a non-Jewish, nonwhite man. When I asked her parents for their daughter's hand (as young men still did then), I had worried that they might turn me down. Instead they were thrilled. As were my parents, who had probably never met a Jewish person in their lives. I think my mother was just happy that I'd emerged from my studies and work long enough to meet someone!

After dating for ten months, Barbara and I were married on the evening of November 20, 1970. We didn't have the time or money for a big, expensive wedding, so we simply went to a justice of the peace. With Barbara's parents and my brother

Ashesh as witnesses, we would be married and then head back to Queens for dinner.

Even that simple plan, however, didn't materialize without some drama. I was scheduled to work that day until five p.m. Barbara was going to come at that time, pick me up, and then we'd drive to Yonkers to be married. She arrived on time, but I was nowhere to be seen. Six o'clock, no Arun; six thirty, still no Arun. Finally, at seven, I came running into the lobby, changing out of my white coat as I did. We'd had a difficult day in surgery; a complicated liver procedure had taken far longer than expected.

When I looked at Barbara, I saw a sense of relief. I realized that in the back of her mind, she might have been thinking that I'd had cold feet, that I wouldn't go through with it. Nothing could have been further from the truth. I knew that I had found the woman I wanted to spend my life with.

The next morning, Barbara and I were off to our honeymoon in the Poconos. We took a Greyhound bus, got off at the wrong stop, and had to hitchhike our way on rural mountain roads to get to our resort. When we finally arrived, we laughed at our misadventure. Happy to be husband and wife, we drank a bottle of Mateus wine and toasted our future. She was twenty-two and I was twenty-six.

When we returned home, we had a proper party at the Swan Club on Long Island's glitzy North Shore. It was hosted by my in-laws, who had taken out a loan to be able to give their daughter such a celebration. Along with Oscar and Frieda, my brother, and Barbara's extended family, my colleagues at the hospital attended—including some of the senior men—as did an old friend, Bijoy, from back at Darbhanga Medical College. Smart, successful, confident Bijoy was now a resident at Kingsbrook

Jewish Medical Center in Brooklyn. Given our schedules, he and I had seen each other infrequently since my arrival. I was happy that he was able to attend my wedding celebration.

"Arun," he said, as we tipped champagne glasses, "I'm proud of you. It looks like you've really made a home for yourself here."

I looked around at my new family, my new friends, my new world.

"You're right, Bijoy," I said. "I have."

Chapter Sixteen

I Want to Heal Hearts

Having come to the realization that I wasn't physically able to do the work required to be an orthopedic surgeon, I was still searching for a specialty in my new profession.

I finally found it in the third year of residency. One morning in the spring of 1970, I heard that Dr. James Malm was operating and that residents were welcome to observe. James Malm! This was a big deal. Malm had not only helped start Columbia's program in cardiac surgery, he was considered one of the true pioneers in this new arena.

I had seen him in the hallways and at meetings. A navy surgeon during the Korean War, he was famous for having performed an emergency appendectomy aboard an aircraft carrier that was part of a convoy being battered by a Pacific typhoon. "The entire Seventh Fleet had to turn into the wind and slow down to stabilize the operating table until I finished," he recalled in an interview years later.

Dr. Malm still carried himself with a military bearing, calm and composed. And distant. One—certainly one lowly resident like me—didn't just go up to James Malm and ask him for surgical tips or to recount tales of his time in the navy.

Seeing him in action, I thought, would be a good opportunity to learn. I took my seat with others in the surgical theater and watched the master at work. It turned out he was operating on a child that day, which heightened the drama.

She was perhaps two or three years old. I remember her holding a stuffed animal as she was wheeled into the operating room by one of the nurses, closely accompanied by the anxious parents.

What Malm was doing that day was repairing a ventricular septal defect—essentially patching a hole between the two lower chambers of the heart. The child had been born with the defect, but while routine today, this was still a risky operation in 1970, particularly when performed on someone so young. The mother was sobbing when she finally released her child and the father and another nurse escorted her from the room. I'm sure the parents had been assured that their daughter was being operated on by the best.

And right on cue, the best arrived.

Malm strode briskly into the operating theater, and his team of eight—nurses, technicians, anesthesiologist, and surgical residents—snapped to attention. A handsome man with chiseled features, he stood about six feet tall and exuded confidence. The child anesthetized, surgery began. He made a precise four-inch incision in the chest, severing the pericardium—the fibrous sac that covers the heart. Released from its natural casing, the child's heart bobbed up to the surface. I could see from where I was standing that it was tiny, the size of a plum, and beating rapidly. Dr. Malm immediately inserted three plastic tubes, each the size of a pencil, into the heart, one in the aorta (primary receiving channel for the blood that the heart pumps) and two in the atrium (upper chamber of the heart that receives blood).

The tubes were then connected into the heart-lung machine—in those days it was the size of a refrigerator—that had been wheeled into the OR.

Dr. Malm then deftly placed a clamp on the aorta and poured a beaker full of slushy ice on the heart to keep it cool and protected during the procedure. Now the child's heart had stopped. I could see a flat line on the monitor—which back then was a vacuum tube–powered black-and-white screen. There was none of the high-resolution imagery we have today!

The child was now being kept alive by the heart-lung machine connected to her by the tubes. It was time to start the repair. While keeping his gaze intently on the inert heart in front of him, Malm put his hand out and withdrew it, a surgical scissor having been instantly placed in his palm by one of his experienced scrub nurses.

He quickly cut open the right chamber of the heart and immediately located the hole. Out went the hand again, and this time a nurse placed a small sheet of Dacron in it. From that Dr. Malm carefully cut a dime-size piece of the tough but elastic synthetic fiber, and then he sewed it into the heart to snugly cover the hole.

I was spellbound by how fluidly Dr. Malm and his team worked and yet how precise and sure-handed he was. *This is why you're doing all that sewing at night*, I said to myself. *To develop hands like this!*

Malm closed up the chamber and removed the clamp. Very soon I could see the tiny heart was beating again.

Today the surgeon would be done, and a resident would close up the chest to finish the procedure. But these were the early days of heart surgery, so Malm did it himself. Again, as smoothly as if he were tying up the laces of his boots.

The child, unconscious but alive, was moved to the recovery room.

Still impassive and every inch the commander, Dr. Malm walked out of the OR to talk to the parents.

What a performance! I thought. Much better than *Oh! Calcutta!*, I would joke to Barbara when I got home later.

Before I had left the hospital that night, I was curious to see how the child had fared. Heart surgery is tough on those on the receiving end. I try never to forget that, and I always caution loved ones about visiting the patient immediately afterward. To put it bluntly, the patient usually doesn't look so good! But it doesn't mean they won't recover fully.

When I went to see the little girl in the children's ward later that night, however, she was sitting up and sucking on a Popsicle, her exhausted but happy parents next to her. Some of this was no doubt due to her youthful resiliency, but much of it could be ascribed to the skill of Dr. Malm and his team. This was a precision procedure. The margin of error was extremely small; at stake was nothing less than the life of a child. If the hole had, say, not been 100 percent covered by the tiny Dacron strip, or if any one of Malm's stitches had not been perfectly taut, or had been misplaced, she could have had big problems. Over the years her own tissue would now grow around the Dacron patch, making it a permanent part of her heart. Chances are, that little girl—who'd now be a woman in her late forties—is alive and well today, thanks to a little piece of synthetic fiber and an enormously skilled surgeon.

"This is what I want to do," I told Barbara that night.

"Heart surgery?"

"That's right. And with children, especially. That's how I can practice these skills at the highest level. And that's how I can still stay true to what motivated me to become a surgeon."

"It isn't the big bucks?" Barbara asked, with a grin. She knew I was making only $19,000 a year at this point.

"No, you know my history. It's a way for me to honor the doctors in India who helped me as a kid. I can't reset bones, but maybe I can repair hearts like Dr. Malm did today."

"Arun," she said, putting her arms around me, "I think it's great. You'd be a wonderful cardiac surgeon. There's just one thing."

"What's that?"

"Didn't you tell me somebody said there's no future in it?"

Barbara was right. Two years earlier, in 1968, I had attended the annual meeting of the American College of Surgeons in Atlantic City, New Jersey. One of the many eminent physicians who spoke was Dr. O. T. Clagett, a former chief of surgery at the Mayo Clinic—the institute founded by the two brothers I had read about in medical school back in India.

I was eager to hear what words of encouragement this leader in the field would have for us young residents.

What we got was cold water poured on our heads.

"I don't understand all you young residents out there who are just starting your training in heart surgery," he said. "The geneticists are going to learn how to prevent congenital heart malformations before birth." He went on to predict that rheumatic fever, a condition that affects the valves of the heart (and which then necessitated the majority of heart surgeries), would disappear like syphilis. And so, he concluded, looking out at the crowd of disappointed young faces, "you simply are not going to have anything to do."

The man from the Mayo Clinic was making this prediction less than a year after Christiaan Barnard of South Africa had performed the first heart transplant. Soon, coronary bypass would become the treatment of choice for millions of patients with blocked coronary arteries. Soon, better artificial heart valves would be developed. And on top of it all, we were on the cusp of a historic rise in heart disease that had nothing to do with congenital defects, and everything to do with lifestyle.

In short, he was dead wrong. Cardiac surgery was about to become the most exciting and competitive field in surgery. And now I was determined to be part of it.

Chapter Seventeen

A Providential Decision

In 1972, after four years of training, working every other night and sometimes for fifty-two hours straight, I graduated from the Columbia University residency program. There were no exams, but all the senior surgeons gave their evaluations, and mine were very high. I was praised for my work ethic, for my willingness to learn, for my growing technical proficiency, and for my dedication to patient care. I was humbled by these kind words from people I respected and also that many of them were happy to recommend me for a thoracic residency program. I passed my American board in general surgery and, in order to expand my potential job horizons, the Canadian board of surgery, as well, becoming a fellow of the Royal College of Surgeons.

Yes, there was still a next step on the ladder of my training. To nonphysicians I realize it must seem as if we doctors never get out of school. And honestly, that's how it felt to me, as well. By that point I had gone through medical school, an internship, a residency—and now I was going to embark on a specialized residency.

Still, there's a reason for all this training, and it's not just so we can memorize anatomical terms. The more advanced you are in your education, the greater experience you have with patient care and the better your mastery of the technical skills needed to perform complex surgeries. The intern simply holds the retractor during a procedure. A first- or second-year resident gets to perform small, simple operations. Senior residents have the responsibility of taking on more involved procedures with an attending surgeon present. The last step is when you can do these surgeries on your own.

If I had opted to be a general surgeon, I would have now been ready to put out my shingle. But there was another step for me. I needed to master the emerging new field of cardiac surgery. This would require another residency of two or three years.

But where? There were only about fifty cardiac surgical programs in the country at the time, each of which had spots for but one or two new residents. It was highly competitive, and again, as a foreign student, and not being a graduate of an American medical school, I was at a disadvantage, despite my strong academic record and the enthusiastic recommendations of my Columbia mentors.

Once again I felt the sting of being a second-class citizen in the medical world.

As graduation approached I was still looking for a place to do my cardiac training. Most of my fellow residents at Columbia had already found their next positions. I felt stuck and frustrated.

Enter Dr. Kenneth Forde.

I had met Ken Forde earlier in my residency, at Harlem Hospital. A New York City native, he had gone to school in Barbados, where his family was from, before returning to attend City College of New York and then medical school at Columbia. Now the associate director of the residency program at Harlem Hospital, he was that rare thing in the upper echelons of surgery in the Columbia system, or anywhere else at that time: a nonwhite face. Forde was an Afro Caribbean flourishing in what was still predominantly a white man's profession. Perhaps because he knew he would be judged differently as a minority, Dr. Forde set the highest standards for himself, starting with his appearance. He was fastidious—his mustache was always neatly trimmed, and he sported a natty bow tie along with his immaculate white coat.

Dr. Forde listened more than he talked. When he did speak, he spoke softly but firmly. He was kindhearted, but he could be tough when he needed to be. And he had, in my mind, been plenty tough on me the first time I met him.

I had encountered Dr. Forde the first week of my surgical residency, when I was summoned to his office.

"Welcome to Harlem Hospital, Dr. Singh," he said.

"Thank you, Dr. Forde," I replied dutifully. "It's an honor to be here, and I'm eager to learn."

"Good," he said. "You'll start by learning a little about how we do things."

"That's great," I said. "I'm sure it's very different than the way they work in Worcester."

His eyes twinkled. He then gave me the names of two patients, both elderly, who were about to have colorectal surgeries. "I'd like you to see these gentlemen, Dr. Singh. Take their histories and examine them. Give them each an enema. Oh, and please shave them in preparation for their surgeries tomorrow."

He then folded his hands and looked at me with an owlish expression that said, "Our business is concluded."

I must have sat there for a full ten seconds before I finally left the room. I was shocked! Enemas? Vital signs? These were things that could have easily been done by a nurse or an orderly. They were exactly the kind of thing they used to have us do in Worcester. It was insulting! And of course I, always on the lookout for any racial slights, interpreted it as yet another offense against a man of color. Except this time, it was coming from an African Caribbean!

"This is work that an orderly could do," I grumbled to my colleagues. "Enemas...shaving. How about having me give these guys a haircut while I'm at it, or shine their shoes? It's humiliating! He's taking advantage of me because I'm a foreigner with dark skin...and what's worse is that he should know better. He's a man of color, too!"

It was one of the rare times I lost my temper. The other residents listened to me fume, but none said a word. At least not to me.

I eventually calmed down and performed the duties I'd been ordered to do. I also tried to be as kind to the two older men as I could be. It wasn't their fault that I'd been stuck with a job that I felt was beneath me.

The next day I was asked to see Dr. Forde again. *Oh brother*, I thought. *I'm in trouble now. He heard about my temper tantrum.*

I entered his office, and there he sat again, mustache, bow tie, dignified. "Arun," he said, this time calling me by my first name. "I heard you were upset yesterday. Talk to me. And you may speak freely."

I took a breath. "Dr. Forde," I said. "I apologize, but yes, I was hurt. I'm here to learn how to be a surgeon, not to be an orderly. And what's worse, you didn't ask any of the other residents to do these menial tasks. Just me!"

"I'm sorry you felt that way," he said. "The truth is, almost all of the residents here have had to do the same thing. Would you like to know why?"

I nodded.

"I believe we must understand what our patients are experiencing. Not only because we want to be compassionate, but because it's sound medical practice. If you had never given an enema, if you had never shaved a patient, how would you know if a patient complained to you…his surgeon…that a nurse or orderly who gave an enema was not right and did not do the right thing?"

He paused and let his logic sink in.

"It's the same thinking behind why the heads of General Motors or Ford often spend time working on the assembly line," he continued. "That way, they can understand the entire process that they are overseeing."

He leaned forward. "Remember, Arun, surgery doesn't begin with an incision. It starts with a consultation and a diagnosis, with us getting as complete a picture as possible of the patient, his or her problem, and then deciding the type of treatment. And part of that treatment includes some of the so-called menial things you were asked to do yesterday. Now you've done these things. Now you'll have a more informed and complete picture of the process. Now," he said, sitting back in a gesture of finality, "you will be a better surgeon."

I'm not sure what impressed me more, his logic or his eloquence. I realized that he was absolutely right. We shook hands, and he has been my friend and mentor ever since.

Three years after my lesson in humility with Dr. Forde, I was again frustrated. But this time it was over my lack of success in finding a spot in a cardiac program.

Time was running out. I had only a few weeks left in my residency at Columbia. I was facing unemployment. That's when Dr. Forde called.

Unbeknownst to me, he'd been telephoning or writing every colleague he knew, at hospitals and universities around the country, singing my praises and seeing if there were any opportunities.

"Arun, I may have something for you," he said.

"Really?" I said.

"Rhode Island Hospital in Providence is launching a new cardiothoracic residency program," he said. "They've been looking for a resident, and I recommended you. I just got a call back that they're interested. Can you get up there tomorrow?"

Dr. Forde was talking about Brown University Program in Medicine, which was affiliated with the hospital in Providence. For them, I certainly could get there the next day!

Once again I was on a Greyhound bus headed to Providence and my favorite luxury hotel: the YMCA. I'd driven through the city once before, during my early search for a residency while I was in Worcester. I remembered gazing out the window of the Greyhound bus at the magnificent Rhode Island State House, the Old Stone Bank with the golden dome, and the other eighteenth-century buildings around College Hill. We certainly had old— much older—buildings in India, but these were more charming and picturesque.

Now I was back on the bus going in the other direction, coming to a place I'd seen fleetingly four years earlier, to possibly start my career.

The next morning I met Dr. Karl Karlson, the head of cardiac surgery at Rhode Island Hospital. By this point I was beginning to understand that Americans were not all alike. As in my country, there were regional differences. Dr. Karlson, a native of Minnesota, was one of the first true Midwesterners I'd met. He had a "Minne-soder" accent and seemed like a man from the heartland: humble, polite, and soft-spoken. He asked me about my training, about my personal life.

Was I married?

Yes.

Did we have children?

Not yet.

I noticed there were no questions about my color, or about being a foreigner. That was refreshing.

He quizzed me about some tough medical and surgical problems, and I thought I answered appropriately, especially watching his facial expressions.

After the interview he drove me back to the Greyhound station. "We'll let you know, soon," he said.

"Thanks, Dr. Karlson," I said, wanting to add, "The sooner the better!"

The next day he called.

"Say, Arun," Dr. Karlson began the conversation (he said "say" a lot), "how do you feel about joining us up here?"

He offered me a job as a resident in their new cardiac surgical program: a two-year appointment starting in July 1972. This would allow me to become board certified and practice cardiac surgery in the United States.

It took me around five seconds to accept. No "Let me sleep on it" or "I'll get back to you." The clock had been ready to strike midnight on my career. But now it was a new day.

My first call was to Barbara, who was thrilled. My second call was to Dr. Forde to thank him.

"Congratulations, Arun," he said. "And don't worry, Karl won't make you do any enemas in your new job."

I laughed, but thanked him profusely. "I was happy to help," Dr. Forde said. "You're a fine surgeon, and a hard worker. You earned this opportunity."

Still, as I would learn later from his secretary, it was Dr. Forde who had worked very hard on my behalf. There were other good candidates for the job in Providence, but on Dr. Forde's say-so,

I rose to the top of the list. He was the reason I got the job, and when his annual Christmas card arrives to this day, almost fifty years later, I give thanks to Ken Forde.

Like Columbia-Presbyterian, my new employer was a teaching hospital, meaning it had been designated by a university. In this case it was another Ivy League school, Brown. The institution's full name at the time was thus Rhode Island Hospital–Brown University Program in Medicine. With that kind of pedigree, you would expect a well-run hospital, and that's what I saw the first day Dr. Karlson showed me around. It was clean, efficient, and financially solid, with a very large endowment. Still, after four years in New York City, the difference in the staff and the patient population was striking: almost everyone I saw on the floor was Caucasian. I was probably the only Indian walking through the corridor.

I was impressed by the hospital and the city, and I told Barbara I thought she was going to like it here, too. Much as she loved New York, she was excited about starting our life together in a new place.

At the time Barbara was at Queens College, finishing up her bachelor of science. She was thinking of going on to law school or a master's in public health. Our plan was for her to finish at Queens and then join me in Rhode Island. But her mother nixed that. "Forget about college," she said to Barbara. "You have to be with your husband."

That was the attitude then, even among progressive people like Barbara's parents.

We found a nice little apartment in the quiet suburb of Warwick, about twelve miles south of Providence. We chose it because it was located a few blocks from Kent Hospital. At the time we had only one car, a 1971 Toyota Corona. We figured that Barbara could walk to work at Kent, while I could drive to Rhode Island Hospital. That way we'd avoid the higher rental prices of downtown Providence.

Very practical, or so we thought. The plan never materialized. Just before she was scheduled to start working, she learned she was pregnant. That was the end of walking to work, college, and her career. But that was OK: Barbara and I both very much wanted her to stay home to raise our children, once they came along. She sacrificed her career for motherhood and family, and my sons and I are the beneficiaries of that decision.

Usually the new doctor on staff just observes on his or her first day in the OR. Not at Rhode Island Hospital. The first time I walked into the operating room, I was handed a saw. "Go ahead and open the chest, Dr. Singh," I was told.

Wanting to make a good impression on them, I carefully but confidently cut through the chest and opened the pericardium. There it was, just as I'd seen during Malm's surgery: a beating heart, freed from the pericardial sac, popped up in front of me.

The attending surgeon now guided me, suggesting that I cradle the heart with my hand to stabilize it and then start inserting what we called "purse strings"—sutures that are sewn very tightly in the aorta and atrium.

Why would we hold this vital organ in our hands? Well, people often forget that the heart is a moving object: holding it to keep it stable makes it easier to work on.

I made small punctures in the aorta and atrium with a stiletto knife, inserted plastic tubes the size of a pen, and connected them to the heart-lung machine. Using a three-inch serrated clamp, I then pulled taut the purse string sutures around the tubing so that blood would not leak and the tubing wouldn't slip out during the procedure.

In this case the procedure was a coronary bypass, the creation of an alternative path to a blocked artery with a vein from the leg or an arterial graft from the chest. Again, like so many procedures that are common today, this was still very new in 1972. The attending surgeon took over the procedure, but that I was even allowed to participate by sewing a few sutures on my first day on the job was quite an honor.

While I'd been well trained at Columbia and felt very confident and welcome, I knew I still had to keep improving.

To that end I kept up my nightly sewing in Rhode Island, although now I had become more adroit with a needle and thread. No longer did the pillows look as if they were covered with large, baseball-like seams. Now the fine patterns I stitched looked more like needlework.

"Just think, Arun," joked Barbara as she watched me sewing away one night, "if the surgery thing doesn't work out, you can always get a job at a dry cleaner's. They always need tailors."

While I could sew, I couldn't type. Part of my responsibility at a teaching hospital like this one was to do research. I had been working on a paper about an unusual form of heart disease that required complex management, and I needed to submit it to a medical journal. While my wife was nearly full term in her pregnancy and feeling very uncomfortable, she had a portable Olympia typewriter and could touch-type.

"Barbara, I really need you to help me with this," I said.

"If you need me to, I will," she said. "But I'm not feeling well."

"I'm sorry, but I don't have a choice," I insisted. "I've got to get this paper to the editor by the end of the week. It's important for my job."

"OK, OK," said Barbara. "Relax, we'll get it done."

That night she typed the paper about a rare condition in

which a fistula (an abnormal connection) develops between the aorta and the esophagus, and the surgical steps needed to correct it. The topic was dense and technical, and on top of it all, poor Barbara—whose physical discomfort seemed to grow as the night progressed—had her husband looking over her shoulder to make sure she got it right.

We finished in the wee hours of the morning. A few hours later, Barbara went into labor.

Our son Arun Singh II was born March 20, 1973. When I saw him, like most new dads, I was intoxicated with joy. Barbara smiled up at me from her bed in the maternity ward. "Well, at least we've got our priorities in order," she said. I looked at her quizzically. "We finished your paper first," she said with a wry smile, "and *then* we delivered your son."

"I'm sorry," I said genuinely. "I feel terrible about being so demanding last night."

"All I can say is that it better be a helluva good paper!" she said.

Happily, the editor of the journal thought it was. The paper was later published in the journal *Chest*, and Dr. Karlson was very happy. Having his residents published looked good for the program.

Chapter Eighteen

London Calling

Soon after the arrival of Ari (as Barbara's father had taken to calling him), I began to realize that I wanted to focus on pediatric cardiac surgery. This is the ultimate test of the surgeon's skill, and because a tender young life hangs in the balance, the stakes couldn't be higher. In pediatric cardiac surgery, each case presents different problems and complexities. I loved that challenge as much as I loved the innocence of the kids themselves, not to mention the long-term rewards of this kind of surgery. (To this day it's thrilling when a healthy man or woman in their thirties or forties with kids of their own walks up to me in a restaurant and says, "Dr. Singh, you may not remember, but you operated on me as a child." There is truly no greater satisfaction as a surgeon.)

Again I was on the hunt for a new hospital. I applied to a number of top pediatric surgical programs around the world. My first choice was the Hospital for Sick Children, located on Great Ormond Street in London, nicknamed GOSH—for Great Ormond Street Hospital. Even in the 1970s, GOSH, as it's now officially known, had a reputation for excellence and innovation that spanned more than a century.

Founded in 1852 in response to the high child mortality rates in London at the time, the hospital had grown from a small facility of ten beds to one of the largest and most important children's hospitals in the world. The names associated with it were dazzling: Queen Victoria, Charles Dickens, and J. M. Barrie, the author of *Peter Pan*, were all among its most ardent supporters (later Princess Diana would be added to that list of famous donors).

The hospital had recorded a number of impressive firsts: The first pediatric surgeon was appointed there in 1928, the first heart-and-lung unit was established there in 1947, and the first leukemia research unit was launched there in 1961. Of particular interest to those of us in cardiac surgery was that Great Ormond was where a heart-and-lung bypass machine had first been used during pediatric heart surgery, in 1962. They were known for innovation, and for excellent outcomes.

Unlike my anxious, nail-biting wait for responses when I'd been applying for a residency before, this process was swift. Great Ormond Street replied straightaway, offering me the position of what it called "house resident" starting in July.

Although I'd been at Rhode Island Hospital for only two years, the staff gave me a warm send-off. They even raised money to pay for our plane tickets to London.

"Say, Arun," Dr. Karlson said, taking me aside at my farewell party. "You know this is a pretty nice position you've been offered."

"I'll be just a junior resident," I said. "I'm probably going to be at the bottom of the ladder."

"Maybe so," he said, "but I don't think you'll end up there. I think you'll impress them in London as much as you've impressed us here."

I was genuinely touched and thanked Dr. Karlson for having so warmly welcomed us. While we were excited about living abroad, both Barbara and I felt we'd found a home in the tiny state that the natives fondly refer to as "Little Rhody."

When we arrived in London, we learned that there, the term *resident* is meant quite literally. We would be living in an apartment building next to the hospital itself. It was a building from the seventeenth century; the floors sagged and creaked. And it came with its own set of residents, who had nothing to do with the hospital. As veteran New York City apartment dwellers, Barbara and I had plenty of experience with cockroaches. She had not, however, been introduced to mice. My first day on the job, I left our apartment at about six a.m., walking across the courtyard to the hospital. When Barbara got up shortly afterward to feed Ari, she went to slide her feet into a pair of slippers at the side of the bed and found herself staring into the face of a rodent sitting on the heel.

Her screams echoed across the courtyard. She jumped up on the bed, grabbed the phone, and dialed the hospital operator. "There's a mouse in here!" she cried.

To Londoners, a mouse showing up in our three-hundred-year-old quarters was probably about as surprising as Big Ben tolling on the hour. Nonetheless, the hospital staff didn't want the wife of their new house resident moving out on the first day. They made a big fuss, sent out an emergency extermination team, and immediately dispatched the offending rodent, with profuse apologies. When I got home that night, I tried to console Barbara with some bromide about how this was just part of the adjustment we would have to make to living in a new country. Why, it could even be seen as part of the adventure!

She wasn't buying any of it. "Arun," Barbara said. "Eating fish and chips, having high tea, visiting the Tate Gallery… that's the kind of stuff we want to experience here. Sharing my bedroom slippers with a mouse is not on my list of great things to do in London." Also, having rodents in an apartment with little Ari was disconcerting.

She was right to be upset. And I had to admit that on my first day on the job I, too, had been disenchanted. At the time Great Ormond Street was still housed in its two original Victorian-age buildings. By the time I arrived, it was an old and tired-looking facility, dusty, dreary, and with much of the equipment shockingly outdated. Not at all like the American hospitals I was used to.

Mice, decrepit buildings, outdated equipment—had we made a mistake coming here?

Early on the afternoon of my second day, Dr. Jaroslav Stark, the Czech-born chief of surgery, invited me up to his office.

"Mr. Singh, we're glad to see you," he said. (In Great Britain, surgeons are not addressed by the honorific *Doctor*. I was mister, just like every other guy.) "How was the trip?"

Just fine, I told him. We had flown in on TWA with no problems.

"Splendid!" he said. "And the accommodations...?"

I cleared my throat and shifted in my chair.

He chuckled. "Oh, don't worry, Mr. Singh. We'll have our mouse patrol on high alert. You and your wife won't be bothered again."

I had to laugh. Word spread quickly.

"Seriously," he said. "I've spent a lot of time in the States. I've lectured and toured all the big hospitals, including Columbia. I know what you're probably thinking about us after your first day. All I'll say for now is please don't judge an old book by its cover."

I knew enough to realize that good medicine started with good doctors and good staff, not necessarily the shiniest hospital corridors. I nodded.

"You're right, Dr.... er, Mr. Stark," I said. "I know there's a lot I can learn here, and I'm eager to get started."

"Excellent," he said. "And now, before you go back to your orientation"—he reached down behind his desk and produced a bottle of sherry and two glasses—"a toast! To your success here."

Tippling on the job was not prohibited in those days. At the time, however, I didn't drink. I told him that I would raise a glass of water if that was OK.

He grinned. "That's fine, Mr. Singh. Either way, welcome!"

It didn't take me long to realize the truth of what Dr. Stark had said. The staff at Great Ormond Street Hospital was exceptional, incredibly warm and caring to the children and their parents. This attitude extended from the lowest-paid orderlies to the highest-ranking administrators. I had rarely seen such compassion and commitment. It was inspiring and brought out the best in everyone there, including me. I found myself quickly at home at Great Ormond, warts and all, and I think my willingness to learn and to work long and hard, and my kindness toward the patients and their families, soon ingratiated me with the staff, as well.

Within three months of my arrival, there was an opening for a higher position, and Dr. Stark immediately promoted me to senior registrar. Not to be confused with the job of the same name in the American higher educational system (where the registrar's office is responsible for class schedules and grades), this was the second-highest surgical rank in the hospital. In this position I would now have the opportunity to work alongside some of Great Ormond's famous names, such as Dr. Richard Bonham Carter and David Waterston, the cardiologist and pediatric surgeon, respectively, who had established Great Ormond's thoracic unit in the 1950s and were still running it together when I arrived. The staff had various nicknames for them. When I was there, the dynamic duo and their operation were referred to as "The Dick and David Show," which made the eminent medical team sound like a West End music hall act.

Although, as its original name suggests, Great Ormond had been established to help sick children from anywhere—many straight off the streets of London—by the 1970s it was evolving into what it is today: a so-called tertiary referral hospital, mostly treating complex cases referred from other hospitals.

For a young surgeon it was a tremendous opportunity. Working alongside some of the world's greatest pediatric surgeons was a priceless experience. In fact, I would stick around the hospital even when I wasn't on call. I enjoyed seeing the challenging problems and surgeries and how senior, expert colleagues solved them. And solve them they invariably did, saving the life of child after child. Could there be any occupation more rewarding?

As our first Christmas season in London approached, Barbara suddenly developed a serious medical condition: a ruptured ovarian cyst that required immediate surgery. We had a baby and no family in London to help, so our neighbors graciously took care of Ari for a few days while Barbara was still recuperating and I was working. I was frustrated, depressed. We just didn't seem to be getting a break. Mother-in-law to the rescue! Barbara's mom flew in from New York and took care of things until she recuperated.

The hospital had a special connection with the yuletide holiday. One of its main early benefactors, Charles Dickens, had lived on nearby Doughty Street (now the site of the Dickens House Museum) and frequented the Lamb, a pub just east of the hospital on Lamb's Conduit Street that was still popular with the hospital staff in the 1970s. The legend I had heard while there is that Dickens wrote *A Christmas Carol* while sipping punch at the Lamb. While that is probably not true, Dickens did frequent the pub and, according to Great Ormond Street Hospital archivist Nick Baldwin, he did do a public reading of his famed holiday novel as a hospital fund-raiser in 1858.

On Christmas morning of 1974, I stepped out onto our little balcony and was greeted with a scene that could only have been described as Dickensian. There in the courtyard was a band of Christmas carolers, decked out in red scarves and various colorful winter hats. Hospital volunteers who serenaded the staff and patients every year on the holiday were singing "Joy to the World" and "Silent Night." Their beautiful renditions rang through the courtyard. To this day it is the most magical Christmas moment I have ever experienced. Barbara was on the mend. Our baby boy was healthy. I was happy and productive in my work—and finally seemed on track to success as a surgeon.

～

Three months later, in March 1975, I was on a flight to far-off San Diego to take my board examinations in thoracic surgery.

Just to be clear, the term *thoracic* refers to the heart, lungs, and esophagus. The heart specialty was (and remains) housed within this branch of medicine. Passing this exam would give me the coveted title of board-certified surgeon in my specialty. This would enable me to land a better position at more prestigious hospitals.

At the time the boards were given twice a year by the American Board of Thoracic Surgery. One was in the spring, the other in the fall. I chose the earlier option. I wanted to get a leg up on my next step, which, I hoped, would be a position as a full-fledged pediatric surgeon in the heart unit of a major American hospital. By taking the boards earlier, I'd be able to put "board certified" on my résumé.

Providing I passed, of course.

As usual, I was on a tight budget, so along with taking a cheap flight, I decided to stay in my favorite hotel: the YMCA. Generally I had had pleasant experiences staying at the Y, but on this particular night in San Diego I was kept up by an intoxicated young couple in the next room (the Y had just changed its policy to allow female guests). The two of them bickered and fought and complained about their parents, their friends, and their lot in life until the wee hours—while one of them strummed a guitar, no less.

Bleary eyed, and having heard more about the lives of these two young miscreants than I wanted to know, I arrived at the hotel near the airport where the boards would be held. In addition to completing a written exam, each candidate would be interviewed by three pairs of examiners over the course of the day. I went from conference room to conference room, where I would sit down and get bombarded with new questions by the examiners, senior and nationally recognized surgeons all. Despite jet lag and lack of sleep, I did well. I had lugged some of my textbooks on the plane to review during the long flight and had anticipated some of the questions likely to be asked. My year in London, working alongside some of the best, had also prepared me thoroughly.

During a break in the interviewing, I went to use the restroom in the hotel. One of the examiners was just leaving when I entered. I recognized him: a prominent surgeon in Chicago, he had quizzed me earlier. I acknowledged him with a polite nod, but nothing more, as I didn't want to break any protocols about not speaking to the examiners outside of the testing rooms. To my surprise, he addressed me. "Where were you trained, Doctor?" he asked. I told him: Columbia and Great Ormond Street.

He nodded thoughtfully. "They did a good job. You know your stuff. Well done today."

I had a big smile on my face the rest of the day. I learned soon afterward that I had gotten a high score on the exams. I was now a board-certified surgeon.

On my way back to London, I stopped in New York to see my in-laws and then took a bus to Providence to meet with Dr. Karlson. He seemed happy to see me, and even more pleased when I told him that I was now board certified. "Say, Arun, that is fantastic," he said. I later learned that I was the first resident from his program to have passed the boards. We chatted briefly and then, just before I left, he asked me if I'd be interested in coming back to Rhode Island Hospital, this time as an attending surgeon.

I told him I'd be happy to return to Little Rhody. He looked pleased. "No guarantees," he said. "But we're going to try and make that happen."

When I returned to London I found a letter from Peter Bent Brigham Hospital in Boston. Brigham (now Brigham and Women's) was then one of Harvard's teaching hospitals. The department had one of the biggest names in the field on its staff: the brilliant Nina Starr Braunwald, the first board-certified female heart surgeon. Dr. Braunwald had also designed the first artificial heart valve. I was offered a position at $35,000 a year—a lot of money in those days—and the letter explained that part of the job would be in her research lab. That's part of the deal in an academic hospital: you're expected not only to practice surgery, but to help advance the field through research, as well.

"This is Harvard," I told Barbara, about the Brigham offer,

"and she's one of the best cardiac surgeons in the country. I have to take this offer seriously."

The next day's post brought a letter from Dr. Karlson. He was offering me the job as he'd hinted, and at the same salary as Brigham.

For the first time in my life, I was in demand! Still, while Harvard is usually more prestigious than almost any other institution, I trusted Dr. Karlson, and Barbara and I liked Rhode Island.

I accepted his offer.

Once again, I anticipated smooth sailing ahead. And once again, I struck an iceberg.

A month later, another letter arrived from Dr. Karlson. "Dear Arun," it read. "I'm afraid I have some bad news." He went on to explain that because of a budgetary crisis at the hospital (what about that big endowment? I wondered) they had to rescind their original offer. The original salary of $35,000 had been "adjusted." The best they could do now was $19,000, with a bump to $21,000 the second year.

Some adjustment!

It got worse. Originally they had offered to pay part of my moving expenses. No longer. On top of that, I would have to pay for my own malpractice insurance, my office, my own secretary, even my own postage stamps and typewriter paper!

Also, I was restricted to operating on children under two years of age.

The new "adjustment" meant that I'd be making the same salary I had earned as a resident—except that I was now a board-certified surgeon. It was humiliating and infuriating, but I had no choice. The bad-news letter arrived in May. My contract with Great Ormond Street Hospital would be finished on June 30,

1975. The Brigham position, I knew, had already been filled by someone else, and in the pre-internet age, there was no way to find another job on such short notice.

I played around with the idea of returning home to do cardiac surgery. One evening at dinner I brought this topic up to Barbara.

"Honey," I said, "what do you think of us going back to India? I might have better luck there. And my mom will be around to take care of Ari."

For a moment there was silence, and I could see the concern in her face. I'd already dragged her from New York to Providence to London. Now I was proposing that we move around the world to a place with which she had no experience?

She knew nothing about India. She had no friends there.

Then she met my eyes with a determined expression. "If that's what you think is best for your career, I'm with you all the way. We're family and we stay together."

A few days later, I realized that going back to India was unrealistic. There was no open heart facility anywhere near my home state of Bihar, nor did I have the money or political connections to start a new program. But I was reminded yet again of what a strong, loyal spouse I had. While I'm sure she was relieved not to be jetting off to India with a two-year-old, I knew she would be behind me no matter what I decided.

And what we decided was to bite the bullet and accept the offer in Providence.

We would make the best of it, and I figured I'd do what I'd been doing since medical school: I'd outwork everyone else, and through persistence (or was it stubbornness?) I would force them to recognize my value and pay me what I was worth.

We took the *QE2* ocean liner back to New York. It sounds like an extravagance, but at that time it was the cheapest mode of transatlantic travel for a family of three that had accumulated a large collection of baby toys and accessories. Besides, there was no Greyhound bus service from London to Providence! With mixed emotions we said goodbye to the good people of Great Ormond and the other friends we'd made during our twelve months in London. Despite the occasional mouse, it had been a wonderful experience for both of us—a year we'd never forget. In fact, had Great Britain's economy not been in such dire straits at this period, I would have considered staying on. I believe Dr. Stark would have liked that, but he knew he couldn't match even the reduced offer from Rhode Island.

On June 29, 1975, we boarded the magnificent *QE2* for our seven-day passage home to America. Our accommodations were not quite as magnificent as the ship itself. We sailed in steerage, the cheapest accommodations, located in the lower decks. It consisted of small compartments, each with just a tiny window near the ceiling. All we saw for the whole trip was the water coursing along underneath the ship.

Despite rough seas, we arrived in New York as scheduled, on July 6, 1975—my thirty-first birthday. The night before, I listened on a shortwave radio set up in the ship's passenger lounge to Arthur Ashe's historic Wimbledon victory over Jimmy Connors. I had started to follow sports while in the US, and like many people of color, I was inspired by Ashe, a classy, intelligent athlete who had succeeded in tennis, a sport previously dominated almost exclusively by white males.

The day we arrived in New York, everyone gathered on deck to watch as we steamed gracefully into the harbor. There was the lower Manhattan skyline looming in the distance, growing ever larger as the *QE2* glided along. There were Ellis Island and the Statue of Liberty. Seeing them, I thought of all the immigrants who had come this same way in decades past. And at that moment I realized: I was one of them. I had arrived here on a jet plane, not a cramped sailing ship; I'd come through customs at JFK, not Ellis Island; but I had probably been just as scared and desperate as many of those who arrived in the nineteenth and early twentieth centuries from Ireland, Italy, and eastern Europe.

Also like many of those earlier immigrants, I'd endured setbacks and frustrations. But they had worked hard, often in the worst jobs and under the most deplorable conditions. Despite that, and despite the discrimination they endured for being Irish, or Italian, or Jewish, or whatever they were, many of them had succeeded.

I thought intently about those "huddled masses" as we stood on the deck in the growing shadow of the Statue of Liberty's beacon. I was humbled by their example and determined to complete my own immigrant's journey.

The next morning I was on the bus to Providence alone to start my new job as a full-fledged heart surgeon.

Chapter Nineteen

Redemption in Little Rhody

I had my beautiful growing family, a new job at Rhode Island Hospital, and a home in America. I was now determined to pursue US citizenship and prove that I belonged in the nation where I'd built my life.

However, in order to become a US citizen, I would have to renounce my Indian citizenship. My native country, for some reason, did not allow dual citizenship. This decision burdened me; people in my family back home would be hurt. Besides, India had given birth to me, and its culture had instilled my core values about everything, from duty to family to work ethic. I will always be indebted to my homeland for everything it gave me and for the precious memories I have of growing up there. India holds my first family—my parents, grandparents, siblings, and so many others with whom I share an everlasting bond. This decision would be devastating to them all, but most of all to my mother.

When I called Mom to tell her the news, for a moment there was painful silence, as if I'd lost her on the other end of the line. Then her sobbing broke through. "Babul, how could you turn your back on your family? Your culture—your country?" Her pained voice reverberated in my head and broke my heart. "Who have you become?"

She was saddened, disappointed, and struggling to come to

terms with the possibility she must have dreaded since I'd first left India—that I wasn't coming home. The news was like a death sentence to her.

"Mom, I would never, ever abandon the family and you," I tried to explain over her cries. "You got me to where I am. I have a chance to really succeed, and like you and Dad, I have a responsibility to my own family now."

When the emotions settled, I reassured my mother that I was only a phone call away. I would work hard to make her proud. We cried some more, reminisced about old times, and laughed together, and in the end she understood and gave me her blessing.

Prior to naturalization I had to take a civics test, and I was relieved to correctly answer all the questions. On the day of naturalization, after performing surgery, I rushed out to the federal courthouse for the swearing-in ceremony. I wish Barbara could have been there to share in the momentous occasion. Still trying to get on our feet, we'd struggled to afford a babysitter at the time, and she was pregnant with our second child and not feeling well.

The courtroom was decorated in red, white, and blue and was filled with people of different nationalities, all wearing American flag shirts, pins, or scarves. There was excitement, optimism, and hope in the air. I donned an American flag tie Barbara had given me. The chief judge, Raymond Pettine, gave a beautiful speech about his family's personal immigration history and discussed the duty and rights of US citizens. He invoked the words *e pluribus unum*, the motto printed on US currency. The phrase is Latin for "out of many, one"—descriptive of the makeup of the United States, which includes people from many countries working together. (I'd later perform heart surgery on the judge's wife, and we'd all become good friends.)

That day, when I raised my right hand to take the oath of citizenship and to pledge allegiance, I was humbled and touched beyond belief. As we concluded the pledge, the words "so help me God" had barely escaped our lips before the room thundered with cheers and applause. People were clapping, hugging, shaking hands, waving flags, grinning widely, or openly crying. It looked like a concert hall.

A school choir began to sing "America the Beautiful," and I couldn't contain my own emotion as I considered how many people had sacrificed everything for the life and liberty of all Americans. I felt incredibly lucky and like an American from that moment on. This was the next chapter of my American dream, and I felt responsibility toward my adopted home. I would never take this opportunity for granted. When I returned from the ceremony, Barbara greeted me with a cake she'd made to look like an American flag. We held each other and wept tears of joy for having finally made official my long-held desire to be part of this country.

While there were many trials and tribulations ahead for me and my family, I have never really lost that sense of gratitude for what this country has provided me. I think it's a little harder to understand for those of my friends who were born here, accustomed as they are to the opportunities provided them as Americans. My feelings were best summed up by former president Obama, who spoke at a citizenship naturalization ceremony in Washington. "We don't simply welcome new immigrants, we don't simply welcome new arrivals—we are born of immigrants," he said in his remarks on December 15, 2015. "That is who we are. Immigration is our origin story. And for more than two centuries, it's remained at the core of our national character; it's our oldest tradition. It's who we are. It's part of what makes us exceptional."

It took me nine years to transition from J-1 visa holder to green card resident to naturalized American citizen in 1976. I experienced my share of struggles along the path to citizenship—and after—but looking back, I know it was worth every bit of it.

After the exhilaration of citizenship, it was now time to face the cold reality of my situation.

With Barbara and Ari staying temporarily with her parents before joining me. I had to sort out how to make ends meet with my drastically reduced salary and overwhelming costs. I had no car, no place to live. Little Rhody was presenting me with some big problems indeed.

The folks at Rhode Island Hospital Trust National Bank (later acquired by Bank of Boston)—once owned by the hospital—were sympathetic. They gave me a low-cost loan that allowed me to buy a grass-green, two-door 1975 Dodge Dart and to rent a two-bedroom apartment in a run-down part of town, West Warwick.

It was a far cry from our digs in Warwick. My first night in the empty apartment, I listened to loud voices and glass breaking outside, and I held my head in my hands.

All our hard work and all the things I'd achieved—board certifications, fellowships to prestigious international hospitals, and exemplary reviews from my peers—for what? Once again I allowed myself to slide into self-pity over the difficult circumstances I faced. But as in the past, the wallowing didn't last long. I responded the only way I knew how: by throwing myself back into my work. So they were going to limit me to working on infants, eh? Well, I'd make sure we had the best damn pediatric cardiac surgical department on the East Coast.

I worked twelve-hour days and launched into research at the hospital lab. I was interested in how to preserve infants' hearts during open heart surgery—and in new procedures for some of the congenital heart defects that were the primary reason for many pediatric heart surgeries. Still, research requires resources, the kind I might have had at Brigham Hospital in Boston. But I'd turned that down, I reminded myself, for this.

Resources, as it turned out, were very few. Not just for my research but for my practice. Barbara was my secretary, and my office was the trunk of my Dodge Dart, in which files and papers soon shared space with my spare tire.

Still, we had to start somewhere. I began to assemble a team around me. I tried to put into practice what I'd learned at Great Ormond Street Hospital in London. In the nurses and technicians I recruited for our new program, I looked for something beyond competence. I wanted compassion. I wanted people who cared about these children, not to mention their parents and siblings.

Besides a team, I needed the tools. When you're operating on an infant, you need very fine, very precise forceps, vascular clamps, and retractors. When I approached the hospital administration about this, they shrugged. "No money," was the mantra. "Make do."

I tried to explain that I couldn't make do. Using adult-scale surgical tools on an infant weighing less than five pounds was like taking a sledgehammer to a pebble. It was going to do more harm than good.

I needed an ally, and she showed up just in the nick of time.

I was sitting in the hospital cafeteria with a cup of coffee, trying to figure out my next move, when a woman who appeared to be in her sixties, wearing glasses and dressed in civilian clothes, walked up to me. She was tiny—about five feet tall—but something about her suggested a purpose and energy that belied her stature.

"Dr. Singh, my name is Lena Lonardo," she said, offering

her hand. "I've heard that you're starting an infant heart surgery program here."

"Yes, that's true," I said.

"Well, I'm here to help you," she said. "I want children from Rhode Island to get taken care of *here*."

"I appreciate any help I can get, Mrs. Lonardo," I said. "Do you work here at the hospital?" I thought perhaps she was a nurse, or maybe an administrator or staffer.

"No, you've got plenty of good people here already. I'm here to offer something you don't have."

"What's that?"

"The ability to raise money."

I raised my eyebrows. "Please, go on," I said.

"First, let me tell you why."

"Mrs. Lonardo," I said, smiling, "if you can help raise the money to start this program, you can tell me your whole life story."

Which, in essence, she did. Over coffee I learned in particular about her grandson, who had had a serious congenital heart defect that required surgery. There was no place in Providence that could perform the surgery, so the family had had to deal with the emotional and financial stress of traveling to Boston constantly during his treatment.

Fortunately, her grandson had survived the procedure, but Mrs. Lonardo didn't want others to go through the same thing. She wanted Rhode Island to have a first-rate pediatric cardiac surgery department.

"We need your program here," she declared. "And I'm determined to help you get what you need to make it happen."

I was genuinely taken aback. After a chorus of *no*s and *cannot*s in response to my requests, Lena's positive energy was refreshing.

"I...I...don't know how to thank you, Mrs. Lonardo," I said. "You are truly an angel."

"Save that until I'm handing you a large check," she said with a laugh.

I liked her style. It turned out that Lena was not someone who traveled in the upper echelons of Providence society and could call on wealthy donors to open their checkbooks. She was a grassroots fund-raiser. That meant bake sales, raffles, and tables set up at the local church or at community organizations. Within days I'd start seeing her and some of her volunteer friends in the lobby of the hospital, urging all those who passed to "help Dr. Singh save children's lives."

It took time, but the money began to come in. One morning, about six months after we'd met, she called to ask me specifics about the cost of the instruments I required.

"How much will you need, Doctor?" she asked me in a phone call one morning.

I had an itemized list ready. These finely calibrated tools weren't cheap. "Ten thousand dollars," I said. I expected silence, an audible gasp, or maybe a dial tone after she hung up on such an outrageous request.

"No problem," she said cheerfully. "We can pay for them."

I was floored. Ten thousand was a year's salary to some people in 1976. I was hoping that perhaps she'd have raised enough to fund a fraction of the cost. She'd far exceeded that.

"Lena," I said, "you and your friends are amazing. May I ask you a question?"

"Of course!"

"How many cookies and muffins did you have to sell to raise this money?"

"A lot," she laughed. "A lot."

Of course, it was more than the bake sales that netted the money. It was generous people in the community—many of them working class—who opened their wallets to support what we were doing, who could not resist Lena's passion and enthusiasm for the cause. That ten-thousand-dollar donation was just the beginning. Through her grassroots efforts, Lena had laid the groundwork for what would become the Rhode Island Association for Cardiac Children, a not-for-profit organization that raised money to purchase equipment, support children's cardiac treatment and research, and help Rhode Island families whose children were undergoing surgery for cardiac disease.

Lena continued this selfless work for many years. She died at age ninety-eight—a valued friend to me and many others. I had been right about Lena Lonardo: she was an angel.

◌━

Few surgeons have had the awful experience of losing their first patient. Fewer still would admit it or dredge up that painful memory.

My first patient, Jason, was only five days old when he was brought to me. He was what was called a "blue baby" because of the pallor of his skin, and he weighed only five pounds and two ounces at birth. Little Jason suffered from a condition called tetralogy of Fallot, a cluster of problems that appear simultaneously. (This was the same condition, in fact, that Lena Lonardo's grandson had.)

Jason had a hole in a lower chamber of his heart, and excessive heart muscle tissue was obstructing blood flow from the right ventricle to the lungs. That was why his skin, nails, and lips were turning blue when he cried or fed or got agitated (these episodes are called "Tet spells" and are caused by a rapid drop in the amount of oxygen in the blood). Untreated, he would have died within days. As was the standard protocol at the time, Jason had been administered a medication called propranolol to prevent the fainting and Tet spells. Propranolol, a beta-blocker, was designed to prevent spasms of the heart muscle. This relieves the obstruction and helps promote the flow of blood to the lungs.

Now he would need urgent surgery to repair the hole in his heart and remove some of that extra heart muscle to open up the blood flow from the right ventricle to the lungs.

This was my first surgery as staff attending surgeon. It was complicated and technically challenging, and the stakes could not have been higher—for the child, the family, for me, and for Rhode Island Hospital.

Jason's parents carried him into the operating room, kissed his blue cheeks, and handed him to me for surgery. They knew the severity of their child's disease and the complexity of the procedure. But they had faith in God and in the surgeon, and they wanted the surgery done in Rhode Island.

"We'll be praying for Jason, and for you," said his mother as she handed me the child.

"Thank you," I said nervously. "I will do my best."

Jason was anesthetized, then wrapped in ice and cooled to 20 degrees Celsius (68 degrees Fahrenheit), which stopped the circulation of the heart. I sawed through his breastbone, cut open the right chamber of the heart, and carefully patched the hole with a piece of Dacron graft—just as I'd seen James Malm do five years earlier, in the procedure that had inspired me to become a cardiac surgeon.

The surgery lasted four hours. It was tense, but my team performed well, and I was proud of them.

After the operation, Jason was brought to the intensive care unit on a respirator. I was cautiously optimistic, but when I spoke to the parents, I told them the first twenty-four hours would be crucial. After the first twelve hours, my fears were confirmed. Jason's blood pressure began to drift slowly and inexorably downward. He became cold and clammy; his urine output was scarce, and his body got puffy—signs of kidney failure and in turn a clear warning that his heart was not functioning properly.

I tried everything, but in those days there was little we could do but stand helplessly by. Two days later, as I sat beside him, Jason stopped breathing. We tried desperately to resuscitate him, but to no avail. He was seven days old.

When we had to pronounce him dead, I stood by his bedside in disbelief. My first patient, this poor little boy—dead! I put my hands to my face and had to hold back tears. I was devastated. After a few moments I gathered myself and disconnected him from the respirator. Holding the lifeless infant in my arms, I carried him to his mother and father in the adjoining room. All I could think as I took these somber steps was that a few days ago this young couple had given me a live baby—*their* baby—and now I was handing them back a corpse.

As unprofessional as it may have been, tears began streaming from my eyes. "I'm so sorry," I said. "I tried everything we know."

Through her own tears, Jason's mother forgave me. "We know you did your best, Dr. Singh," she said. "This was God's will."

Maybe so, I thought later, but I knew there had to be another reason. I went back over everything that had been done for this child. Why had it happened? What had we overlooked? Should we have operated here at all? Maybe our hospital wasn't ready and should have sent him to Boston for the procedure instead.

Maybe, I thought darkly, *I* wasn't ready.

These were the thoughts that kept popping into my mind. As I went back over everything we'd done, I finally spotted what I thought might be the culprit: the propranolol he had been administered prior to surgery. Its effects might have lasted until after the operation; the beta-blocker would have continued to block the heart from pumping as vigorously as it should have. While propranolol was routinely administered in these cases, I couldn't help but think that the medication had essentially sabotaged Jason's recovery.

A few months later, I was proven right. A bombshell study appeared in a major medical journal, implicating propranolol in a number of similar cases and warning against its use in surgeries such as the one I'd performed. While the drug was (and still is) used safely for other conditions, we would never administer it to an infant with Jason's condition today.

This was cold comfort to his parents. And to me, for that matter. While it confirmed my post-op suspicions, it didn't change the outcome of my first surgery. Nor has it prevented me from thinking for the last forty-one years about Jason, his parents, and what I could have or should have done differently. A small part of me has never recovered from seeing the emotional pain his parents had to endure.

I tried to move on. A few days later a newborn, John, was brought to me in the middle of the night. Poor John was very sick. He had multiple defects in his heart, holes in both the lower and upper chambers, and a narrowed valve. He needed a complicated surgery, which we did. He survived. And yet when I think back to John, it is not with satisfaction at a job well done. It turned out he had major chromosome anomalies, including Down syndrome, and other congenital problems, such as a missing kidney. In the late 1970s, his prognosis—even with the repairs to his heart—was not good.

With John's case, I came face-to-face with something we hadn't discussed much in medical school. We are taught to perform surgery in order to save a life, but what about quality of life for those we are saving? In John's case, what lay ahead was years of physical pain for him, as well as emotional and financial strain for his parents. We knew it and they knew it. And that's exactly how it played out. Although his heart had been repaired, he suffered from a host of other illnesses, ended up in a long-term care facility, and died, most likely intubated and sedated, at age seventeen.

He lived that long in part because of my surgery and the intervention of other physicians along the way. Good for us! But did we really help him or his family? The question plagued me early in my career, but after some soul-searching, I realized that I had to put it out of my mind. Who was I to deny anyone life, no matter how wretched or limited that life might turn out to be? It was admittedly an oversimplified answer to a complex question, but I couldn't have functioned as a surgeon if such issues weighed on my mind before a procedure.

The terms of my employment at Rhode Island Hospital were clear. I could practice only on children two and under. The reason for that was business, and had nothing to do with medicine. The other surgeons didn't want a new guy coming in and taking patients. But sometimes all that goes out the window, as was the case one hot weekend in the summer of 1976, about a year after I'd returned to Rhode Island.

I was at the hospital catching up on paperwork when I got a call from the cardiologist in the emergency room. A forty-seven-year-old male had been brought in by ambulance with severe chest pain and dangerously low blood pressure. Tests showed all his coronary arteries were severely blocked, and without bypass surgery he had very little chance of survival.

"Looks like a heart attack," the cardiologist said. "I think he needs urgent surgery."

"He's an adult," I said. "I'm not allowed to touch him."

"I know," he replied. "It's ridiculous. But you're the only surgeon available right now."

"I'm on my way." *Screw their stupid rule*, I said to myself. This man's life was at stake. The least I could do was examine him, and if need be maybe we could transfer him to another hospital. When I got there, I could see he was in severe pain. His EKG continued to show what we call "progression." In other words, the heart damage was continuing. His arteries were all blocked, and without surgery he had no chance.

"We can't transfer him," his doc said as I looked at his chart. "He needs urgent resident surgery. And you're the one to do it."

He was right. "Urgent resident surgery" meant that a procedure had to be done right here, right now by someone in residence. Me. Restrictions or no, the decision was clear. An emergency was an emergency. He was rushed to the OR and I went to scrub up.

The man, who was called Tom, would require a triple bypass. Tom had a family—a wife and two children ages thirteen and fifteen. I performed the surgery, and it seemed to go smoothly. I allowed myself the luxury of a pat on the back afterward. Despite having worked exclusively on small children for the past two years, I felt I had performed well.

My congratulations were premature. The next morning I got a call. Tom was dead.

Apparently he had gotten up to sit in a chair in his hospital room. He told the nurse, "I don't feel so well." According to her account, he then closed his eyes and slumped in his chair. He had a ventricular fibrillation—an irregular heartbeat. Sometimes an electrical current in the heart muscle misfires and the heart seizes up like an engine. That's what had happened here. The heart attack he'd suffered had probably contributed to it, but there was no surgery then or now that could have prevented it.

It was bad luck, bad karma, and for me (not to mention poor Tom and his family) a bad outcome. I sank into depression.

Two patients lost in a few months. At this point I began to second-guess my career choice. Maybe I wasn't as good a surgeon as I'd thought. Maybe I should switch to another branch of medicine. Encouragement came from an unlikely source. One of the senior surgeons at the hospital—perhaps one of the same men who'd demanded that I be restricted to operating on children so as not to (no pun intended) cut into his business—must have felt bad for me. There had been no official reprimand. Even the administration realized that my efforts to help save a life had been appropriate. But the senior man made a point of seeking me out in the cafeteria a few days after Tom's death.

"Arun," he said, "we've all lost patients. I'm sure you did your best."

I nodded wearily. "Thanks," I said.

"Really," he went on, putting his hand on my shoulder. "I've seen you work. You've had great training and you're a damn good surgeon. Between you and me, I also know you've gotten a raw deal here, but trust me, it's going to change. You're going to end up being one of the most successful surgeons in this hospital. I mean it."

I was touched by this unexpected show of support. I decided to stick with it.

Still, the stress of my situation—the poor outcomes, the struggle to make ends meet financially, the long, punishing hours I was determined to put in—took its toll in other, frightening ways.

I was driving home from the hospital one night when I realized the road in front of me was blurry. At first I thought my car headlights were malfunctioning, or that I was on a poorly lit stretch of road, but that wasn't the case. It turned out I had edema—swelling—under the retina of my right eye. My mother had the same issue, I learned. My ophthalmologist told me that while we're not sure why, the condition is exacerbated by tension and stress. "I've got plenty of that," I said with a rueful laugh when he gave me his diagnosis. "What can we do about it?"

In the twenty-first century, laser treatment might have corrected the problem. But in 1976 the answer was: nothing. I was left with a permanent blind spot and blurred vision in my right eye. I learned to compensate for it; my ocular muscles were still strong, I believe, from the hours of staring up into the sunlit skies of India as a kite-flying kid. Still, it was a problem I certainly didn't need, especially at that point in my life.

That wasn't the only sign that I was fraying. It was the crack of dawn, and I had just come off a long shift taking care of a sick baby. I remember rolling down the window of the Dodge Dart to get some cold air that might reinvigorate me. It wasn't enough, apparently, as I entered Route 95 via an exit.

I was now driving the wrong way on one of the nation's busiest interstate highways.

Suddenly I saw headlights approaching me, fast. A tractor trailer truck was barreling toward me! I realized my error as he began blowing his horn. I screeched on my brakes. He did the same, and with only about fifty yards separating my little green

Dart from the cab of a monster-size sixteen-wheeler, I pulled off the road.

At that point the trucker did something remarkable. As I recovered from my initial shock and began to maneuver my car to turn around and proceed back the right way on 95, he deliberately jackknifed his truck on the road behind me. With much hissing and creaking and roaring, he essentially formed a protective barrier from any ongoing traffic, allowing me to safely reverse directions. As I finished my three-point turn, I leaned out my window and called up to him. "Thank you, sir!" I said. "I'm sorry. I'm a doctor, working late. I'm not drunk!"

I could barely make him out behind his windshield, but I thought I saw a barely discernible nod. He probably didn't believe me. Regardless, I was grateful he hadn't gotten out of the truck and beaten me to a pulp for putting both of our lives in danger.

When I got home and related my story to Barbara, she was beyond upset. "That's it," she said. "We're moving." I thought she meant leaving Rhode Island. She'd finally realized that her husband had no future here. "No, no," she said, when I asked her if she wanted to go back to Queens. "I mean that we're going to move closer to the hospital. I don't want you doing these long drives home anymore."

Barbara was right. We had our son Ari to consider. My long drives weren't the only issue, either. A few weeks prior to my near-fatal mishap there had been an incident in our apartment complex when a drug deal had apparently gone bad. Shots had been fired, and one of the bullets had accidentally gone through the window in our bedroom while my wife and Ari were sleeping.

Clearly it was time to go.

We moved into a small house in Cranston, a lovely town that

was much closer to the hospital. It was a house we really couldn't afford, but the people at the Old Colony Bank graciously waived the down payment.

A few weeks later—July 30, 1976—we welcomed our second beautiful son, Michael, into the world. I didn't see much of my children in those early years, but when I did they lit up my life, which seemed, at that moment, as cloudy as the view from my right eye. After two years in Rhode Island, things were not looking good at all. We were in debt, my practice was suffering, and I was plagued by self-doubt.

When I thought things couldn't get worse, they did: in April 1977 the hospital informed me that it could no longer afford to pay my salary, period. The position that had looked so promising when it was offered to me had steadily shrunk and was now about to vanish altogether. As of July, I was informed, I would not have a job.

I went to the chief of surgery.

"Dr. Randall, you brought me here to build a program," I said.

"I know, Arun, and I'm sorry. It was a mistake," he said. "We just can't afford it."

I tried to make my case the best I could. I reminded him of the need for such a program in Rhode Island. I pointed out the community support and the fund-raising efforts of Lena Lonardo. Was there any way, I asked, that I could stay and practice?

"I'll be honest with you," he said. "I don't think there's any future for you here. My best advice is to move to a bigger city— Boston, New York, wherever. I'm sure you'd be able to find something there."

In other words, *Get lost, Singh.*

I was furious. But I fought back. I pestered the hospital administration; I made my case to my colleagues, to patients, and to anyone who would listen.

My lobbying efforts must have worked. A few months later I received a letter stating that I had been given unrestricted privilege to practice heart surgery—on adults as well as children—with one major caveat: the hospital would not pay me a salary or provide any benefits. Any money I earned would come from my practice.

While I think my badgering of the higher-ups helped, I've always suspected that maybe some of the senior surgeons and cardiologists, who'd expressed support for me after Tom's tragic death, put in a good word themselves. Regardless of how it happened, I'd been given a second chance. Now I had to make the most of it. While I had been given permission to practice on adult patients, it didn't mean I had any patients. I would have to drum the business up myself. I became the equivalent of a surgical hustler, trying to find work wherever I could. That summer, I worked in the emergency room, sewing lacerations and treating broken bones from car accidents. I was willing to cover for every surgeon who went on vacation. (Needless to say, I took no vacations!)

People began to notice. One day, I was approached by one of the cardiologists. "Arun," he said, as I was racing down the hall to cover for another surgeon. "I see you're working hard around here. Very good."

"I'm trying my best," I said.

"I'm wondering if you have any time to take on a few new patients."

Before I could reply, he added that they had no insurance.

These were people who needed heart surgery but couldn't really afford it.

I couldn't have cared less. Even if my compensation would be considerably lower, they were patients. I had learned from my earliest days of medical school that nobody wants to be sick, it's not their choice. As physicians, it was our duty to help alleviate their suffering.

"Absolutely," I told him. "I'd be happy to take them on."

I saw this as an opportunity to prove myself. I ended up performing surgeries, on these and other patients, in less time and with better outcomes than some of the other, more established surgeons.

Word spread quickly, and soon others were referring people to me. Over the next year, I began performing more heart surgeries, and with excellent results. My confidence grew. Maybe things were going to turn around, I thought. They did—and with an unexpected boost from the most bizarre of circumstances.

Around this time, the hospital moved its surgical facilities into a new building on Eddy Street in Providence. The facility had been opened with much fanfare, a sign that the hospital's financial crunch might be easing at long last. The Davol Building, as it was dubbed, had multiple operating rooms, all equipped with state-of-the-art technology of the time. Soon after it opened, I was doing a coronary artery bypass surgery. It was one of our first times in the new facility, and both the team and I were excited. The patient was placed on the heart-lung machine, the heart was stopped, and I was ready to get to work: I was going to sew a bypass graft—a routine but still delicate procedure that had to be handled with care. As I was making an incision on the coronary artery, a deep-throated boom rumbled from the bowels of the building, and everything went dark.

When I say dark, I mean pitch black. I couldn't even see my hand in front of my face—not a good thing for a surgeon whose hand at that moment happened to be inserting a surgical instrument into a human heart!

My first response was unprintable. I had learned to curse like an American by now, although I rarely did. When the lights went out that day, however, I admit that a few f-bombs flew. But quickly I took hold of myself. *Better to remain calm and try to make the best of it*, I thought.

I spoke to the team, which had reacted much like me. "OK, folks," I said. "Let's just stay cool and do the best we can. I'm sure they'll fix this soon. In the meantime, can I get a light over here?"

At that moment, as if on cue, staffers came running into the OR with flashlights.

We learned later that other operations in process had been halted in midincision. This made sense. You could close and come back later and finish repairing a hernia with no real danger to the patient. But we couldn't do that. The patient's heart was stopped, and what was keeping him alive—the heart-lung machine—had also shut down because of the power failure. Our perfusionist and some other hospital techs did yeoman's work that day: they had to hand-crank the machine, like the engine of an antique car, to keep it circulating the blood. It was laborious physical work, and, taking turns, several men did it over what seemed like an eternity, keeping the blood flowing through our patient.

Meanwhile, working by the light of about half a dozen flashlights held as still as humanly possible, I performed three bypasses on the patient. It was no substitute for the usual floodlit operating room, but we made it work. *Light is light*, I thought to myself. *And I've got a little of it . . . enough to work.*

After forty-five minutes of pitch darkness, the electricity was restored, greeted with sighs of relief and then apprehension. The main part of the operation had been successfully completed. Still, we were all worried: Would the patient recover? Had something been overlooked in the chaos of the blackout? Would we be sued if the outcome wasn't good? What would happen to the hospital? And what about the adverse publicity? This was no doubt going to make the news, and it wouldn't be good for the reputation of the hospital.

We were wrong about the last part. That night there was a brief story on the local TV news about the blackout. It turned out that there had been a fire in one of the new generators, and the brand-new, high-priced backup power system had failed.

More importantly, the patient survived and went home a few days later. I forget his real name, because to everyone on my team and in that room, he went by another sobriquet. From that day forward, we called him the "Miracle on Eddy Street."

What happened subsequently was rather miraculous, as well.

~ *Chapter Twenty* ~

"The Best in Heart Care..."

A few weeks after performing surgery during the power outage, I was summoned to a meeting with the hospital administrator. To my surprise, when I arrived, I was warmly welcomed and introduced to other people in the room, including the hospital's director of marketing. It was explained to me that I had been chosen as one of the "faces" of Rhode Island Hospital. They wanted to use me in an advertising campaign promoting the new facility and our dedicated staff.

"We're going to leverage some of the visibility from this blackout crisis to break through the clutter and make a real impact on our target demographic," said the marketing guy.

I had no idea what he was talking about, but it sounded good. "Sure," I said. "If I can help the hospital, I'm happy to. As long as we make sure to recognize the rest of my team."

Well, as it turned out, we didn't really recognize the rest of my team that day—at least not in the advertising campaign. What did happen was that big, full-color photos of me were produced: one of me with a surgical mask over my face, supposedly working intently (it was actually me in a photo session, leaning over an empty operating table), and the other a headshot of me smiling. These images were plastered all over billboards and buses and on television commercials throughout Rhode Island and southeastern Massachusetts for the next few months.

When the campaign was first launched, and a couple of hospital staffers joked that they now saw me every day on their way to work, I got in my car and went back up 95—which I had avoided since the near collision with the truck—to see what they were talking about. I almost drove off the road again when I saw a gigantic image of myself smiling over the interstate.

The tagline (the marketing guy explained to me that's what they call the punchy phrase at the bottom of an ad) was something like "The best in heart care…Dr. Arun Singh," and next to it was the hospital logo.

That's rich, I thought. *A few years ago, they cut my salary. Then they wanted to eliminate my job altogether. And now I'm the best?*

My cynicism was quickly cast aside, though. People started recognizing me on the streets; patients and their families lit up when I walked into the room for a presurgical conference. "You're the doctor on TV!" they'd say. It was surreal.

My son Ari was excited. Some of his classmates had seen his dad on billboards and in commercials. And of course, Barbara was so proud of me. "Arun, after all we've been through," she said, "you're finally getting the recognition you deserve."

As Barbara knew, my team deserved the recognition as much as I did for the "Miracle on Eddy Street" (and let's not forget the patient that day)! Still, she was right. For someone who had scraped and stumbled along the bottom for so many years, having a fourteen-foot-high, forty-eight-foot-wide image of yourself towering over a major US interstate highway certainly put things in a different perspective.

By the early 1980s, my practice was flourishing. I was doing two to four operations per day. My mornings would start at five, and on some evenings I'd be leaving the hospital at eleven p.m. This was what I'd worked for, and I was determined to make the most of it. As clichéd as it may sound, however, there was a price for my success. My two sons were growing up, and I was never around for them. I rarely made a birthday party, never attended a parent-teacher conference, never saw them play any sports, and hardly ever took a vacation with them.

Fortunately Barbara was there for all these things, and for my sons' many academic and other successes. Despite my absence, thanks to her warm and wise parenting skills, they were growing up just fine—en route to becoming the outstanding young men they are today.

Why was I an absent parent? I guess I was just too afraid to leave the hospital. It had taken so much for me to get to this point. I lived in terror that just around the next corner was a calamity that could take it all away: a stern-faced administrator with some dire news about budget cuts; a patient threatening to sue; or, my worst nightmare, a patient I was unable to save. They were specters that haunted me through my career.

Gradually, as the successes began to pile up, and my skills as a surgeon continued to improve, I allowed myself to loosen up. One of the smartest things I did was take on an associate. I had resisted, but after I'd been successfully performing an average of two to four operations a day for so long, it was time. That is not something any surgeon should be doing regularly—even a driven, determined surgeon like me. As I slumped into my chair after the fifth operation one night, I realized that I needed help.

I found it in the person of Dr. William Feng.

Bill had been born in Shanghai and had grown up in Hong Kong. He was a Harvard graduate who had attended medical school at Brown University and then trained under me as a cardiac surgeon at Rhode Island Hospital. Bill was smart, hardworking, skillful, and dedicated to his patients—just the kind of surgeon I wanted in my practice. He joined me and together I think we made a formidable team as we performed many heart surgeries—routine and complex—successfully for the next twenty-four years. Bill eventually had his own issues with what was by then a new hospital administration. While he didn't go too far away—he became a successful heart surgeon in the neighboring state of Connecticut—I felt his loss acutely.

There's a line in the hit hip-hop musical *Hamilton*, in which Hamilton and Lafayette—neither of whom was born in America—congratulate themselves for having helped win the American Revolution by rapping the line "Immigrants, we get the job done!" I felt that way about Bill and me. One of us Chinese, the other Indian. Together we saved a lot of American lives. We got the job done, and I'm proud of it.

The working and personal friendship between us was effortless. That's how it goes with some people, isn't it? You're just in sync; you complement each other. That had never been the case with my father and me. And around the time that Bill joined my team, my parents arrived for a visit.

This would be their third trip to the United States. The previous visit had come shortly after we had returned from London. Barbara and I had been struggling to make ends meet at that point. We hadn't even had an extra bed in our small, cramped house. I had taken the mattress from our bed and put it in the basement for my parents to sleep on while Barbara and I slept on the bed frame. My father had mellowed somewhat with time and the aftereffects of his stroke. He'd never criticized or made any comments about the substandard arrangements or the fact that we were in dire financial straits. Still, his mere presence in that situation had been enough to shame me. I'd felt once again like the errant boy whose failure had been predicted by this man.

When they visited for the last time, in the mid-1980s, the situation was much different. By this time we had moved into our brick colonial house in a quiet, historic neighborhood of Providence, I had gotten rid of the Dodge Dart, and I was driving a Mercedes.

And Barbara showed them photos of the giant billboards and tear sheets of the ads with my picture on them. Through that campaign and my growing practice, I was a now fairly well-recognized person in Providence. When we went out to dinner, colleagues, friends, and patients would often drop by our table to say hello. My mother was delighted to speak with them all and tell them how proud she was of her Arun.

Although much more reserved, I knew my dad was noticing this, too.

Their situation had improved, as well, by this point. My two brothers and I had pooled our resources to buy Mom and Dad a spacious house with all the modern amenities in a posh neighborhood of Patna. They even got a cook and a driver—which may sound like crazy-rich luxuries in the US but are actually amenities that many comfortable Indians have. That's exactly what my parents were at that point: comfortable grandparents, living in a spacious house with a lush garden behind that was filled with mango and guava trees. They were finally able to live the kind of life that we felt they deserved.

I had endured my own dark periods, my own bouts of desperation and hopelessness. Now, with age and experience, I saw my own father's black moods a little more sympathetically. He had lost everything early in life: his first family in the tragic train accident and the affection of his parents for having married out of his caste. His once-promising career had stalled, forcing him and his family to live on the charity of his father-in-law. Finally, the stroke had robbed him of much of his remaining dignity and reduced his power of speech. And on top of it all, he'd had an eldest son who did nothing but get in trouble and bring shame to the family. I realized that my behavior as a boy had made this already broken man look, to himself at least, like even more of a failure.

By contrast, my father was wonderful with Barbara. He had been since the first time he met her. Despite cultural and religious differences, he (and, less surprisingly, my mom) got along famously with her and my in-laws.

One of my parents' earlier visits had happened to coincide with the Jewish High Holiday of Yom Kippur. You could have knocked me over with a feather when this pious Hindu happily marched off to synagogue with his Jewish daughter-in-law (and enjoyed the service). He was also warm, loving, and affectionate with his grandsons.

Still, his coolness to me, the awkward silences between us, rankled. So it meant a lot to me on his final visit to the US when, as we sat together in our usual quietude after dinner, he turned to me and said words that I'd been waiting to hear for many years:

"I was wrong about you. I'm very proud of what you achieved… and I love you."

Four years later, he died of a heart attack on Kartik Purnima— one of the most important holy days on the Hindu religious calendar. When my mother called me with the news, I said a prayer for the complicated, sad, sometimes difficult but ultimately good and honest man who was my father.

Chapter Twenty-One

Survival at a Horrible Cost

One afternoon in the late eighties, Barbara noticed a lump in her breast.

I took her to a general surgeon. That was the norm then; not many surgeons specialized in breast diseases, but he had been recommended by colleagues, and I was assured that he was the top man for this in Providence. When we met him, he comported himself very much like a top man of that era. Obviously competent, successful, and experienced, he was also condescending to Barbara and imperious. After his examination and the test results, he spoke not to someone as inconsequential as the patient, but to somebody he deemed nearly his equal and worthy of his attention, for at least a few minutes: me.

"It's nothing serious," he said confidently, and I breathed a sigh of relief. "But you should understand what's going on here."

I was puzzled. What, besides my wife's having found a lump in her breast, was transpiring?

"She wants attention," he said, as if this were obvious. "Trust me, I've seen this before, and often with the wives of successful men. Look, you're known for working long hours, aren't you?"

My reputation had preceded me. I admitted that was so.

"OK, so you're gone most of the time, the kids are getting older, she's in the house alone. She feels neglected."

This sounded strange to me. Barbara didn't seem to act as if she felt neglected. Nor did she ever seem to have any trouble getting my attention.

"And she should stop drinking coffee and quit smoking."

I started to say that she had never smoked, but he went right on talking. He explained to me that she had fibrocystic disease, not uncommon in her age group and, he assured me, easily treated. "We'll put her on hormone therapy for that," he said. "That will also help sort out her moods. Anyway, I've got another surgery, Arun. We'll speak again."

With that our consultation was over.

To this day Barbara gets livid when I bring this man up. She's right. To my everlasting shame and regret, I allowed myself to go along with this diagnosis. I rationalized it at the time; who doesn't want to hear good news? I'd been told that the cyst was benign and not to worry. But in my heart I knew that the independent, confident, beautiful woman who is my wife was not simply seeking attention. On the other hand, I should have paid more attention to the fact that there was a history of breast cancer in her family.

The logical next step would have been to schedule an appointment with a specialist in Boston or New York, preferably someone who did not take a nineteenth-century view of women. But we never did that. A year later, the lump was not only still there, it had grown to the size of a golf ball.

This time, I found a surgeon in Providence who took her case seriously. He sent Barbara for ultrasound and CT scans, and even though the imaging then wasn't that good, the results—when combined with his examination—seemed clear to him. This wasn't some kind of midlife crisis or childish acting out. Barbara had malignant breast cancer. She would have to undergo radical mastectomy—an extensive surgery in which the chest wall muscles and lymph glands are removed.

The night before her operation, she and I lay together and cried together. I wept because the woman I loved was about to undergo surgery. I wept because I could not begin to contemplate my life without her. I also wept because of what could go wrong in that surgery. I knew the risks and the complications; I knew the inexplicable things that can sometimes happen, even in the best hospitals and with the most highly skilled surgical teams. And in this case the outcome would be in the hands of someone else. I had no control. Just like my patients.

The procedure on Christmas Eve went well, but there was more bad news: another cancer was detected on her left breast. Four months later, she would have to go through this all over again. Her left breast was removed, and Barbara was then submitted to massive doses of chemotherapy.

This was 1989. Chemo has come a long way since then. When my wife went through it, no effective antinausea drugs were available in those days as part of the "cocktail." My memories of those days are of Barbara curled up in the bathroom next to the toilet. She also lost her hair, but she never lost her spirit or her sense of humor. "Go to the hospital, Arun, will you please?" she would say, when I expressed ambivalence and guilt about working while she was so sick. "I'll go nuts if I have to deal with you moping around the house all day."

She'd manage a smile when she ribbed me, but she was right. While Barbara was trying to stay as positive as possible, I was mired again in despair, much as I'd been during my tumultuous first five years at Rhode Island Hospital. Now I thought, *My career is flourishing, but my wife is dying.*

Ari and Michael were real troopers during this period. Ari

was sixteen and Michael was thirteen when their mother was diagnosed. They might have been young, but they knew the score. We were friends with a family in which the mother had died of breast cancer at a young age a few years earlier.

There would be more complications and setbacks ahead, but Barbara's indomitable spirit ultimately prevailed. That, along with the good treatment she'd gotten from the second surgeon, I am convinced, saved her life. She even managed to pull me out of my gloom once again. And I needed it, because it was around this time, as we were dealing with Barbara's treatment, that one of the great fears I'd always suspected was just around the corner in my career suddenly materialized.

One night while I was on call, I got called to do an urgent bypass surgery. The patient was a fifty-two-year-old man who had severe blockages in all the coronary arteries. His name was Don, and he had been in another area hospital for five days. There he had been administered heparin, a blood thinner, to dissolve the clot that had developed in his narrowed coronary arteries. He was transferred to our hospital the night before surgery. When I met Don, he appeared otherwise healthy, despite periods of chest pain. I was told by the surgical resident that everything was fine and ready to go in the morning.

The next morning, surgery began. We opened his chest and harvested a vein from his leg and an artery from his chest wall. We were just about ready for him to go on the heart-lung machine when blood work came back. "You better look at this, Doctor," said one of the nurses.

She handed me the lab report: Don's platelet count was dangerously low. Normally platelets (the cells in the blood that help the clotting process) measure about 120,000 to 150,000. His were around 30,000.

"This is really low," I said. "Is that an error?"

A repeat blood test reconfirmed it.

Now we were faced with a dilemma. Without surgery this man would likely have a massive heart attack and die within a day, if not a few hours. He was already prepped for surgery, and his chest had already been opened.

I was frustrated that we were even in this situation. I doubted that some precipitous drop in his platelets had occurred in the time it had taken to transfer him to Rhode Island Hospital from the previous one. Why hadn't they picked this up in their testing? We had to find out now, with the patient on the operating table? Later it would turn out that a number of errors had been made along the chain. But there was little time to debate that now. We proceeded to perform the operation and hope for the best.

We performed triple coronary artery bypass surgery without any problem. I crossed my fingers after the operation. Six hours later, when Don woke up in the ICU, he could not move his legs, which had turned blue. I knew right then and there what we were dealing with: a clot had formed in his abdominal aorta and cut off blood flow to the lower body. We took Don back to the OR immediately and removed a large white clot from his aorta. It was too late to save his legs, though. We had to perform a bilateral amputation and immediately put him on kidney dialysis. Had we not done that, toxins released from his damaged leg muscles would have stopped his heart within hours.

His survival came at a horrible cost, however. Don had permanently lost the use of both legs and his kidneys. The devastating prognosis was that for the rest of his life he would require dialysis, be wheelchair bound, and would need to wear a colostomy bag.

What had gone wrong? I went through every step of the

procedure, and the culprit was clear: the heparin. We figured out that the low platelet count was the sign of a reaction to that drug, which led to a rare disease called HITT (heparin-induced thrombocytopenia thrombosis). A blood test for HITT confirmed the diagnosis. We would eventually write and publish a journal paper about Don's case. And in doing so we may have helped others to avoid the same fate.

But that wasn't going to help Don. I couldn't help but think that if we had not been aggressive, if we had not insisted that he get back into surgery just a few hours after his first procedure, he would have died, and we would never have known about the HITT. As with the baby with complications whose life I prolonged, I wonder sometimes in retrospect what choice the patient himself would have made had he been given the option: to die in a hospital, or to live the rest of his life with a colostomy bag and unable to walk?

I suspect he would have chosen the latter, and, as he is still alive today, I pray that the quality of his life has been sufficient to make up for the awful consequences he suffered from his surgery. Had he received the proper blood test at the other hospital, had his low platelet count been spotted before he was on the operating table, and had we known the result earlier, we possibly could have prevented what happened. But even if we had known, I have to be honest: there were no guarantees. He had to be operated on, low platelets or not. Otherwise he would have died.

After the surgery Don's family was very appreciative of what we'd done and how hard we'd worked to save him. But they knew that it had come at a catastrophic cost to their loved one. When he was ready to be discharged, his wife came to me. "Doctor, how we are going to take care of him? Who's going to pay for all the medical expenses?"

I felt terrible for her. She recognized what was ahead for Don, for herself, and for the rest of their family. Her husband was now disabled. He would need constant and expensive treatment for as long as he lived. As a result their lives would be upended. He'd need to live in a house designed for someone who was wheelchair bound. He'd have to have a special vehicle to drive. His days would revolve around dialysis treatments. Don would not likely be able to hold a job, and this was a middle-class family. How *could* they pay for this?

I guess it was no surprise when, a few months later, I received a letter informing me that I was being sued for malpractice. Not only me, of course: both hospitals, his cardiologist, the surgical resident, and others were also named in the lawsuit.

Meanwhile Barbara recovered from chemotherapy, our kids settled back into our normal routine, and I returned to my busy practice. Despite the lawsuits, things were looking better. Or so it seemed.

Then, in April 1992, Barbara and I decided to attend a cardiac surgery meeting in Los Angeles and spend some quality time together. One afternoon, while we were returning from Universal Studios, we suddenly heard sirens and saw black smoke rising up in the distance. We rushed back to the hotel and turned on the TV to find out that riots were breaking out across the city as a result of the acquittal of white police officers who had been captured on video viciously beating Rodney King, an African American.

For three days we were confined to our hotel as the city shut down and the National Guard was called in to restore order. I have a vivid memory of that time from when a group of hotel guests were standing together watching images of the fires and looting and shooting on the TV in the lobby. A little girl turned to her parents and asked, "Mommy, what country is that?"

In the midst of this chaos, I got an urgent call from Barbara's doctor. The CT and ultrasound she'd had before we left for LA had revealed what was likely a large tumor in her uterus. "We have to take it out, Arun, and soon," her oncological surgeon said.

I remember staring at the phone after I hung up with him. I really felt as if the sky were falling down on us: my career was in jeopardy because of the lawsuit, and my wife, battling cancer, was heading back into surgery. It took us three days to get a flight home, and it was one of the longest plane rides of my life, because I knew what was ahead. The day after we returned to Providence, we met with the oncological surgeon. The day after that, Barbara had her procedure. This time it was a removal of her uterus and ovaries—a total hysterectomy.

Throughout the ordeal Barbara remained strong, always positive. She never lost her spirit, and she kept the family together. I, on the other hand, was a nervous wreck. I couldn't bear the thought of a life without Barbara. But her optimism proved well-founded: when the pathology report came back, it showed that the cancer had not spread. Barbara now had a good shot at a complete recovery.

Meanwhile, the malpractice suit moved along slowly. It took years of multiple depositions, discoveries from the plaintiff's lawyer, and expert opinions before the case was set for trial.

One night during that time, when the stress of the suit was dragging me down, I took my son Michael out to dinner at a Chinese restaurant we liked in Providence. At this point he was about seventeen. As we were sitting studying the menu, I noticed a gentleman roll into the restaurant in a wheelchair. I recognized him right away as Don. He didn't notice me; he might not have even recognized me if he did. And while there was a part of me that wanted to speak with him, just to see how he was doing, I knew that wouldn't be wise.

I ruminated over the situation and then looked up at my son. "Michael," I said, "let me ask you a question."

"Sure, what, Dad?" he replied as he continued to scan the menu.

"If someone did surgery on me, and it didn't go right, and I ended up like that man over there...in a wheelchair...what would you do?"

His eyes rose from the menu and met mine. "I'd sue the son of a bitch," he said, without hesitation.

I knew right then how this should end. So did our attorneys. The case never even went to trial. A few months later, an arbitrator ruled in Don's favor. And I don't mind saying, for the record, that he deserved that ruling. Not because of any mistake I'd made—there's really nothing I would have or could have done differently—but because, again, his wife was right. This wasn't his fault. Somebody had to pay for this man's treatment. Who would that somebody be? You? Me? The others involved in his care? The hospital? The insurance companies? The manufacturers of heparin?

Well, in the end, of course, it is all of us who pay. The malpractice system in this country is deeply flawed, in my opinion, and rife with abuse. But if you ask me for a better option, I confess that I don't have one. And as I've told others, including some of my colleagues, I don't blame patients like Don when they do sue. If I were he, I would have done exactly the same thing.

Still, the malpractice suit was a black mark on my record for years, and it took a huge emotional toll. Every time I renewed my license or reapplied for a hospital appointment, I had to explain the particulars of the case and the settlement yet again. Plus the uncertainty of it, the agonizingly slow wait for some kind of legal closure, not to mention the anxiety over the suit's impact on my career, led to many sleepless nights, and a few points when I again contemplated leaving the profession. As she had in the past, when I got to the end of my rope, it was Barbara—this time from her sickbed—who talked me back, reminding me how hard I'd worked to get where I was. I'm glad she did, as my practice continued to flourish and brought me great satisfaction.

Thank God there were few cases like Don's—for all our sakes.

As with so many tribulations, there was the proverbial silver lining: being the spouse of a cancer patient and seeing the awful consequences of Don's surgery gave me a new perspective. Not on my practice, but on my patients. The agonizing wait before hearing how Barbara's surgeries had gone, and the desperation in Don's wife's voice when she pondered their future—these things changed my thinking. I had always tried to be kind to my patients. But now I empathized with them and their families in new and deeper ways. I also realized that as well trained as I was, and as much education as I had, the patients and their families were my teachers.

It is those people and those lessons, I feel, that must now come to the forefront of my story.

— *Chapter Twenty-Two* —

Please Make My Heart Better

During my years here, I've become a fan of American sports, Major League Baseball and the National Football League in particular. It was one of the great American baseball players, Hall of Fame pitcher Jim Palmer, who once said something that struck me as relevant to what I had been doing over a long career as a surgeon. During a TV interview, Palmer said he could remember every pitch he'd thrown in a major league game.

Even if he was speaking metaphorically, I can believe that.

While I certainly don't recall every stitch I've made in every operation, I can describe the basic details—patient history, surgical procedure, and outcome—of each of the more than fifteen thousand cardiac surgeries I've performed.

Those memories are etched in my mind even though my surgical routine was, well, *routine* throughout my career. When I got home from a day's work at the hospital, I would have a late dinner, and then, usually at around 10 p.m., I would start preparing for the following day. This entailed looking at all available information (lesson learned from Don) about the next day's patients, worrying (as is my nature)—and praying.

My prayer the night before surgery was always the same: "Let the complicated become simple and the simple not become complicated."

When my prayers were answered—as they usually were—the surgeries ended up being less memorable—a good thing. But there were exceptions: maybe the patient's condition was unusual, or the outcome was unexpected, or something surprising happened in the operating room. It's hard to forget those latter cases, in which surgery or its aftermath didn't go as you'd hoped.

One of the most memorable surgeries of my career involved the simple becoming complicated. The experience was so draining that it made me reconsider the profession I'd devoted my life to—and not out of anger or disgust with the system, as had been the case with the malpractice suit.

In this case it was the sheer emotional weight of the case. In the aftermath of a straightforward operation gone terribly wrong, I thought, *I can't do this anymore. It's time to retire.*

The night before surgery, I always reviewed the charts of the person or people I'd be operating on. This took about forty-five to sixty minutes per patient. A lot of surgeons wait until the morning of the operation to do this review. Then they might say, "Something's wrong here, I'm not going to do this operation today." I never did that. I never canceled an operation at the last minute unless something happened with the patient overnight, such as their having a stroke or contracting a cold with a high fever and infection. I have been blessed with the ability to function at a high level on not much sleep, so I didn't care if it was one a.m. and I was scheduled to be at the hospital in five hours. I wanted the information then. I wanted to see everything in place.

I took this approach not just for my sake, but also for the patients'. They trusted me to keep them alive. They were the bravest people, giving me that trust, and I didn't want to lose it. I wanted to do everything I could for them.

Even after I assured myself I'd done everything possible to

prepare, I worried. Just as patients and their families were filled with often conflicting emotions before surgery, so was I. I worried whether the next day I'd make someone a widow or have to tell someone they'd lost a parent. It was also impossible not to think about the aftermath of surgery, that someone I'd successfully operated on might develop complications hours later. What might I do the next day to lessen the chance of something like that happening? These sorts of thoughts went through my mind before every operation, in addition to the technical aspects of surgery.

As an aside, here's something I never really told patients about. Everybody wants surgery first thing Monday morning, because they think the surgeon will have had a nice weekend and show up refreshed. I did better surgery later on in the day and week than early Monday morning. At the start of the workweek, I felt all the stress about the upcoming operations, because it was part of my job to imagine every possible thing that could go wrong. People don't want to have the second or third or fourth operation of the day, but that's when I was at my best. Part of that was because I was warmed up and had better mobility in my hands. But there was also the emotional aspect, which weighed most heavily on me early in the morning.

Once I was in the operating room, those emotions almost always vanished. I was completely focused on the work at hand. That's why the case of a young man I'll call William is so vivid in my memory. It was a rare instance when wrenching emotion pervaded the operating room.

William was a twenty-two-year-old who came to me for evaluation as a candidate for open heart surgery. He was a tall, handsome, well-built college senior who was to graduate in the spring. He already had a job lined up in Boston at the investment bank UBS. His future was bright.

But William was having shortness of breath when doing things like playing basketball or jogging. A physical exam done in preparation for his impending job had revealed a heart murmur. I had operated on his mother twice—the first time for an ascending aortic aneurysm and the second time, ten years later, for a leaky aortic valve. The aortic valve connects the main chamber of the heart to the aorta, the main artery in the body. There was a chance that William had been born with similar defects.

Sure enough, an echocardiogram showed that William had a leaky aortic valve. Also, his aortic valve had two flaps instead of three. About 2 percent of the population have two flaps in their aortic valve. For most of these people, the aberration doesn't significantly affect cardiac function, and they can go on to live a normal life to age seventy or eighty with no issues. But about 10 to 20 percent of young people with two flaps have the problem that William had: a mild or moderate leak in the valve and a dilated aorta (William's measured 5.2 centimeters diameter—more than 2 centimeters larger than normal). In such cases there's a 2 to 4 percent chance each year of the aorta rupturing. Over ten years that means a 20 to 40 percent chance of rupture, which could have serious consequences, including death.

So even though William was doing fine, these odds in combination with his mother's history made him a strong candidate for surgery. He was a little scared but trusted my judgment and consented to surgery. Because his situation wasn't an emergency, we agreed I'd perform the operation after William had graduated from college.

I recommended, and William agreed to, what's known as a David procedure. This would entail replacing his ascending aorta with a Dacron graft, as well as repairing and then re-implanting his own aortic valve inside the graft. I explained to William that it was a more involved procedure than replacing his valve, but that I'd been doing it for twenty years with excellent outcomes. The advantage is that you retain your own valve rather than live with an artificial valve, which can fail and requires that you be on a blood thinner for the rest of your life. I told William the procedure would allow him to live a much more normal life. He liked that option. He was eager to actively enjoy the many years ahead of him as much as possible.

The morning of William's operation was like most others. I talked with him and his mother, going over once again what exactly the procedure would entail, giving an estimate of how long it would take, and patiently answering any questions they had. I always encouraged patients and their families to write down questions they might have. They're afraid, they're preoccupied, and they might forget to ask you something important while you're with them. I always answered honestly, but I also always tried to reassure them that, although there's always risk, we'll do our best to minimize it.

Although I told William and his mother how long the surgery would take, I followed my usual practice of not being too precise. I might say I'd be done around noon when, if things went as expected, I'd be done at more like eleven a.m. The purpose of building in this extra cushion was to ease the family's minds, so that they wouldn't start worrying if I hadn't shown up by 11:10. Of course, sometimes I would come to the waiting room at eleven and not be able to find the family because they were all wandering around! But usually they would be there waiting, eager to get the news.

There's always the possibility surgery will last much longer than anticipated. If what I had estimated would be four hours became more like seven hours, or if a patient was doing poorly,

I thought it was important to keep the family updated. I'd have a social worker, nurse practitioner, or physician assistant find the family and explain to them that we had encountered a little problem, and that I'd be down to see them as soon as possible.

When that happened, I would adjust the rest of the day's schedule as needed. Just as I didn't want to be like surgeons who reviewed a patient's chart the morning of an operation and decided then to cancel it, I didn't want to let an early operation gone long lead to canceling someone else's surgery. Of course, sometimes we don't have a choice despite all our best efforts. The patient and their family have their mind set on it, and are emotionally prepared for that day. I felt obligated to respect their bravery. If it meant operating late at night, I'd do it.

Many times I entered the operating room consumed by thoughts about an upcoming operation, but once surgery was underway, those emotions disappeared. Everything else gets blocked out while you focus completely on the problem in front of you.

In addition to your own work, you have to manage the rest of your team. Depending on the procedure, you might have with you as many as nine people, and a minimum of six. There could be two or three assistants, who might be your associates, resident doctors, physician assistants, and/or registered nurses. There's a perfusionist, who operates the heart-lung machine, which temporarily takes over the work of the heart and lungs during surgery to keep the patient's blood and oxygen circulating. There's also an anesthesiologist, a circulating nurse (who manages the area outside the sterile area of the operating room), and a scrub nurse (who assists the surgical team with donning gear and passing instruments). There could also be any number of medical students on hand. Everyone present is a highly trained professional, of course, but still, it's up to you as the surgeon to control the environment. You become demanding to make sure everybody's doing things the way you want them done.

I always gathered the team before surgery to brief them on what I expected. Everybody knows their responsibilities, but there are always details to go over, such as whether it's predicted the patient will need two or five bypasses. Over time, others learned how I liked to work and adjusted accordingly. During surgery you keep communicating, but there isn't as much conversation as many people might think. Working with a good crew, you become like a well-practiced football team, everybody knowing what to do on a particular play, or a good orchestra, everyone working together to produce something greater than the sum of their parts. To offer one more metaphor, my role in the operating room was to be the captain of the ship. Even though the outcome depended on the crew, I was the one making the decisions.

William's procedure went as smoothly as anyone could want. Over the course of four hours, we put him to sleep, opened his chest, replaced his aorta with a Dacron graft, repaired his aortic valve, and re-implanted his native coronary artery to the graft. His heart function was normal and he had no trouble coming off the heart-lung machine. At about eleven a.m., I stepped out of the operating room to dictate my notes about the morning's work. My team was to take the final steps: finish closing his chest and put a dressing on his wound.

Suddenly William's heart started fibrillating, meaning that it was quivering instead of contracting. He had no blood pressure and was under cardiac arrest. He was expiring, and quickly.

We started CPR, we shocked him, but the heart wouldn't come around. I was in distress—just a few minutes ago I was thinking how well everything had gone, and now this wonderful young man, whose mother was expecting me in the waiting room, was dying before my eyes. And I didn't know why!

Compounding the problem was that the heart-lung machine had been dismantled. Typically patients come off the machine when we're confident the body is ready to support itself. We then watch the patient—blood pressure, echocardiogram, and so on—for half an hour before dismantling the machine. The reason for this watch period is that before an operation, the patient receives heparin (yes, the same blood thinner that in rare cases can cause the kinds of problems my patient Don experienced). For most patients, heparin is critical; without it the heart-lung machine will form clots, and the patient will die. When the patient is off the machine, you reverse the blood thinner with a clotting agent, protamine, so that the patient doesn't bleed extensively from even the smallest cut.

Once you've given the protamine, you can't simply return the patient to the heart-lung machine if there's a problem. You have to start that part of the process from scratch, which takes time.

So with our other methods failing, I had no choice but to cut open his chest again. The heart was flaccid, not moving. He was close to death. I grabbed William's heart between my two hands and started pumping it myself, squeezing the heart rapidly to simulate its own action. In essence I was keeping this young man alive with my hands, pumping his heart for nearly ten minutes while my team prepared the heart-lung machine to once again take over the job. I prayed quietly to myself that this young man would not die while I literally held his heart in my hands.

⌒

After several of the most stressful minutes of my life, we were able to get William back on the heart-lung machine. It took

another two and a half hours in the operating room to suffi-
ciently support his heart and get him back to baseline activity.
Finally we were able to reclose his chest and take him to the
intensive care unit. I accompanied him to make sure he was stable. Meanwhile, I had sent a nurse to tell his mother why there
was a delay, and that I would speak with her as soon as William's condition allowed me to.

I was satisfied the heart had come back, but of course I wanted
to know what had happened. It's possible small air bubbles inside
the chambers of William's heart had dislodged when we moved
him at the end of the operation. Usually these little bubbles clear
up, but they can cause trouble if the air rises to the brain, causing
a seizure, or goes to the coronary artery, causing fibrillation. William's case is a reminder that sometimes things seem to happen
for no reason. We were fortunate that it happened in the operating room, where the team was already assembled and where
we could quickly open his chest and support his heart. If it had
occurred half an hour later, he might well have died.

Even though William seemed to be doing well, I remained
distraught. The big concern was that he would develop complications. Because we'd had to rip open his chest, would the bone
fail to heal properly? Would he contract a severe infection, or
have a stroke, or suffer kidney failure? I thought, *If something
happens to this young man, this may be my last operation.* I shared
that sentiment with some of my team. The emotional toll was so
great because you don't expect an incident like this with such a
young patient, someone who represents the future.

When William's condition was stable, I went to the waiting
room to talk with his mother. She grabbed me and started crying
into my shoulder. I think she felt some guilt over her son's situation, because of the possibility of having passed on a congenital

heart defect. I told her what had happened and that I didn't know why it had happened. I said that most likely, he would be OK, but that I couldn't tell her that for sure for another four to six hours, until he was awake and we knew how his kidney and other functions had come out. I remained at William's bedside for a few hours, delaying my other operation scheduled for that day until late in the evening. At around six p.m. he woke up. I brought his mother in to see him. He gave her a thumbs-up. She started crying again, but I think this time the tears were of a different sort.

Anytime something bad happened with a patient, I would get angry and frustrated. Endless questions would go through my mind: *What did we do wrong? Could we have done something differently? Should we not have done this? Should we have instead done that?* You do the best you can, based on your knowledge and experience, but in those situations it's impossible not to question yourself. When the outcome is poor, it really hurts, because you've failed, and your failure has affected so many people. It's no real consolation to tell yourself how ill the patient was before the operation or that, as in William's case, it might have been some one-in-a-million set of circumstances. Even though I was grateful that this young man had survived, the circumstances haunted me. How could we prevent this from happening again? Because there was no clear answer, I kept myself from becoming incapacitated the way I always did, by jumping right back into my work rather than avoiding it.

There was always another patient waiting, another life we had to take carefully into our hands.

I said earlier that, on a typical day, one thing I did when I got home from the hospital was prepare for the following day's surgeries. Another thing I did was worry about the patients I'd worked on that day. You can imagine what a relaxing home life this made for! Here, while Barbara might want to sit down and watch television with her husband, I'd be distracted and brooding. I often called the intensive care unit at eleven p.m., asking the staff on duty how my patients were doing. What were their vital signs? Were they bleeding? How was their kidney function? Had they had a stroke or heart attack? After all, my team and I might have done a great job on the operation itself, but what good is the surgery if the patient doesn't wake up? In the big picture, things aren't over just because the operation is finished. Those kinds of worries were always in the back of my mind. It wasn't until forty-eight hours after surgery that I was able to relax a bit. Anything can still happen after that, but it's a lot more likely to be routine.

The day of William's surgery was anything but typical. When I checked in on William again, he was awake and alert, and his heart and kidney function were normal. Between that good news and the fact that he had been off a heart-supporting drug for six hours, I was fairly confident he was going to be fine. Only then did I feel that it was OK to go home.

When I saw William the next morning, he looked perfectly normal. He had recovered from the near-fatal experience of less than twenty-four hours earlier. He was kept in the hospital for seven days instead of being discharged after the typical five days, but all his tests were normal, and his heart function was good. Within a few weeks he had recovered completely. Three months after surgery, he was back to normal activity and had returned to his job. One year after that horrible day in the operating room, I saw him for a follow-up visit, and his condition was perfect. His care was transferred to a local doctor, in Boston, where he'd have yearly checkups.

William's case is a great example of how even during a straight-forward operation, unpredictable things can happen suddenly. These are humbling experiences that remind us that we go from day to day never knowing what's going to transpire. William's case was an extreme example, one of the few times I was ready to walk out the hospital doors and never return. I thank God that William—and I—recovered. His success inspired me to stay with my profession, and I went on to perform many more complex and successful operations.

As I mentioned earlier, my prayer before surgery was, "Let the complicated become simple and the simple not become complicated." What does *complicated* mean in this context? One aspect is the nature of the operation. You might do multiple procedures at the same time, as when a patient needs not only a bypass but also a valve repair or implant. Then there's the condition of the patient before surgery: What state is their heart in? How much is it damaged? What about their general fitness and lifestyle? Are they overweight? Do they smoke? Do they have diabetes or a kidney problem or dementia? All these factors can add up to a much higher average risk than if you're operating on an otherwise healthy person—like active, twenty-two-year-old William.

While most surgeries are routine, in the sense that they are likely to be common procedures, all surgeries have potential complications. That's especially the case with open heart surgery, which has so many aspects: the heart-lung machine, blood transfusion, medications, and so on. In addition to the technical components, there's the unpredictable matter of the human being who's the patient. Presurgery testing should give a good indication of what you'll find once you start an operation, but there are no guarantees. Many times I expected patients to do poorly because they had a bad heart muscle, they'd had a heart attack or diabetes or lung problems, they were overweight, two or three of their valves were leaking, or some combination of those factors. And then I'd do the operation and the patient would recover beautifully and quickly, with no complications.

Other times, presurgery testing wasn't able to give the complete picture, as was the case with William. For example, I might find that the valve I'd planned to put in wouldn't fit the patient's aorta because the aorta was too small or too much calcium had built up in it. More often the patient's unique physiology meant a bad reaction to some part of the procedure, whether a blood transfusion, the blood thinner, drugs and anesthesia, or the heart-lung machine—the nonorganic elements used in surgery.

There's no such thing as straightforward surgery because there's no way of predicting how it will go. That's why I say the patients and their families are the bravest people. The best I can do is explain to them all the potential risks; then the choice is theirs about how to proceed.

That was always my method, whether I discussed the possibilities with parents of an infant, middle-aged professionals, or elderly retirees. I can still picture having this conversation with the oldest person I ever operated on, a ninety-nine-year-old man whose aortic valve was progressively closing. His name was Walter. He was thin and frail and looked every bit of his age. He had complained of severe shortness of breath, and I could tell during our conversation that he wasn't exaggerating. He had to catch his breath between words while we were talking. But mentally he was very sharp. I asked Walter if he lived alone and he nodded. He told me he would like to live a little longer, and to be able to breathe better. I told him his options: go home, take medication, and live a couple of months before the heart gives out, or try open heart surgery. I quickly added that at age ninety-nine, such a surgery would carry a high risk for stroke and complications. But I knew it could be done, and I was willing to do it.

He burst into tears when I told him this. What was wrong? Slowly, pausing after every few words, Walter said these were tears of relief. He was happy that I had examined him, listened, and paid attention. This had not been the case with the first surgeon he had consulted. A few months earlier, Walter had gone to a large academic university medical center in Boston for a consultation with a highly recommended heart surgeon. While he was sitting in the waiting room, he overheard the surgeon chastising his secretary behind the frosted glass walls of his adjacent office. "You made an appointment with a ninety-nine-year-old man?" he heard the surgeon say. "Are you crazy? There's no way I'm doing surgery on someone that old."

Afterward, the surgeon had walked into the examination room and brusquely told Walter to go home. "I'm sorry we had to waste your time, sir, but to be honest, there's nothing I can do for you," the surgeon said. According to Walter, the man never examined him, never even gave him an opportunity to speak.

Walter was right to be upset with that first surgeon. That's no way to treat someone who is sick and desperate, no matter their age. You should have some compassion, humility, and respect. Walter wasn't asking for surgery in some vain attempt to live forever. The poor man could barely breathe.

Fully aware of the risks, he came to the hospital a few days later. I spoke to him before the surgery.

"Walter," I said, "I'm going to do my best to give you some quality of life in your remaining time. But I must tell you one more time. You know there's a high risk here and that you may not survive, right?"

"I know," he said, slowly, pausing after each word. "And I appreciate you doing this, no matter what happens."

"You do have your will in order and all arrangements made, just in case?" I asked.

"I do," he said. "But I have faith in you, Doc."

I shared with him my opinion that, all things considered, dying under anesthesia isn't the worst way to go. Such philosophical discussions are not the norm with a patient right before surgery. But Walter was not the norm. He agreed and managed a smile.

"Doc," he said. "I may surprise you."

He certainly did. The following year, I attended Walter's hundredth birthday party.

He lived to be 102.

Let me be clear: I'm not advocating surgery for nonagenarians. But Walter's case is a great reminder that you have to treat patients like unique human beings, not anonymous, generic numbers based on their age. If you refuse all elderly patients, someone will be denied a chance to live—to celebrate, perhaps, another birthday with friends or family.

Walter's case raises a timely issue for the medical profession. As we enter the twenty-first century, the baby boomers are getting older and living longer. With that longevity comes higher incidences of heart problems. What do you do for them? Because they often have other complications—diabetes, high blood pressure, depression, fragility, and so forth—their operations are going to be high risk. Currently the mortality rate for patients under seventy years of age who undergo cardiac surgery is about 1 to 4 percent. For those older than seventy, that risk skyrockets to 10 to 20 percent.

Even if they survive the surgery, the older folks require lengthier stays in the hospital and are more prone to complications. Also, unlike Walter, about half of elderly patients who undergo heart surgery end up going not home, but to extended care facilities.

Those are the facts. Moreover, I'm fully aware that the pressure is on surgeons and hospitals to refuse to perform on older, high-risk patients, because it negatively affects the hospital outcomes we love to advertise as proof of how wonderful we are.

So yes, I understand all the arguments against doing these surgeries. Arguments that are likely to grow louder in the coming years, as more and more old patients come to us with conditions that might—might—be treatable with surgery.

And despite all the reasons we should not, my philosophy is still that we should.

I look at it this way: if I can save 50 percent of these people and give them a chance to live, it is worth the effort. Who am I to deny them the chance to live? You've got to have hope!

Congress has recently passed the "Right to Try" bill to allow the use of nonapproved FDA drugs as a last measure to help terminally ill patients get the potentially lifesaving investigational treatment they need, before it is too late.

The change is already taking place. Over the past decade or so, new and less invasive technologies and procedures have been allowing us to replace heart valves in elderly, frail, and high-risk patients, or safely do a coronary artery stent or repair an aneurysm with less trauma to the body. My sense is that it won't be long before the idea of surgery for a ninety-nine-year-old isn't nearly as radical as it sounded when I operated on Walter.

Another major league great, Edgar Martínez, is widely credited with saying, "Learn to control your emotions or they will control you." In the operating theater, I certainly learned to do that. You try to focus on the procedure, not the person. But that doesn't mean I was indifferent to the suffering of my patients. After all, I don't just work on hearts—I have one, too. And believe me, it was tested, particularly in my early years.

Which is why I will always remember Shawn Johnson. His story, like his life, is much shorter than that of William or Walter or most of my patients, but it affected me in a more fundamental way than almost any other.

When his parents brought him to see me again in 1977, Shawn was four years old. He had been born with a number of heart problems. He had no spleen, and his heart was twisted, with one chamber missing. But he had a keen intelligence and an endearing personality. Even at his young age, I recall being impressed by how articulate and perceptive he was. He was also compassionate—he had met other children in the hospital, and he was always asking me what I could do to help them, just like I helped him after his palliative surgery.

Shawn's parents were dedicated and supportive, even as his condition worsened. They also tried hard to keep things positive, which I applauded. With the help of his mother, Shawn created a coloring book, in which he drew pictures of his surroundings in the hospital. There were little childlike renderings of IV machines, crash carts, and small figures in beds, some with smiley faces and others sad. He also wrote about his feelings on blood draws, intravenous fluids, and his interactions with the doctors and the nurses. The title of his booklet, written in big letters on the first page, was *Please Make My Heart Better*.

I made that my mission. I so wanted this brave little boy to survive. His condition, however, was very precarious and complex— well beyond our hospital's capabilities at the time. Shawn, who was in a great deal of pain by that point, needed to go to a place that would give him the best chance of survival. I recommended to his parents Children's of Alabama, affiliated with the University of Alabama School of Medicine at Birmingham. It was also one of the nation's preeminent centers for pediatric cardiac surgery at that time.

His parents agreed, and with their help and support, I made arrangements for Shawn to be admitted. He was operated on just a few days later. The pediatric surgeons at Alabama were some of the best in the country. Yet despite their prodigious efforts, Shawn didn't survive the operation.

I got a call from one of the surgeons immediately afterward. He told me they had done their best, and I knew that was true. I thanked him and got off the phone. For a moment I tried to remind myself of the importance of keeping my emotions in check. There was nothing more I could do for Shawn, and I had other patients who required my attention. But I couldn't help it. Shawn had given me a copy of his little coloring book before he had left for Alabama.

After the call, I sat in my office, clutching that book, and I cried and cried.

I still have it on my desk, forty-one years later. *Please Make My Heart Better.*

I certainly tried, Shawn.

That brave little boy had a bigger impact on my life than almost anyone realized, and still does. In the days and weeks after Shawn's death, I thought about what he and his parents had endured. Bleakly I pondered the randomness of life, of a universe that would doom a bright young child like Shawn to such a premature death. Although his condition was rare, I thought to myself, *Who's to say the next child born won't have it? Who's to say* my *next child won't have it?* That was chilling. At that point I was the father of two healthy children. I discussed my fears with Barbara, and told her that I couldn't bear the thought of a third, running the risk—however slight—that the baby would be born with a condition like Shawn's or any life-threatening condition.

I realize it was not a logical decision, but for once the emotions that I was supposed to keep under control were simply too powerful. The thought of seeing another kid that I loved suffer as Shawn had was just too much to bear.

Barbara agreed. We did not have any more children.

Chapter Twenty-Three

Your Heart, My Hands

For the surgeon, focus is everything. It must be unwavering and absolute on a task that is sometimes mechanical and rote, occasionally creative and daring. In my line of surgery, at least, focus is almost always a matter of life and death for the person on the operating table.

True, the medical team can, as is sometimes depicted on TV shows, banter about children or weekends or vacations or something in the news over the course of a three- or six-hour procedure. I never disallowed that in my surgeries. But I always felt that the surgeon must remain intent on the task at hand.

Despite our concentration, despite our efforts to stay riveted on the delicate and time-consuming procedures we are performing, it wasn't always possible to avoid distractions completely. Much as I tried to keep it at bay, what was happening in the wider world had a way of showing up in my operating room. Drug addiction, the AIDS crisis, the obesity epidemic, third-world poverty, the ongoing national debate about abortion, and, of course, the equally passionate debate about health care.

I have faced all of these formidable challenges, armed only with a retractor!

But they couldn't be ignored. Not only because of what these issues mean to our society but because of what they mean to the most important people in my life outside of my family: my patients. It was through the realities of their lives, the circumstances or behaviors that had sometimes caused their conditions or brought them to me in the first place, that these often contentious societal issues managed to elbow their way into my surgery. I'd like to share with you some of their stories and how my life and my attitudes changed because of them and how I altered and impacted theirs.

One day I received a call from another hospital. It was transferring a young Caucasian woman from nearby Fall River, Massachusetts, who needed urgent care. Twenty-three years old and twenty-four weeks pregnant, she had contracted a staph infection that had spread to her heart.

Angela was her name, and I visited her in the ICU.

"Hello, Angela, I'm Dr. Singh," I said. "How are you feeling?"

She responded as most septic patients do. The fever that accompanies these infections leaves them disoriented and gasping for air. Their words are slurred and garbled, emitted in short staccato bursts as they struggle for breath.

"Can't breathe...Not feeling well...I can't lie flat...Make me better...Get me out of here."

Angela also had a tale of woe to relate, which she gasped out to me in semicoherent pieces. She had recently broken up with her boyfriend. He had now abandoned her, even though she was pregnant with his child. She'd lost her job at a local factory. She lived alone. And when I posed the question to her, she admitted that she'd started to use drugs.

Clearly Angela had issues, and I felt for her. But my first concern was saving her life. Imaging showed that her heart was enlarged and that her mitral valve—which allows blood to flow into the left pumping chamber of the heart—was seriously damaged. Instead of having a normal, smooth surface, the valve looked like a cauliflower, lumpy and bulbous, with an irregular surface. When the valve has deteriorated like this, small pieces of it can break loose. We call them snowflakes because that's what they look like on an ultrasound. But despite their whimsical name, they are anything but benign. These small clumps can end up blocking arteries to the vital organs, leading to stroke, heart attack, kidney failure, and many more.

Angela needed surgery fast. But because she was twenty-four weeks pregnant, there was a high risk that we could lose the baby.

This presented a dilemma: Should we terminate the pregnancy, or proceed with the operation and hope for the best? Such a decision is obviously not one the surgeon can make on his own. I called her obstetrician and we discussed the options. But events quickly outpaced us. As I'd feared, one of those clumps from her diseased valve broke off and landed in her brain, causing a stroke.

Surgery was postponed while she was treated for the stroke. It took about two weeks, but she responded well, recovering fully. Her speech improved and her mind cleared. I now felt it was imperative to move ahead with surgery as soon as possible, before another snowflake could go floating down her bloodstream and cause further havoc. She would require a mitral valve replacement with an artificial valve—unusual for someone of this age, but it had to be done.

By now a team of physicians was consulting regularly together on Angela's case: in addition to her obstetrician and me, an infectious disease specialist, a psychologist, and a social worker were involved—not to mention her parents, and Angela herself.

We had to do surgery. That much was clear. But what about the fetus? Among the medical consultants, the recommendation was unanimous: the pregnancy needed to be terminated before we proceeded with the operation. Otherwise there was a risk Angela could die as well as the baby.

It was up to me to present this to Angela and her family.

I entered her room along with her obstetrician and the social worker. Angela's parents sat nervously by her bedside. I remember their faces, creased by years of hard work and struggling to make ends meet, and now by anxieties about their daughter and unborn grandchild. Angela had mentioned her strong Catholic faith to me earlier, and I noticed her mother had rosary beads that she fingered nervously as I sat to talk to them.

Angela looked understandably drained and distraught, although her eyes, clouded when she had first been brought in, were now clear. She listened intently as I began to explain what her team was recommending.

"Angela," I said, "you dodged a bullet here. You recovered from a stroke, and quickly. That's very good. But in your current condition, there's a high risk you could have another. That could be lethal, and if you die the baby will die, too. The safest way to proceed"—I paused, carefully choosing my words—"is to take the baby away."

She sat upright in the bed.

"You mean abortion?"

"Yes."

She shook her head vigorously. "No way!" she said. "Sorry, Doctor, I can't do that."

I tried to explain that the odds of the baby dying during surgery would be one out of three. "I know this is a difficult issue," I said, "but do you really want to risk that? Do you really want to deliver a dead baby, even if you survive?"

Angela looked at her parents. Tears were flowing from her mother's eyes, and I could see her praying silently to herself. Her father looked grim. This was obviously a very difficult decision for them. I didn't want to force anything on a family that had already seen enough troubles.

"Think about it," I said. "Talk it over with your parents."

"I will," she said. "Thank you."

Two days later I returned with the rest of the team.

"So, Angela," I said, "what have you decided?"

"Doctor, I know it may sound crazy to someone who didn't grow up the way I did, but we just can't go through with the abortion," she said. "It's against my religion. So I'm willing to take a chance." She paused and smiled. "Besides," she said, nodding over to her parents, who were still at their bedside vigil and looking at me intently, "we have faith in you."

I appreciated her confidence, but a part of me thought, *How can you let a tenet of your faith stand in the way of your possible survival? Do you think God really wants to put your life in jeopardy?*

I realized almost right away, though, that this was not my decision to make—or second-guess.

"OK, we will do our best." And we prepared for a high-risk surgery.

The next day Angela's chest was opened and she was placed on the heart-lung machine, which now had the responsibility of keeping both mother and unborn child alive. I opened the chamber of the heart and, as expected, found a mitral valve completely destroyed. As I was replacing it with a porcine valve, the anesthesiologist who was monitoring the fetus called to me. "Arun," he said, "the fetus's heart is dropping."

A normal heartbeat for a fetus is around 140 beats per minute. I looked at the monitor and saw that it had already dropped to one hundred. *Beep-beep-beep*, then *beep.... beep... beep.* I watched it slow down before my eyes to forty, then to twenty, and then silence and an ominous flat line.

We tried giving Angela various medications, but that didn't work. The baby's heart had stopped beating. There was nothing I could do now but try to finish the valve replacement as quickly as possible. All the while I imagined myself having to tell Angela and her family, without adopting an "I told you so" tone, that the fetus had died during the surgery.

But then, just as I was closing, the anesthesiologist spoke up again. "Arun, look, it's coming back," he said. Sure enough, the ultrasound machine started transmitting again, slowly at first, but the beeps were soon back to normal. The fetus had somehow survived.

I breathed a sigh of relief. But we weren't out of the woods yet. During the time the heart was stilled, the vital organs could have sustained damage due to the lack of blood. This could have affected the brain development or caused other problems. Would Angela's unborn child suffer from developmental disabilities? There was a good chance of that now.

Normally a patient getting a valve replacement like Angela's would have been out of the hospital in five days. But because of her situation—the stroke, the infection, the pregnancy— she ended up staying two weeks. The obstetrician followed the baby closely after Angela's discharge and reported to me that it seemed to be doing well. Angela was progressing, too. Her heart and valve function soon returned to normal.

She soon came back to the hospital to deliver her baby, a beautiful, blue-eyed, blond girl. I visited mother and daughter in the neonatal ward. "Thank you, Doctor, for saving my life," she said. "And my baby's."

"She's so pretty!" I said. "What's her name?"

Angela looked up at me and smiled. "Hope."

In the months following the surgery, I learned that Hope had beaten the odds twice. Not only had she survived high-risk surgery, she was developing normally. Last I heard, Mom had started a new life outside of Fall River.

My experience with Angela and Hope confirmed two important truths. First, despite all our advanced medical technology and experience, my team and I still could not predict with certainty the outcome. Most of the time we made the right decision based on the evidence at hand. This time we didn't, and I'm glad we were wrong.

The other lesson: it is the patients and their families who have to make the final decision. They must do what they feel is right for them, and that decision may involve factors beyond what I can see in a blood test or on an MRI.

Ultimately, Angela's case attests to the fact that while it may be my hands at work, it is *your* heart, and *your* life.

Angela's involvement with drugs was only part of her story. But for more and more of my young patients, it became the somber, one-note symphony that echoed through their often-abbreviated lives.

These were young adults who, under normal circumstances, would never have met me; they would have had healthy hearts and, I'm certain, far happier outcomes. But because they'd succumbed to narcotics—particularly opioids like heroin—they would arrive in my surgery with infected heart valves and virulent organisms growing in their bloodstreams, usually the result of sharing dirty needles.

I never refused these patients treatment, and I tried not to judge them. But it was frustrating to see the hold that this stuff had on them. They shared some behavioral traits, too. At first these patients always denied that they were using. I'd confront them with medical evidence to the contrary and they would invariably swear they'd never do drugs again.

It was so sad to see these young lives destroyed. No case was sadder than that of Luciana, a strikingly beautiful young woman who lived in Central Falls, a working-class community outside of Providence.

Luciana was Venezuelan; she'd come to the US as a teenager and spoke English with what I must admit was a charming accent. In her late twenties when I met her, Luciana seemed to have it all. She was young, tall, blue eyed, with high, supermodel-like cheekbones. She had an engaging, vivacious personality and a good sense of humor. And yet her life was the proverbial train wreck.

She came to me, like Angela, in gasping, confused distress. A cherry-size mass had formed on her tricuspid valve, located between the right atrium and the pumping chamber. The growth was the result of staphylococcus, a virulent form of bacterial infection.

This usually responded to penicillin, but Luciana's was resistant, and for a predicable reason. She was using heroin, which of course she refused to admit.

We performed the surgery, removing the mass and replacing her tricuspid valve with a bovine version. It went well, and a couple of days later I visited her. I realized that in some ways this was going to be the hardest part. I finally had to confront her about her drug problem.

"I would never use drugs!" she said when I raised the issue. "I'm a mother, I have two little boys. I couldn't do that to them."

I knew from the social worker that she'd had two boys from two different men, both of whom had arrest records and were heroin users. I explained to her that the nature of her infection was likely due to using infected needles. I tried to underscore the severity of the situation.

"Luciana," I said, "without this surgery you could have died. If you go back to drugs, this will very likely happen again, and I can't guarantee that the next time it won't be fatal."

She began to cry. "I didn't mean for this to happen. I want to be a good mother. I can't leave my boys alone." She admitted that not only had she used heroin, she had also become so desperate for money to afford her habit that she had resorted to prostitution.

That day Luciana promised me that for the sake of her children, she would never use drugs again.

I saw her annually over the next several years. She'd bring the boys with her—they'd sit in my waiting room with coloring books or, later, handheld video games. I was pleased: Luciana looked healthier and seemed to have put narcotics behind her. She was, as they say, "clean."

Until one afternoon about seven years after her surgery. When she arrived for her annual follow-up, I could see the difference right away. She had always been thin, but now she looked emaciated, her eyes were sunken, and her skin was sallow. I watched her as she sat down in the waiting room with her boys. The normally attentive mother seemed distracted and jumpy.

I knew Luciana pretty well at this point, and I also knew the signs of addiction. I didn't mince words. "Tell me the truth," I said when she sat down in my office. "Are you using again?"

She looked insulted. "Dr. Singh!" she said. "I can't believe you'd ask me that. Of course not."

"You've lost a lot of weight, and you don't seem like yourself."

"It was the South Beach Diet," she said, waving her hand dismissively. "A mistake. I'm back to my normal eating."

"Really? You're not using drugs?"

"I swear to Jesus Christ!" she exclaimed theatrically.

"OK," I said skeptically. "You're sure? You know it will turn up in the blood test if you have."

She looked down at her knee-high boots. "Well, I haven't been using them recently," she said.

Luciana came back one more time, a few weeks later, to discuss the results of her blood test, which had confirmed my suspicions. This time I noticed that the boys' demeanor had changed, as well. They were old enough now to be aware that something was not right with their mom. Even though they sat quietly in my waiting room doing their homework, I could see by the way they looked at her that they were concerned, too.

When I presented the results of the tests to Luciana, she cried. She then recited a familiar, but not unreasonable, tale of woe. There was no means of support for her boys. Her family back in Venezuela was poor. The two fathers were gone, probably in jail. She finally confessed that she had gone back to heroin use "once in a while," and that on occasion she had again resorted to selling her body for sex to support herself and the boys.

She also acknowledged that, with this kind of behavior, she was putting her life in jeopardy. "I know the next time it might be too late for you to save me," she said. "But what choice do I have?"

I wanted to tell her that options might be open to her, and that she needed to go back to social services and talk with a social worker to figure out how she could avail herself of them. But I knew that she had gone that route once, and while it had worked for a while, she would probably dismiss it this time.

For once I really had no answer. These were problems that my medical training had not prepared me for.

I walked her out to the waiting room to say goodbye to the kids. I had a feeling this was the last time their mother would be visiting me as a patient. "Mom's taking us to McDonald's after this!" said the eight-year-old excitedly.

I subsequently lost touch with Luciana and her family. A few years later, I did inquire with a social worker who'd known her. She said that as far as she was aware, the boys—by then in their teens—were doing well. Their mother was alive, but like so many others caught in the grip of addiction, she was still struggling with her demons.

While it started in the 1980s, AIDS was still prevalent in the late 1990s and early 2000s. Whether care should be provided to these patients was a hot topic of discussion among health-care workers. Part of this, I'm sure, was the result of homophobia, at least in the initial stages of the epidemic, when it was seen as a "gay disease." But later the debate turned on the dangers to those of us treating the afflicted. There were stories of EMTs, nurses, and physicians who had contracted the disease because they were accidentally exposed to an HIV-positive patient.

I recall several of my surgical colleagues saying at a meeting that they would refuse to operate on a patient with AIDS. While I respected these men as professionals, I was outraged by this attitude. "So what are they supposed to do?" I asked. "Just go off somewhere and die? Or maybe we should put them on an island somewhere, like a modern-day leper colony?"

Things got heated, although at Rhode Island Hospital it

was mostly hypothetical until the day an AIDS patient was brought in for surgery. His name was Robert. He was thirty-five years old, Caucasian, and an army veteran who had served in the first Gulf War. He also happened to be gay, and had probably contracted the disease from his male partner. Sadly, he had also been using drugs. As a result his aortic valve (the valve between the left pumping chamber and the main artery, the aorta) was leaking severely and his heart was quite enlarged. He could neither breathe nor lie flat due to severe heart failure.

I met with the infectious disease specialist. Given the nature of AIDS treatments at the time, he told me that surgery could likely prolong Robert's life another four or five years. If he didn't have the procedure, he'd surely be dead in another month or two.

It was our responsibility to help Robert. I gathered my team and told them that we'd be working on an HIV-infected patient. They weren't happy. I understood their concern. In cardiac surgery we are awash in blood. It was not uncommon to get accidentally pricked by a surgical needle or splashed with blood during a long surgery. The fear at that time was that the slightest exposure could result in contracting the disease from the patient.

"Arun, why should I put my life on the line for him?" asked one of our technicians.

"For a lot of reasons," I said, explaining that this man worked full time and had served his country honorably. "And maybe the most important reason," I said, "is because it's our job. We're here to save lives."

It was the closest thing to a locker room speech I ever gave in my entire career. And I think it had the desired effect. The team reluctantly went along because they knew that, as the surgeon, elbow deep in this man's guts, I'd be taking the biggest risk.

I won't pretend I wasn't a little nervous, too. How could I not be? But the preparation for Robert's operation was meticulous. We took all the precautions. My entire team of ten donned double gloves, gowns, masks, eyeglasses. We looked like a phalanx of robots walking into the OR that day.

The surgery went smoothly. The valve was replaced and the patient was doing well. As I was putting in the last stitch, I was distracted—looking at the monitor, and asking one of my technicians a question—and the needle pierced Robert's body, right through my gloves and into my finger. Blood began to trickle out.

For a moment we all froze.

Quickly I squeezed my finger to allow it to bleed. I washed my hands with soap and water, then with Betadine, a highly concentrated disinfectant used to cleanse patients before surgery. And I prayed.

As the team somberly finished up, I tried to cut the tension. "Well," I said, "the patient will survive. We'll see about the doctor."

I don't remember if anyone laughed.

I tried to reassure myself that the odds were very slim that I would contract the virus, because I had been stuck by a solid needle rather than a hollow one. But I was worried enough that I didn't tell Barbara. I just didn't want her and the boys worrying.

Of course, I could never completely get it out of my mind. I now had to be tested periodically for HIV. A half dozen negative tests and ten years later, I was told that I could stop worrying.

As for the patient, he returned to work. A few years later he moved out of state (not uncommon because of the stigma associated with the disease, particularly in that era). It is my fervent hope that, with the advances in our treatment of AIDS, Robert is still alive and well today.

~

Near the end of my career, I was asked to see an Ethiopian girl in her twenties for a serious heart operation. She had just arrived a few days earlier from Addis Ababa, I was told, and had been taken to Providence, where she had a friend.

When I walked in to examine her, I felt transported in time back to Darbhanga Medical College Hospital. There, as a young intern, I had treated the indigent people of the city. They were often stick thin, malnourished, and with an aura of death surrounding them. This was the first time I'd seen someone like that in America. I was shocked by her appearance: she weighed ninety pounds, was missing teeth, and had sunken cheeks and a distended belly. Addisalem was her name, and the friend who was there to translate told me that she was twenty-six years old. I would have guessed forty.

Addisalem was clearly malnourished. But even though she now had access to better nutrition, she had developed serious heart disease because of her long period of starvation and a bout of rheumatic fever, a disease that has long since been eradicated here but is not unheard of in the third world. She was going to require triple heart valve replacement surgery. Her valves were as unsteady as she herself was on her feet. There had been no surgical therapy available for her in Ethiopia, and she had applied for an emergency visa for humanitarian reasons. Her application had been put in a pool for a lottery. She'd won, and had been granted a visa to come to this country, if she didn't die en route.

As her friend explained this to me, I couldn't take my eyes off Addisalem. This girl's appearance reminded me of the sad young women I had seen in India. They'd come in looking much like her, desperate for help. But there had been no surgical treatment available for them in a poor place like Darbhanga, and most of them had ended up dying on the floor of our aptly named casualty room. They had been casualties, I realized now, of a failed society.

Then it dawned on me: by God, this was now my chance to do something I could never do for those unfortunate women.

"...Addisalem wants to know if you can make her better, Doctor," concluded her friend. I snapped back to attention.

"Yes," I said, perhaps with more conviction than she expected, as the interpreter was slightly taken aback. "I mean, *absolutely*. Tell Addisalem that we're going to fix her and make her feel better."

And we did. A triple valve replacement is a long and involved operation, and because of her chronic malnutrition, her recovery took longer than a typical American patient's. But she did recover, and, with adequate nutrition, her health was fully restored. Addisalem subsequently learned English and got a job in a restaurant in Providence. During one of her follow-up visits, I asked her what her beautiful name meant. It was Addisalem herself who answered this time.

"It means *new world*," she said, smiling, "like here."

Addisalem later moved to New York to start a new career. I was so happy to see her making her way in the New World and her American dream.

☙

I was usually glad to see my patients in their follow-up visits. As with Addisalem, in the vast majority of cases, I was seeing improvement. Lives (and internal plumbing) rebuilt, and lives moving forward.

That was not the story with Carl, when I first met him in my office for a consultation. I hasten to add that this was not because I disliked him. On the contrary. While Addisalem had been a victim of the dire conditions of her third-world homeland—where outbreaks of famine were all too common—Carl was a victim of overabundance. You could say that he and similar patients were victims of the American lifestyle. Men, often in blue-collar jobs, who worked hard and played hard, dismissing or simply ignoring the growing evidence and public health warnings about smoking, diet, and sedentary habits.

When I met him, Carl—a machinist by trade—was forty-three years old and had amassed 235 pounds on his five-foot, seven-inch frame. That he needed coronary artery bypass surgery should have come as no surprise to anyone, given his lifestyle, and I suspect that's one reason that when he first came in for an appointment he was anxious, tense, and restless, pacing in my waiting room, while his wife sat quietly reading *People* magazine.

When I examined him, I took a page out of my old medical school professor's book. Dr. Desai's first question to every patient had been about their most recent meal. He, of course, had been using that question to determine who was genuinely indigent and who was merely trying to get free hospital care. In this case I wished to confirm what I suspected already as the cause of Carl's coronary artery disease.

Carl acknowledged that his diet consisted largely of doughnuts, cheeseburgers, and fries, typically washed down by beer. Oh, and he smoked two and a half packs of cigarettes a day. Exercise? "Yeah," he said, managing a weak joke. "As soon as I get off work on Friday night, I run to the bar."

Very funny. Not only was Carl's lifestyle an almost guaranteed ticket to the cardiac care unit, so was his family history. His father had died at age fifty-seven of a heart attack; his mother had been killed by a stroke at sixty-one; Carl, who had three children ages thirteen to seventeen at the time, had not seen a primary-care doctor for a quarter century.

I shook my head as he relayed all this. "Carl," I said, "if you had deliberately made it your mission in life to have every risk factor in the books for a heart attack, you couldn't have done a better job."

He looked sheepish. "I know, I know. She's always on my case about losing weight and all that," he said, jerking his head in the direction of his wife, who sat stonily.

"But…" He threw up his hands in a gesture that suggested he had no control over his doughnut consumption.

Now he could hide from it no longer. A few weeks prior, he had started having chest pain and noticed shortness of breath. He'd tried to ignore it, thinking it might be acid reflux. A week of taking over-the-counter antacids had done nothing to improve the symptoms. One night he woke up with severe chest pain and couldn't breathe. His wife called 911, and he was rushed to a local hospital, where tests revealed he had had a heart attack. They also found that he had high blood pressure, mild diabetes, and elevated cholesterol, for which he'd never received any treatment. Further tests revealed that all his arteries were severely blocked. He was no longer a candidate for a coronary artery stent—the typical treatment for men suffering from this kind of "lifestyle" disease. Now Carl's best chance for survival was coronary artery bypass surgery. That's why he was sent to me. This was a common story.

"I hate to tell you this," I continued after studying his test results, "but on the inside, you look like an eighty-year-old man. You've got advanced heart disease."

He pursed his lips and looked at the floor like an errant schoolboy as his wife glared at him, shaking her head.

"The good news is that I can fix this," I said. I told him that the chance for a successful surgery was 99 percent and that he would probably be able to return to work as a machinist in three months.

He perked up momentarily. "And I have more good news," I continued. "This means you have a second chance at a healthy life. Stop smoking, lose weight, and get the diabetes and high cholesterol under control, and you will be fine."

At this, Carl—seemingly upbeat a moment earlier—broke down in tears. "Whatever you say, I'll do it, Doc," he said. "I just want a chance to see my kids grow up."

I reassured him that he would have that chance, *if* he took his lifestyle change seriously.

As we were about to leave, Carl said he had one last question. A bit embarrassing, he admitted. I reassured him: "You can ask me anything."

"This surgery. How much is it going to cost?"

It turned out that like some of the blue-collar workers I treated—but certainly not all—Carl had very little health insurance. He'd used that as an excuse for not seeing a primary-care physician. While I doubted he would have even if routine annual visits had been covered on his plan, I was concerned for him. The cost of a heart operation varies from state to state, but in Rhode Island at that time, around the year 2000, it was approximately $100,000. That was way beyond Carl's means.

I arranged for him to meet with a social worker in order to get financial help.

A week later I performed quintuple coronary artery bypass surgery on Carl. It went well. A few months later he returned to my office. I almost couldn't believe it was the same person. He had lost significant weight and had quit smoking. He was walking regularly, taking his medication, and eating healthier.

"Carl, you look great," I said. "I'm very proud of you."

He confided to me that money was still an issue, but that he was determined to stick with his healthier lifestyle. His new primary-care physician would now monitor his progress. "Keep up the good work, and listen to what your doctor tells you," I said.

We shook hands, and he departed.

Twelve years went by. I was near retirement when one evening I got an emergency call at home, telling me I needed to get to the hospital right away. "It's an old patient of yours," I was told.

It was Carl. Now in his mid-fifties, he was almost unrecognizable, as he looked like a man in his seventies. Carl had rolled back all the improvements he'd made a decade earlier. He'd gained all the weight back. He'd resumed his two-pack-a-day smoking habit. He had stopped taking the cholesterol medication because, as he'd told his doctor, he couldn't afford it.

There was little I could do at this point. Two out of five of the bypass grafts I had done twelve years earlier were now closed, and all his native coronary arteries were blocked. He was no longer a candidate for reoperation or stents.

While medication eased his symptoms, this script was now pretty much written. Fourteen months later he died in his sleep at age fifty-six, presumably of another heart attack.

Carl's decline and death, after such a promising restart, saddened me. His case is a reminder that patients have to take some responsibility for their own well-being. Surgery can repair a leaky valve or create a bypass to blocked arteries, but it is no match for a lifetime of smoking, poor diet, and an otherwise unhealthy lifestyle.

Carl's situation is also a sobering reminder of what I consider to be our great national shame: the lack of a workable, fair, cost-efficient health-care system. I'm not a health policy expert, and I don't presume to have the answers. But I do think it's just outrageous that in this country we do not have universal health care. It's bad for our economy, our society, and our public health. It must change. How? I don't know. And apparently neither does anyone in Washington.

To be fair, I have lived and worked as a medical professional under three forms of health care: our current system here in the US, which is bankrupting this great country; the national health-care system in Great Britain, which, despite its many fine hospitals (such as Great Ormond Street), is ponderous and inefficient; and, of course, the almost nonexistent third-world health-care system of the India of my youth.

All leave much to be desired.

I think it will be up to the next generation of political and medical leaders to find the solution. And it is about such future leaders I would like to speak.

Those aspiring to careers in medicine were always welcome in my operating room. Whether they were premed in college, medical students, residents, or established medical professionals, such as nurses or physician assistants, I was always willing to take time to teach or show them what I was doing. I also encouraged the young people who visited to stick with their studies. Becoming a physician or surgeon is a long, hard path, but worth the effort. It is, I still believe, a wonderful profession. In how many other professions do you have an opportunity to save lives, contribute to the good of society—and get well rewarded for it?

Sometimes the route that these students took would surprise me, to say the least.

One day in the 1990s, I was performing surgery on an eight-year-old boy named Kyle. The child's condition was one I have mentioned before: tetralogy of Fallot. He had been born with a hole between the lower chambers of the heart and excessive heart muscle in the right chamber.

It was the same procedure I'd performed on Jason, the first baby I'd ever operated on. Fortunately, the outcome this time was better.

The operation was going very smoothly. The child's chest was open; the heart was supported on the heart-lung machine. I opened the chamber of his tiny heart and carved out extra heart muscle blocking the passage of the blood to the lung. As I was ready to apply the Dacron patch to close the hole in little Kyle's heart, I looked around the room. On this day a few medical students from Brown University had been invited to observe. One of them, a lovely young lady with blond hair, freckles, and blue eyes, looked particularly attentive and serious. When I caught her eye, however, she looked down, almost embarrassed.

I asked her a few questions about the procedure. I do this not to put any medical students on the spot, but to help them learn.

"Are you aware of the procedure we're performing here today?"

She was, and she correctly identified it.

"Good. Do you know what we're doing at this point?"

She did. "You're about to patch the hole with a piece of Dacron cloth."

"Very good," I said. I queried her further and was impressed with her answers. "You've done your homework, young lady," I said.

"Well," she said, "I had the same procedure as a child, so you could say I'm pretty familiar with it."

"You did?" I said. "Where did you have it done?"

I expected her to say Boston, since that's where a lot of children had gone for heart surgery before I started the program at Providence.

"Why, right here," she said. "You did my surgery."

I must have stood there, frozen, for almost a minute with my forceps and Dacron patch held in midair.

I couldn't believe it. I asked her name. When she told me, of course I remembered her and her parents. She had been the same age as this patient—about eight years old—when I operated on her. Now she was in her mid-twenties.

"Jenny," I said, "I am so happy to see you here."

Dr. Jennifer Souther, I can proudly say, completed medical school and became a primary-care physician in Rhode Island.

Back in the 1980s, I closed the hole between the lower chambers of the heart of a four-year-old girl named Maria. A few weeks after the surgery, I got a letter, written in the hand of a child. I thought it might be from one of my young patients. But it was from one of Maria's neighbors in East Providence, a nine-year-old boy named John. He had seen how quickly his little friend had rebounded from surgery. She was already running around and playing with the other kids on the block, which she couldn't do before. Young John complimented me for doing such a good job.

"Maria is doing really well," he wrote. "Thanks for taking such good care of her."

I remember chuckling at the time at receiving such a letter. "Fan mail from a patient's neighbor," I told Barbara, handing her the note when I got home that night.

"That's sweet," she said, smiling as she read it. "Isn't it nice to know that a nine-year-old appreciates your work?"

In his letter John also said that he hoped to become a doctor someday and asked me for advice. "Study hard and get good grades" was the stock response. But I also told him that you had to have drive and passion to become a physician. It was a long road, I explained, and it would take many years, but I wished him the best of luck.

I never heard back from him and remember thinking that maybe I had unintentionally dissuaded a nine-year-old by telling him that his medical training would take ten years.

A decade or so later, I was just about to scrub for open heart surgery when an orderly popped his head in the operating room and asked if he might watch the surgery. "Of course," I said (these were the days before HIPAA laws, I hasten to add).

While I was performing the operation, the orderly, who was around twenty-two years old, stood at the head of the patient, approximately four feet away from me, watching and listening intently as I explained every step. After the operation was done, I asked him if he had any questions.

"No," he said. "By the way, you don't know me, right?"

"I don't think so," I said. "Did I operate on you or someone in your family?"

"No, but you encouraged me to become a doctor."

"I did? When?"

He took out a letter and flashed it at me. It was in my hand-writing.

"I'm John," he said. "I wrote you after you did surgery on one of my neighbors, a girl named Maria. I told you I wanted to be a doctor, and you were nice enough to send a few encouraging words to a nine-year-old kid you didn't even know."

"I do remember this!" I said. "Well, how are you, John?"

"Great," he said. "You told me about how I'd need good

grades, passion, and drive. Well, next year I'm starting medical school and I'm psyched."

I was amazed that a note I had scribbled to a kid years earlier had made such a difference in his life. I'm happy to say that John went on to medical school in New York and became a primary-care physician.

Many of my young patients have gone on to successful and interesting careers outside of medicine. I never know when I'm going to run into them. One day I was at a medical conference at the Hotel Providence. There was a lot of commotion in the lobby. I saw TV crews and cameras. I walked over to the scrum of media to find out what was going on. At that moment a beautiful young woman with a tiara on her head and a sash across her red carpet–worthy dress—with the words "Miss RI" on it—was being escorted into the lobby by two gentlemen. She saw me, and, as if by design, the little entourage suddenly veered in my direction. To my shock, Miss Rhode Island came right up to me and planted a kiss on my cheek. I blushed as reporters and hotel staff looked at me quizzically.

"Dr. Singh," the beauty queen said, "my parents noticed you here earlier. Do you remember me?"

She had been a premature baby and I had performed heart surgery on her. She had probably been as big as my hand at the time, and now in her high heels and crown she towered over me.

"You've certainly grown up," was about all I could manage. Her parents then came over, and we enjoyed a brief but pleasant reunion.

And I got my picture taken with Miss Rhode Island!

While they're not all doctors or beauty queens, I do regularly see and hear from my patients of all ages. I can't tell you how gratifying it is, considering the obstacles I've overcome, the hardships I endured as a child, and the challenges I faced in my training and over the course of my career. It's all worth it when those patients or their family members look me in the eye and tell me that they are alive today because of me.

At moments like that, I would not trade my career for anything. But a few years into the new millennium, it became apparent that my career was coming to an end, whether I was ready or not.

Chapter Twenty-Four

Final Cut

Every week I called my mom faithfully. It was usually at night, after I got home from surgery. I'd eat a late dinner and then ring her in India, where with the ten-hour time difference she was just getting ready to start her day.

Mom always answered the calls the same way. "Hello, Babul," she'd say, still using the term of endearment for her son who was by then pushing sixty.

We'd talk about her grandchildren, the family, my work, her health, and Indian politics. But no matter the topic, I always got off the phone feeling good. Mom was that kind of person.

One evening in May 2007, I called her even earlier than usual because I had an emergency surgery scheduled for nine p.m. Upbeat as always, Mom sounded particularly enthused that morning. My brother Dilip, who lived a few hours' drive away, was coming to visit, as was my sister, who lived in Patna. They were bringing my nieces and nephews. She was delighted at the prospect of having her family at the house and told me about the special rice pilaf and vegetables she was making for them. The vegetables would be roasted in her special sauce.

"Mom, stop," I joked. "You're making me hungry. And I've got to go to work."

"So late, Babul?" she said. "You work too hard."

I explained to her that I had to perform an emergency coronary bypass surgery on an elderly woman. She needed it done right away and the earliest available time was that night.

"That poor woman," my mom said. "I sympathize. Getting old is tough, let me tell you."

"Mom, who has it better than you?"

"I am blessed," she admitted. "But I want you to take good care of that woman. She's probably a mother like me, so you tell her your mother wishes her well."

"OK," I chuckled. "I will. I've got to run, Mom. Have fun with the grandkids and say hello to Dilip and Ampali for me."

The surgery that night went well. But when I stepped out of the operating room, there was a message on my beeper. "Call home right away." I felt my heart sink, worried something bad had happened in the household. I rushed to the phone and Barbara answered.

"Are you all right...Are the boys all right?" I said.

"We're fine," she said. "But you better call home...India."

I dialed the long string of numbers. My sister answered the phone. She was crying.

"Ampali," I said. "It's Arun. Tell me what happened."

Through sobs she explained that she, Dilip, and their kids had arrived at Mom's as planned. Mom had prepared the meal; they had all enjoyed her delicious rice pilaf and vegetable dishes and the sweets for dessert. Mom then said that she wasn't feeling well. She was having chest pain and was having trouble breathing. "It's nothing, though," my mom had said, according to my sister. "Finish your dessert, have a good time. Don't worry about me."

This sounded like my mom. But soon it became apparent this was something more serious. My brother and his sons put her in the car and rushed her to a hospital. She lay in the back with her head in my lap.

At the hospital her blood pressure plummeted, and within twenty minutes of arrival, she had died of a massive heart attack.

I was numb and speechless. My mom was seventy-nine, and of course I had known this day would come eventually. But not on a day when she'd felt so good just a few hours earlier. Not on a day when I had kept another, older woman alive but could do nothing for my own mother. I imagined the steps we would have taken had I been on call in Patna that night. I realized that the hospital there had probably tried the same measures (India's health-care system has made great strides in the years since I left). To be fair, the outcome might very well have been the same here.

Still. All these people whose lives I had saved, but I was powerless to do anything for my mom.

It bothered me for days, as I grappled with grief and guilt.

When I arrived home that night, I went out into the back-yard and stared up at the midnight sky. *I wouldn't be in this yard, in this home, in this country, without her,* I reflected. She had put me on the plane to Worcester in 1967 and made sure that the news was trumpeted in the local paper. She'd even somehow managed to imagine my career in cardiac surgery before I did.

As the death of a parent will do, Mom's passing made me reflect on my life. Although I probably would have denied my father the satisfaction of seeing his prediction of my begging in the streets come true, there was no way I would have become a physician or a surgeon, no way I could have sustained the long hours over forty years without the ballast, love, and encourage-ment she'd provided in my life—even from thousands of miles away.

Like so many mothers, she was the rock of the family. And

her cheerfulness, her positivity, and her warmth often kept me from sliding too deeply into my own dark recesses of worry and gloom. The smiling Arun most people knew, I felt, existed largely because of my mom, whether by nature or by nurture. That so few knew the self-doubting, worrywart Arun was largely because she (and Barbara) helped keep that part of my personality at bay.

After a time I gathered the strength to resume my duties. Although I agonized over the decision, I just could not take the time away from my patients to make the long trip home to India for her funeral. However, I was able to pray for her soul with a Hindu priest on the phone before her cremation. Some years later Barbara and I visited Varanasi, the holiest city in India, on the banks of the River Ganges.

While both my parents were religious, I haven't been the most observant Hindu. But I must say, for both Barbara and me the experience was powerful. We walked down the ghat—the sacred steps that lead to the Ganges—where we were rowed out onto the river on a small boat. We placed the clay pot holding my mother's ashes in the muddy, polluted, but oddly beautiful waters. It is said that those whose ashes are placed in the Ganges at Varanasi will achieve *moksha*—nirvana.

That day I prayed for the kind and loving woman who was my mother, and hoped that I could continue to channel her strength and cheerfulness in the years ahead.

As it turned out, I would need every bit of it.

⌒

Throughout my career, I'd tried to focus on the thing I cared most about and the thing I did best: my patients and their treatment. I was never interested in becoming an administrator. I also tried to avoid getting caught up in the politics that are an inevitable part of any large organization.

But change was coming to the medical field, and neither my seniority in the hospital nor the national standing I had managed to achieve in my field could keep me from being affected.

Many of the changes I refer to are familiar to anyone who's read the local newspaper or been in a doctor's office in the last decade: the mergers, the demise of the solo practice, and the rise of large physician groups and networks, as well as the complex new billing systems and the increasing costs of the health-care business.

They were now hitting home. They were hitting *me*.

In the mid-1990s, Rhode Island Hospital had merged with another local hospital, the Miriam, which also had a cardiac surgery program. Together they formed a new health-care entity called Lifespan, a comprehensive, integrated, academic health system affiliated with the Warren Alpert Medical School of Brown University. In 2007 the administration felt that it would be best to consolidate the cardiac programs into one hospital. As I was senior surgeon, the hospital administration came to me and my associate, Dr. William Feng, to sell us on the idea and discuss their vision of the future.

What they explained to us—about saving resources, increased efficiencies, and so forth—made sense. We signed on.

It turned out to be a mistake. Soon afterward the senior administrator who had initiated the merger left abruptly. Things went south very quickly after that. The smooth integration we had been promised proved anything but. Staff felt uncomfortable; technicians and nurses and even some physicians who had long and solid records of service were put out to pasture. There was a ton of resentment and all kinds of accusations were flying. Needless to say, morale bottomed out.

Some of the younger surgeons, including Dr. Feng, my protégé, decided to seek greener pastures. I didn't blame him.

Now I was the only heart surgeon who could be turned to for the high-risk surgeries. Soon over half my caseload—about three hundred surgeries per year—consisted of seriously ill patients.

Keep in mind that *high risk* is a relative term. These aren't Hail Mary procedures in which the odds are long that the patient will pull through. Indeed, 85 percent of those who undergo high-risk cardiac surgery survive. (For those who are younger, below seventy years old, and who are getting routine or elective heart surgery, the survival rate is 98 or 99 percent.) But in the new bottom-line, image-driven world of hospital management, those outcomes—once a testament to the depth of a hospital's resources and the confidence and skill of its medical teams—were now seen as a potential liability.

And thus, as the person doing the majority of these surgeries, *I* was seen as a liability. And an aging one at that.

That's when the whispers began. "Arun's losing it." "Arun's not well." "Arun's skills are deteriorating." The rumor that I was seriously ill started after I had treatment for a perforated ulcer, a result of the stress that the whole situation was causing.

Then a consultant was brought in to observe and interview me and my colleagues. The fact that the consultant's report pointed the finger not at me but at other, hospital-related factors was highly inconvenient to the hospital. (The report was never made public, although I managed to see a copy.) Another and in my view more objective and authoritative statement of my professional fitness was made in 2014, when I was recertified for five years by the American Board of Thoracic Surgery.

Recertification involved a long series of online examinations that tested my cognition and knowledge of the latest changes in the field. Granted, they didn't come and observe me, but my passing that exam demonstrated that I was still competent in my field.

In the end, however, none of this really mattered. At age seventy I was simply seen as too old to be practicing surgery—especially high-risk cardiac surgery. Several decades before, I'd been the face of the hospital, displayed on TV commercials and billboards. Well, that face had aged, and I was definitely no longer the poster boy with a scalpel and a smile.

In the fall of 2015, I was called to a meeting with the chief of surgery and a senior hospital administrator. The chief of surgery said that maybe it was time for me to leave and, in his words, "just enjoy life." And, the administrator added, a little less joyously, if I would not depart voluntarily, the hospital would terminate my privileges to perform heart surgery.

At first I was in total disbelief. How dare they? Just a year before, I had received a lifetime achievement award from the hospital. After all I'd done for the institution and for the people in charge—and in a few cases that had meant actually operating on their hearts! *I don't deserve to be treated this way*, I thought. I was furious. I hired an attorney and was ready to take legal action against the hospital.

But after a couple of weeks, I began to reconsider. A suit like this could damage the reputation of a hospital and a community that I still loved. Not to mention that I could come off like some aging actor who had to be dragged off the stage kicking and screaming.

I didn't want to embarrass them or myself.

After several weeks of talking with family, friends, attorneys, administration, and hospital trustees, I decided that I would retire as of April 1, 2016. To their credit, when I informed them of my decision, the hospital administration agreed to honor the remainder of my contract.

Perhaps the deciding voice in my decision to walk away after forty-one years in the practice came from across the sea and beyond the grave. Old Dr. Singh, my grandfather Nana, had warned me that this day would come. I had long forgotten that conversation in faraway Darbhanga, in his study. But now it came to me like a visit from Nana's ghost.

"The main enemy," he'd said, "is time. No matter how skilled a surgeon you become, you will get older. Like I did."

Nana's eyesight had deteriorated along with his dexterity. I honestly did not feel that any of my skills or senses had noticeably diminished. But it was going to happen at some point. Would the extra two or three years that I could still practice at the top of my game have really been worth it? I imagined days spent with lawyers, giving depositions, sitting across a table from grim-faced hospital representatives. To say nothing of going to work every day to face what would have become a hostile environment.

No.

That wouldn't have been healthy for me or my team—and certainly not for my patients, whose needs always had to come first.

I explained my thinking to Barbara and my sons, as well as to my attorney, and to a few trusted colleagues at other institutions. They agreed with my thinking.

In a way I also understood the hospital's point of view. It wanted to get younger. This happens in the world of sports all the time. Aging stars are released or traded off. Younger players are signed for far less money. They wanted to do the same at our hospital. Fine. Yet I still couldn't help thinking that it could have been handled so differently—not only in my case and not only in my hospital, but with many other aging professionals.

Had they asked me to begin to phase out over a couple of years—maybe gradually reducing my caseload while increasing the time that I spent mentoring the younger surgeons—I would have said yes, and the whole situation would have been resolved far more amicably, without lawyers and without my getting an ulcer!

⌒

My last day of surgery was March 10, 2016. I timed it so that I would still be around the hospital for a few weeks in case there were any complications. Fortunately, there weren't.

That day I worked on an octogenarian patient—a woman who needed aortic valve replacement and a triple coronary artery bypass. "They needed a seventy-one-year-old surgeon to work on an eighty-year-old patient," I joked to one of my team members. "They told me to do this, and then I can go home."

There weren't too many other laughs my last time in the OR. I'd worked with many of these people for decades. Saying good-bye to them was going to be tough. I am reluctant to start naming them, because there were so many. But two who had been with me the longest were Eric Swanson, my physician assistant for thirty-one years, and Lydia Rodrigues, my "scrub tech"—the person responsible for handling the instruments during surgery. Lydia was with me for forty years.

Eric was there for my last surgery. By that time Lydia had already retired. She had seen the handwriting on the hospital wall that had taken me longer to decipher.

As I was scrubbing in the sink, looking out through the glass window at the patient lying on the operating table, I thought about how many times I'd gone through this ritual.

Forty-one years and 15,160 documented open heart surgeries. In the hospital's announcement of my retirement, they would credit me with twenty thousand surgeries. Once I counted in the thousands of lung, vascular, and blood vessel surgeries I'd performed, and the surgeries that I'd actively assisted with, I realized that they were right.

Regardless of exactly how many times I had operated in my surgical career, one thing was certain: it was all coming to an end today.

I walked into the room, the large operating room lights were turned on, I put on my glasses and headlight, and the nurse gowned me for the last time.

The emotions I had, the nostalgic thoughts that had entered my head, vanished with the first incision. I focused one more time on the patient, her heart, and the surgery. During the latter part of the four-hour operation, I sensed some movement and heard whispering behind me. I turned my head slightly to see that the physician assistant was recording me with his cell phone.

"Smile!" said one of the nurses standing next to him. "We're recording the final stitches of Dr. Singh's last heart surgery for posterity."

Let the video record show that my hands were still steady performing that last surgery. But you can see that my right index finger is crooked—a result of grasping instruments and sewing sutures for all those years.

The patient was moved to a stretcher; the lights were turned off. I removed my mask and glasses, put down my scalpel. In keeping with an old OR tradition, someone on the staff wrapped up the handle of the scalpel and presented it to me. Now I have the knife from my first heart surgery in 1975 and the knife from my last heart surgery in 2016. With tears in my eyes, I thanked, kissed, and hugged my team and other friends from the hospital who had come by to wish me well.

Then I touched the door, knowing this would be the last time I'd be passing through. I walked out of the operating room and didn't look back.

It had gone well. The surgery. The career. And, on balance, the life.

Epilogue

About a month after my retirement, I got a call from Dr. Boyd King, medical director of the Physician Assistant Program at Bryant University. "How would you like to teach for us?" he asked. "We have some bright young people who could learn a lot from you."

I was flattered and accepted the offer, although with some reservations. As a senior surgeon at a university medical center, I'd done my share of teaching before, working with medical students and residents over the years. I'd enjoyed the former—talking them through the procedure, quizzing them about what they were seeing—but the latter had presented problems for me. If, for example, I saw a resident was doing something incorrectly during a surgery, I would take over, for the good of the patient. The residents didn't like that. "This is how we learn," I was told. "Sorry," I replied, "someone's life is on the line."

For that reason I wasn't winning any popularity contests with the residents. Would the PA students feel differently?

I'd been working with PAs, like Eric Swanson, for years. I also knew that they, along with nurse practitioners, were becoming a larger and larger part of the new medical landscape.

In August 2016, I delivered several lectures on cardiac surgery to the PA students and gave some demonstrations, including one in which I used the heart of a pig. They got a glimpse of the real

Dr. Singh that day when I got so lost in the surgery I almost forgot it was a demonstration—and on a porcine organ!

The Bryant PA students were well prepared and knowledgeable. I was also impressed with their experience. When I started at medical school, I was a seventeen-year-old kid who could barely apply a Band-Aid to a cut. Many of these students were a little older. After college they had been EMTs, lab technicians, or medics in the military. Now they were taking the next step.

They tell me that I'm well liked by the students, so I intend to continue teaching part-time at Bryant for a couple more years.

Since I retired, along with the positives in my life—my grandchildren, my travels with Barbara, and my teaching—there has been something else. I wouldn't label it a problem, but it concerned me enough to seek professional help.

I dream about surgery, almost every night. These are not nightmares. No scalpel slips out of my hands and severs a coronary artery. No spirits of departed patients point accusing fingers at me. No one complains about their bills. (They better not. If anything, I always undercharged.) Nor are these dreams even particularly dramatic. But they are vivid and detailed. I'll have a conversation with another doctor. I'll scrutinize an X-ray. I'll insert a valve.

Night after night, I go to work—at least in my mind. I was concerned enough to see a psychiatrist, who suggested that my recurring dreams were a form of parasomnia. One journal article defines parasomnias as undesirable behavioral, physiological, or experiential events that accompany sleep. Sleepwalking, for example, is considered one form of parasomnia. My recurring dreams fall under the rubric of REM sleep behavior disorder, which is characterized by vivid and intense dreams. Some patients with this condition talk in their sleep, or punch, kick, or flail at imaginary demons.

Fortunately for Barbara, I'm not acting out surgery in my sleep. But my mind is working overtime, churning away and replaying scenes from a life in the OR. The psychiatrist explained to me that the dreams were a result of my hippocampus, the brain's repository of memories, constantly firing impressions and remembrances of my time as a surgeon. For fifty years I was so consumed with surgery that my brain can't seem to stop retrieving and replaying those memories again and again.

The problem is that I wake up as tired as if I really had performed surgery!

Am I doomed to repeat these memories, night after night, for the rest of my life? I'm not sure. But on one level I really can't complain. As a twenty-one-year-old medical student in India, reading about the Mayo brothers and Dr. William Halsted in far-off America, I dreamed of becoming a surgeon.

Half a century later, two years removed from my last surgery, I'm still dreaming about it.

Arun K. Singh, MD
Providence, Rhode Island, April 2018

Acknowledgments

For their guidance, wisdom, friendship, feedback, and encouragement I am grateful to my friends and colleagues Girard Visconti, Christine Jabour-Visconti, Neil Brandon, MD, Dr. Edward Iannuccilli, Paul Ruggeri, MD, and Betty and Jared Aaronson.

I would especially like to acknowledge two longtime colleagues and mentors, both of them giants in the field: Toby Cosgrove, MD, who not only inspired and challenged me during my long surgical career but took time out from his busy schedule to read the book and offer his kind words in a foreword; and Kenneth Forde, MD, who helped guide my first steps on the road to becoming a cardiac surgeon.

I remain indebted to the super heart team at Rhode Island Hospital and my secretary Cindy Santucci, whose unflagging efforts, enthusiasm, and personal sacrifices made everything possible from day to day. It is not possible to mention each and every person from my four-decade career, but I know who you are, and your names are etched in my heart forever.

A special thanks to the bravest people—my patients and their families. You trusted your hearts to my hands. I wish I could say that I saved each and every single one of you. I didn't, but I gave it my all.

I have dedicated this book to my mother, my wife, and my sons. But I would also like to acknowledge my siblings Dilip, Ampali, and Ashesh and my daughters-in-law Sujin and Shalini, and grandkids Maya, Krish, and Ian for their love, their gratitude, and their support. As always, you remain the center of my world and I cherish all of you.

Finally, thanks to my cowriter, John Hanc, who worked tirelessly to make *Your Heart, My Hands* a reality. This book would not have been possible without his help, and I am indebted to him forever.

Also, thanks to my patients and colleagues who gave permission to use their names in order to tell their stories. Words cannot say enough about my working team: Hannah Phillips, Mari C. Okuda, Kristin Roth Nappier, Rudy Kish, Katie Broaddus, and others at Hachette Book Group for their support. Finally thanks to Gary Hallquist, Prime Time, for editing the photographs for the book.

Arun Singh and John Hanc would like to thank:

Our literary agent, Linda Konner, for her wisdom, support, and loyalty; our editor, Virginia Bhashkar, for believing in this book and for her valuable input in the editing process; book coach Lisa Tener and writer Scott Douglas for their important contributions in the early stages of this project; and Andrew Hanc for his help in manuscript preparation. Also thanks to Nick Baldwin, archivist of Great Ormond Street NHS Foundation Trust, for sharing his vast knowledge on the history of that great medical institution.

About the Authors

One of the preeminent heart surgeons in American history, ARUN K. SINGH, MD, performed over fifteen thousand open heart surgeries on infants and adults and another five thousand related procedures over his forty-one-year career.

Born in India in 1944, he was trained in surgery at Columbia University College of Physicians and Surgeons, Brown University Program in Medicine, Rhode Island Hospital, and Great Ormond Street Hospital in London.

From 1975 to 2016 Dr. Singh practiced at Rhode Island Hospital, Brown University, where he helped to build a nationally recognized cardiac surgery program. A member of the faculty at Brown University's Alpert Medical School since 1976, he is now professor emeritus.

Dr. Singh has published more than 150 scientific papers, has authored many chapters in medical texts, and has given lectures on heart disease and cardiac surgery to professional and lay audiences both regionally and nationally.

He is a fellow of the American College of Surgeons, the American College of Cardiology, the American Heart Association, and the Royal College of Surgeons of Canada, and is a member of the Society of Thoracic Surgeons and the American Association of Thoracic Surgery.

Dr. Singh has earned numerous awards as a physician, including a Hero at Heart Award from the American Heart Association.

He was voted Rhode Island's "Top Doc" in heart surgery for twenty years running by *Rhode Island Monthly* magazine.

In 2017 he was inducted into the Rhode Island Heritage Hall of Fame. The Singhs, who have two grown sons and three grandchildren, support a number of charities, including Rhode Island Community Food Bank and the Ekal Vidyalaya Foundation, which develops schools in rural India for underprivileged children.

JOHN HANC's seventeen books include the award-winning memoirs *Not Dead Yet*, coauthored with cyclist Phil Southerland, founder of Team Type 1, and *The Coolest Race on Earth*, an account of Hanc's participation in the Antarctica Marathon. He is also the coauthor of *Fighting for My Life* with Jamie Tyrone and Marwan Sabbagh, which is being published in spring 2019 by Thomas Nelson, an imprint of HarperCollins.

A longtime journalist, Hanc is a frequent contributor to the *New York Times* and *Newsday*. His work has also appeared in such publications as *Smithsonian*, the *Boston Globe*, *Runner's World*, and the *Columbia Journalism Review*. He teaches writing and journalism at the New York Institute of Technology.